TYPHOON ATTACK

Norman Franks is a past master at bringing out
the personal aspects of the airmen themselves.
In this work, he follows the action to the
Normandy beach-head, the break-out into
France, the Falaise battle onwards.
The Daily Telegraph

... an excellent, authentic and fascinating
collection of experiences from some of the
stalwart and courageous characters who
struggled with the Typhoon's early vicissitudes
and later fought the fierce and successful battles
of the Typhoon war in support of the liberation
of Europe by our combined forces.
Roland Beamont, *Aerospace*

If you want a combination of first-person
episodes of battle – both interception in the
beginning, and ground attack under strenuous
conditions over Europe – then this is your book.
Aircraft

This well-written book proves that truth is once
again stranger than fiction. A truly exciting read
and the nearest the armchair WW2 buff will
come to participating in the real thing.
Torquay Herald Express

Typhoon Attack

Norman Franks

GRUB STREET · LONDON

Published by
Grub Street
The Basement
10 Chivalry Road
London SW11 1HT

British Library Cataloguing in Publication Data
Franks, Norman L.R. (Norman Leslie Robert), 1940-
  Typhoon attack. – New ed.
  1. Great Britain, Royal Air Force – History
  2. Typhoon (Fighter plane)
  3. World War, 1939-1945 – Aerial operations, British
  I. Title
  940.5′44941

ISBN 1 904010 33 4

Edited by Amy Myers

Printed and bound in Great Britain by
Biddles Ltd, Guildford and King's Lynn
www.biddles.co.uk

NB: This is an updated and amended edition of an original
volume published by Wm Kimber in 1984

Contents

		Page
	Foreword	7
	Acknowledgements	9
I	Premature Birth	11
II	Hit and Run Raiders	28
III	On the Offensive	39
IV	Operations 1944	65
V	Dive-Bombing, Rockets and Engines	74
VI	Build-up to Invasion	98
VII	Invasion	115
VIII	Into Normandy	128
IX	The Breakout	134
X	Forward into Holland	149
XI	The Other Ways of Landing	163
XII	The Winter of 1944-45	173
XIII	Tactics and Flak	193
XIV	Trains, shipping and Bridges	207
XV	Operations 1945	216
XVI	Victory	233
	Recollections	248
	Epilogue	252
	Index	253

Foreword

by

Air Commodore C. D. North-Lewis DSO DFC & bar

The significant part played by the Hawker Typhoon in the defeat of the German Army during the Normandy campaign and the subsequent battles until the final victory has largely been ignored by military historians. Norman Franks in this book *Typhoon Attack* has, therefore, played a valuable part in helping to rectify this omission.

After an inauspicious start to its operational career as a fighter, the Typhoon when armed with bombs and then rockets became a formidable fighter-bomber. By D-Day, eighteen squadrons with around 350 Typhoons, the majority fitted with rockets – the remainder with bombs – were available for the close support of 21 Army Group. The Typhoons had played a major part in the establishment of the bridgehead in the run up to D-Day by knocking out the German coastal radars. The Typhoons continued to give decisive and invaluable support to 21 Army Group in their victorious campaign which culminated in the destruction by the Typhoons of the German armoured counter-attack at Mortain followed by the rout of the German 7th Army at Falaise.

In order to achieve the necessary accuracy the rockets were released at low level. As the targets were often heavily defended by light ack-ack the casualty rate was high. During the four months of the Normandy campaign, including the run up to D-Day, 151 Typhoon pilots were killed, 36 were taken prisoner and 274 Typhoons were lost. But these losses were not in vain. General von Luttwitz, commanding the 2nd Panzer Division said: 'The intervention of the Tactical Air Forces, especially the rocket-firing Typhoons, was decisive.'

After Normandy the Typhoon force continued to provide close support to 21 Army Group in their drive to the Rhine and in their advance to the Elbe. They played a major part in all the battles fought, especially in the defeat of the German counter-attack in the Ardennes over Christmas 1944. With the defeat of Germany in May 1945, the Typhoon had had its day and it was withdrawn from operational service. Today the only Typhoon in existence is on display in the Royal Air Force Museum at Hendon.

The Typhoon pilots came from all the Allied countries. During the four years the aircraft was in service, 666 of these pilots from the following countries lost their lives: Argentina 2, Australia 42, Belgium 17, Burma 3, Canada 150, Ceylon 1, France 2, India 1, Ireland 1, Italy 1, Jamaica 3, New Zealand 48, Norway 2, Poland 3, Rhodesia 21, South Africa 19, Trinidad 2, USA 6 and the UK 311. In addition, 169 were taken prisoner of war. The average age of all those killed was 22. To mark their memory a magnificent memorial has been erected at Noyers Bocage, near Caen.

This book is the story of the Typhoon told in the unemotional words of the pilots who flew the aircraft and of the groundcrew who kept it in the air, often working under very difficult and sometimes dangerous conditions. It is a story which shows their courage, fighting spirit and devotion to duty. I am very proud to have been a member of that Force.

Acknowledgements

When I decided I wanted to write about the Typhoon, it soon became apparent that to do justice to the subject and to differ from other books about an aeroplane, I needed to approach it in a different way from my other books. I therefore decided that I needed to talk at length with the men who had flown Typhoons. I had been encouraged when writing my book *The Battle of the Airfields* (Grub Street, 2000) to have contacted a number of Typhoon men who had been eager to help. I was fortunate that they not only agreed to help me with a book on the Typhoon, but were equally happy for me to interview them in their homes. These, and a number of others, all assisted me greatly and it was a personal pleasure for me to be able to meet every one of them, or nearly all, and be able to talk over their experiences to achieve what I desired for this book.

The only notable exceptions were the two men in New Zealand, two in Australia and one in South Africa. Luckily, each one of them sent a wealth of information and interpreted my requirements almost as if I had interviewed them. To them and to everyone listed below, I give sincere thanks. I have used their words as they spoke or wrote them. I had no desire to try to improve or to comment on what they experienced flying the Typhoon in action. It is what they did, what they felt and what they thought. This is the story of the Hawker Typhoon, but it is also their story, and the story of their many contemporaries, many of whom did not survive to see victory. Gentlemen, I thank you.

Air Chief Marshal Sir David Evans GCB CBE CBIM: 137 Squadron
Air Commodore C.D. North-Lewis DSO DFC*: 175, 182, 181 Squadrons and 124 Wing.
Group Captain H.S.L. Dundas DSO* DFC: 56 Squadron

Group Captain D.E. Gillam DSO** DFC* AFC: Duxford Wing, Leader 146 Wing.

Group Captain F.W.M. Jensen CBE DFC* AFC AE FBIM: 195 & 181 Squadrons

Wing Commander H. Ambrose DFC*: 257, 175 & 181 Squadrons

Wing Commander S.J. Eaton DFC: 257 Squadron

Wing Commander G.J. Gray DFC*: 181 & 182 Squadrons

Wing Commander L.H. Lambert DFC AFC: 168 Squadron

Wing Commander P.H.M. Richey DFC*: 609 Squadron

Wing Commander B.J. Spragg DFC: 257 Squadron

Wing Commander A.G. Todd DFC: 56, 164, 193 and 257 Squadrons

Squadron Leader G. Clubley DFC: 181 and 137 Squadrons

Squadron Leader H.G. Pattison DFC OStJ: 182 Squadron

Squadron Leader A.H. Smith DFC*: 486 and 197 Squadrons

Flight Lieutenant R.W. Cole DFC: 3 Squadron

Flight Lieutenant V.C. Fittall DFC: 486 & 198 Squadrons

Flight Lieutenant R.E.G. Sheward DFC: 137, 164, 263 & 266 Squadrons

Flight Lieutenant J.G. Simpson DFC: 193 Squadron

Flying Officer T.T. Hall DFC: 175 Squadron

Flying Officer R.W. Pottinger: 3 Squadron

Flying Officer A. Shannon: 257 & 197 Squadrons

Flying Officer W.R. Speedie: 175 Squadron

Pilot Officer N.B. Wilson: Tech Adj

LAC K.F. Figg: 182 Squadron

LAC D.C. Shepherd: 137 Squadron

LAC D.N. Macdonald: 121 Wing

Thanks are also due to Mrs Phyllis Russell, Martyn Ford-Jones, Chris Thomas, Geoff Thomas, Chaz Bowyer, The Keeper of the Public Records Office, Kew; Amy Myers and all at Grub Street, and not least my dear wife Heather, and as always my two coffee-making sons Rob and Mike.

CHAPTER ONE

Premature Birth

It is often thought that the Hawker Typhoon was a product of the Second World War. Its origins, however, began in 1936, when Air Ministry called for an eventual successor to the Spitfire and Hurricane day fighters. Although these two aeroplanes were still new and in many ways revolutionary for their time, they might prove of only limited life. The future has always to be prepared for, if sometimes only on paper.

However, Hawker's brilliant aircraft designer, Sydney Camm, already had ideas for a successor to his Hurricane design. This in itself was the natural development from the Hawker Hart and Fury biplanes. The new aeroplane had naturally to be faster – the Air Ministry specification said 100 mph faster – and have a heavier armament, possibly the new 20 mm cannon. In actual fact Camm's idea for the successor to the Hurricane, the Tornado, was being designed even before the first production Hurricane Mark I, had its first flight.

The Air Ministry's specification (F. 18/37) went out to aeroplane manufacturers in January 1938. Apart from the question of armament (Camm himself preferred .303 machine-guns to cannon) the specification suited Camm's design ideas admirably. It was, therefore, no surprise to anyone that Hawker's tender was accepted in April 1938.

The airframe design itself was satisfactory but it was the big engines required to achieve the desired speeds that caused the main concern. There were three contenders; Napiers had the Sabre, a 24-cylinder engine with four rows of six cylinders in an H layout driving two crankshafts. Rolls-Royce had its Vulture engine, Bristols their Centaurus. In the event, the Centaurus was considered not far enough advanced, the Vulture underpowered, weighed too much and had mechanical problems. This left the Sabre, but this too had mechanical problems as little development had been carried out. This was to cause a major headache in the Typhoon's progress and dog the whole of its early life in squadron service. However, once the decision to use the Sabre had been made, it had to be lived with, much to the consternation of the next generation of fighter pilots who had to fly with it.

When the Second World War began in September 1939, the Typhoon was well advanced and in fact it made its first flight on 24th February 1940. (The Tornado made its maiden flight in October 1939, powered by the Vulture engine.) Air Ministry had already put in an order for 1,000 of Hawker's new Tornado and Typhoon fighters, the first to be delivered in July 1940, the 500th by September 1941. Finally the Typhoon emerged ahead of the Tornado, which was finally killed off when Rolls-Royce had to concentrate on its new Griffon engines. The Vulture engines already produced were transferred to the new Avro Manchester bomber project which in turn, because of the low performance of the engine, led to the famous Avro Lancaster design, but powered by Rolls-Royce Merlin engines.

The change slowed down Hawker's programme and when the Battle of Britain put urgent demands on the company to replace battle losses in Hurricanes, further production delays had to occur. When the battle was over and production of the Typhoon was able to continue, Britain very quickly had a new shape and sound in its skies.

When at last the Typhoons were rolling off the production line, the first squadrons to fly them had to be selected. Air Chief Marshal Sholto Douglas, C in C Fighter Command, gave the task to his Squadron Leader Tactics at HQ Fighter Command, Paul Richey DFC and bar. Richey had fought in France during 1940 with No 1 Squadron until he was wounded. In the Battle of Britain he'd been a fighter controller until able to return to operational flying in 1941. In the meantime he had written a book on his experiences in France which became a classic of its time.

I'd been in 609 Squadron as a senior flight commander from March 1941 to August. Then I'd been in command of 74 Squadron. While with them at Llanbedr we received a signal that Sholto Douglas was going to visit us which was a rather curious place for him to go to. He landed and talked to the boys, then questioned me for an hour. The next day came a signal posting me to HQFC. I tried to get out of it but couldn't so off I went. I heard later that Sholto had gone into one of his morning conferences with my book *Fighter Pilot*, which had just been published, under his arm and threw it on the table and said to his 'P' Staff chap, 'Find out who wrote that,' – it was anonymous of course. Then he said he wanted everyone to read it. When it was discovered who had wrote it, Sholto said he wanted that chap in his HQ.

After I'd been there about a month I went to him and said I didn't like the work and may I go back to the squadron? He said certainly not, I want you here for six months! So six months later to the day I went to him and he asked what I'd like to do. I said I'd like, if possible, to take over 609 Squadron, having heard that their CO was about to go on rest. As 609 had just got Typhoons I'd like to be with them. Sholto said OK, and I was sent as Supernumerary to 56 Squadron, then when Gilroy left 609, I was in the chair. So that was how I came onto Typhoons, a decision I was to regret! It was interesting but I rather regretted not going back onto Spitfires.

Squadron Leader P.H.M. Richey, HQFC

While at Fighter Command, Paul Richey had in fact been instrumental in not only selecting the first three squadrons to fly the Typhoon but he also chose its first base – RAF Duxford. He selected this station on the basis that it had hard grassy ground to help reduce the landing run of the fast and heavy Typhoon and that its distance from the coast would help security; fewer prying eyes from German reconnaissance aircraft. Duxford was also in an operationally quiet area which would avoid premature action being forced upon it and its squadrons. The three squadrons Richey selected on the basis of experience, standard of flying and availability. He chose 56 Squadron and later 266 and 609.

The first squadron, 56, commanded by Squadron Leader P.P. Hanks DFC – who had been in France with Richey in 1940 – began changing its Hurricanes for Typhoons in September 1941. Duxford's Station Commander was Group Captain John Grandy DSO who had commanded 249 Squadron in 1940.

There were problems with the Typhoons right from the start.

Squadron Leader Prosser Hanks listed some on 26th September. Even at this early date the view from the cockpit gave concern and also the starting procedure. The engine tended to cut out when on the landing approach, which was disconcerting rather than dangerous, and the squadron also hoped that before they were made operational the aircraft armament would change from machine-guns to 20mm cannon as promised. Then in December, Hanks became Wing Commander Flying at Duxford, his place as CO of 56 taken by Squadron Leader H.S.L. 'Cocky' Dundas DFC, who had fought in the Battle of Britain and until recently had been with the Bader Wing flying sweeps over France.

When I arrived at 56 Squadron just before Christmas 1941 I was, of course, very excited to be commanding the first squadron to get the great new fighter but I must say I was slightly horrified, perhaps that's too strong a word, but was astounded by what I found.

It seemed like an absolutely enormous aeroplane compared with the Spitfire. One sort of climbed up, opened the door and walked in! There was absolutely no backward visibility at all in those very first aeroplanes. They had armour plating behind one's head, right up to the side of the aeroplane. Unlike the Spitfire, where one could see behind, with this thing you simply couldn't, it was quite opaque, so that wasn't very good!

Then we were having a lot of trouble with the oil. Just after take-off the oil temperature tended to go off the clock; the oil cooler seemed to get blocked up in some way. You then had just about two minutes to get round and in again before the engine stopped. Something to do with viscosity, but one would take off and then watch the oil temperature gauge like a hawk and if you were unlucky and the needle rose rapidly then that was the signal to get moving.

The Typhoon had a Coffman starter system which was not terribly easy, particularly in the extremely cold weather, because with 24 sleeve valve cylinders, it used to get a bit sticky.

So these were the sort of immediate problems we had. I gave it a few weeks, then went to Group or Fighter Command and said, look, really I think there are certain things that have got to be done about this aeroplane, but the most important thing is the rear view. If it's going to be used as a fighter you simply can't send it into action like this because people can't see sufficiently behind them.

I remember later there was a great conference arranged at Duxford at which all the big-shots came down from Fighter Command and 12 Group. Sydney Camm came along and people from Air Ministry and so on, and there was I, poor little 21-year-old squadron leader, faced by all these senior officers and god-like creatures like Sydney Camm. But I just stuck to my guns and said that this had got to be put right. Eventually they made modifications, put in some armour plated glass either side and the rear opaque section they made transparent.

Sydney Camm was very put out when I was arguing so vehemently that this was a bad design and we couldn't go into action with it. I remember him saying something to the effect, 'My bloody aeroplane's so fast you don't have to see behind you!' [Paul Richey remembers this comment too. NF] Things got quite heated I remember, and I recall it so well because I was such a 'bog-rat' compared to everybody else, but I'm glad to say I got my way.

So all the aeroplanes, one by one, went back to be modified. They gradually got the oil business more or less right during the early months of 1942. Then came the trouble with the tails.

Squadron Leader H.S.L. Dundas, OC 56 Squadron

The second squadron, 266 (Rhodesian) Squadron, began receiving Typhoons in February 1942. It was commanded by Squadron Leader C.L. Green DFC, himself a Rhodesian. Charles Green was to become a famous Typhoon leader as well as pilot. 609 Squadron didn't get Typhoons until April 1942, just before Squadron Leader G.K. 'Sheep' Gilroy DFC handed over to Paul Richey. Once this three squadron Typhoon wing was in being, it was commanded by Wing Commander D.E. Gillam DSO DFC & bar AFC.

Denys Gillam, a pre-war pilot, had received his AFC in 1938 when flying from Aldergrove on weather recce flights often in extremely hazardous conditions and for flying in urgent supplies to the residents of Rathlin Island, isolated by a gale for three weeks. In the Battle of Britain he had fought with 616 Squadron (as had Cocky Dundas) and before being given the Duxford Wing had been flying at the head of 615 Squadron attacking shipping in the English Channel with cannon-armed Hurricanes.

I was very pleased to get the first Typhoon Wing. I thought they were a terrific advance, although I must say I never thought they'd be a good fighter to fighter aeroplane. They could hold their own certainly, if someone was misguided enough to try to outfly them downhill, when they were in for a surprise, but they were a terrific gun platform. They were much steadier than a Spitfire or a Hurricane. Where a Hurricane was very good a Typhoon was rock steady and when you fired your guns your aim wouldn't shift at all, whereas the Spitfire gave a lot of vibration which chucked you all over the place. It could dive and hold its dive without swinging or messing around; you could hold it and then pull it out.

Wing Commander D.E. Gillam, Wing Leader, Duxford Wing

However, the Typhoon was having a number of problems still and accidents which gave some concern for the future of the aircraft to say nothing of the concern felt by the pilots who daily had to fly them. It was also becoming apparent that the Typhoon as a pure day fighter was leaving much to be desired. Denys Gillam continues:

Originally I was involved in a very big discussion and I crossed swords very much with Harry Broadhurst on this. He of course was an Air Vice Marshal and I a Wing Commander. He wanted to make Typhoons become night fighters and they weren't good for night fighting because the exhaust outlets were right in line with the eye of the pilot and however much he battled it he got a terrific amount of flame there.

Broadhurst, for his part, could see that the Typhoon as a fighter had limitations and argued that it should not be used in large formations. If it was used in formation, it negated the advantage of the Typhoon's relatively high speed and exaggerated its relatively poor manoeuvrability.

There continued to be a number of conferences about the problems and the future of the Typhoon. There were also any number of reports written by those concerned, that went to either Group or Fighter Command. The minutes of a meeting at Duxford on 10th February 1942, chaired by Group Captain H.I.T. Beardsworth of HQFC and attended by, amongst others, Cocky Dundas, Hawkers, Napiers, Glosters, and the Ministry of Aircraft

Top left: Wing Commander D. E. Gillam DSO DFC AFC, leader of the Duxford Wing 1942.

Top right: Squadron Leader H. S. L. Dundas DFC, OC 56 Squadron.

Right: Squadron Leader P. H. M. Richey DFC, OC 609 Squadron.

Production, reveals the extent of the problem: the oil system, fuel system, oxygen and R/T connections as well as rear view; cockpit fumes, poorly fitting cockpit door, cockpit heating, hydraulic pumps and of course the engine.

Problems with the Sabre engines increased as 1942 progressed, resulting in more reports and meetings with Fighter Command and Napiers. In July there was further discussion, with Sydney Camm and T.O.M. Sopwith from Hawkers, where the rear view and the Typhoon's speed were again under review. But by now they had the other, more dangerous problem mentioned by Hugh Dundas. The tails began to come off.

Squadron Leader H.S.L. Dundas, OC 56 Squadron

My recollection of that is quite clear. We were asked to do some tests which involved going up to maximum altitude at full throttle and although I can't remember what it was all about, two or three of these accidents took place when people were coming down from this. I always had the impression that what had happened was that the people, having got up to very high altitude, and the Typhoon didn't go very high – 28 or 29,000 feet and you were wallowing about like an old cow. So then they just rolled over and went down nose first. Then at a certain point you found yourself going very fast indeed and I thought what happened was that we were getting into the nose going under and then people would begin to throttle back. They would wind back on the actuating gear and in coming out would be getting near the effect of reaching the sound barrier. So I always believed that was what was happening. I can't recall that anybody really accounted for it very satisfactorily, one just avoided that kind of manoeuvre. It was a heavy aeroplane and it had a very powerful engine and if allowed to dive in a vertical position it built up speed terrifically.

Squadron Leader P.H.M. Richey, OC 609 Squadron

Apparently it was the bushing. The mass weight balance was on an arm with the bush at the pivot. The bushing was just rimmed out, it wasn't a properly fitting bush and when the thing got a bit of vibration on it, it would waggle about and the vibration increased (and became harmonic), then it broke off. When it broke the elevators just went up and caused the tail to snap off. The shock invariably knocked out the pilot. The tail problem

Squadron Leader P.H.M. Richey, OC 609 Squadron (continued)

usually followed a half roll and a dive, then pulling up. I think once you put the loading on the elevators, that's probably what did it. But it was a disgrace, in my view, to put the Typhoon into operations with these problems.

Wing Commander D.E. Gillam, Wing Leader, Duxford Wing

We started to get a series of accidents, probably happening about once a month or occasionally twice. Aircraft flying along in formation would suddenly nose dive straight down and either disintegrate before hitting the ground, or hit the ground and disintegrate. The prevalence was such that there was obviously something technically wrong. At first this was felt due to monoxide poisoning and new exhaust manifolds were tried, sealing the fire damp between the engine and the cockpit to make this more secure. We then tested for monoxide evidence but nothing of any consequence was found. The accidents continued and it was then felt that the tailplane was structurally weak because in most accidents the tail just came off before the rest of the aircraft broke up. They then riveted a band round the tail just in front of the fin, reinforcing the whole of the tail skin. This didn't stop the trouble and we had further fatalities. It was only when taxi-ing out one day, my Number Two said his stick had gone forward and was hard up against the instruments and it was very heavy to handle. He taxied back and we found the mass balance weight which was inside the tail of the aircraft, which was about a ten pound lump of lead on an 18″ strut, had fallen off. Examination of the other aircraft found cracks in this unit. It was concluded that the cause of the trouble was harmonic vibration caused by the length of this particular strut and the weight. This was altered by making a strut of different construction and different length and we never had any more trouble. The amount of fatal crashes this had caused was really rather horrific.

At last in mid 1942, the Typhoon was made operational and the wing began flying fighter sweeps over the Channel. As yet they were not allowed to fly the new type over enemy-held territory. The first operational casualties occurred and the first moments of operational tragedy.

We lost a flight commander on a take-off – Francois de Spirlet. The chap formating on him was on his left – Cheval Lallemant. There was a tyre burst and the two aircraft collided. De Spirlet's tail was cut off and his aircraft went straight in and burst into flames, while Lallemant, who was his best friend – they shared a room together – could only watch. Poor chap was in a state of shock.

I was on a 48-hour leave in London but I rushed back. Lallemant was in his room on his own, and wouldn't see anybody and was apparently through with flying.

So I left him till next morning and he still wouldn't come out so I went in to see him and said, come on Cheval, you've got to come and fly with me. I eventually persuaded him that he should and I made him take off exactly in the same position he had on de Spirlet. I had my No 2, Christian Ortmans, on my right and the three of us took off and of course, Cheval stayed about 500 yards away for about a quarter of an hour. I kept calling him closer and closer, and eventually he finished up in very close formation. We did a very nice formation landing and he never looked back; in fact he got a DFC and bar by the end of the war and commanded the squadron later.

The Typhoon did swing on take-off. In fact I brought out a written order for the squadron, on how this should be counteracted. The way was not to bring up the tail too soon. Everyone was brought up to get the tail up as quickly as possible, to accelerate fast, but the Typhoon swung before it got proper speed because of the torque. The thing to do was to take off with the stick more or less central, start the take-off run with the stick not back but central so that the tail didn't come up straight away. Then when you got enough speed on – enough speed to keep the thing straight – then let it come off the ground. I sent a copy of this order to Grandy who said he'd re-distributed it to all Typhoon pilots so they should do this.

Squadron Leader P.H.M Richey, OC 609 Squadron

De Spirlet's crash was on 26th June 1942. Just a month later, on 24th July, Paul Richey himself was in trouble. 609 had been asked to fly a demonstration flight over Fighter Command HQ at Bentley Priory. Richey, flying his usual R7752 'G' – he always flew aircraft lettered G – was right above the HQ when it happened. Richey continues:

I don't know exactly what happened but the engine back-fired and blew a chunk out of the block, followed by flame and smoke. I was very lucky to get down on Hatfield with the aid of a half gale.

I did a half circuit, the wind was in the west over Bentley Priory, so I turned left, which one always does in an emergency, I don't know why, looking for an airfield, searching rapidly for something to land on. Then I saw an airfield which happened to be Hatfield, pumped everything down and landed. The rest of the squadron just went home and at Fighter Command, they didn't even bother to find out what the fix was!

As if the pilots didn't have enough to cope with, the new Typhoon did unfortunately look a bit like the equally new German Focke Wulf 190. This was to cause a number of tragic accidents when other Allied fighter pilots attacked and shot down Typhoons, sometimes with the loss of their pilots.

On a fine sunny 1st June, 56 Squadron sent out a two-man patrol that was then vectored onto a suspect aircraft. Some Spitfires were also sent to intercept the 'bogey', ran into the two Typhoons and shot them both down. Sergeant K.M. Stuart-Turner (R8199) and Pilot Officer R.H. Deugo (Canadian) (R7678) were the two unlucky pilots, the former being killed, Deugo baling out of his burning Typhoon.

The first wing sweep which flew to Mardyck, took place on 20th June led by Wing Commander Gillam and included Group Captain John Grandy. Ten days later another 56 Squadron pilot was shot down by a Spitfire. Flying Officer Erik Haabjoern (Norwegian) had reported a rough engine during an escort to six Bostons raiding Abbeville. Cocky Dundas told Haabjoern to return to base, turning himself to escort him. A Spitfire bounced him and he went down into the sea off Dungeness. Luckily he survived to become a Typhoon commander and Wing Leader later in the war.

No 266 Squadron opened the Typhoon's credit account on 9th August when they shot down a Ju88, followed by a Me210 four days later.

The Duxford Wing flew support Channel sweeps during the Dieppe operation on 19th August and again scored victories, a

Top: Gillam's personal Typhoon at Duxford – R7698.

Middle: Paul Richey's personal Typhoon, 609 Squadron – R7752.

Right: Denys Gillam planning a sortie for the Duxford Wing, 1942.

Dornier 217 shot down by Flight Lieutenant R.H.L. Dawson of 266, while Pilot Officer Munro probably got another, and the Wing Leader damaged a FW190. As the Typhoons flew back towards England, one section was attacked by Norwegian Spitfires and shot down the victorious Roland Dawson, who went to the bottom of the Channel with his Typhoon.

> The crux came at Dieppe when a Typhoon was shot down by Spitfires who mistook it for a Fw190 and in the post mortem afterwards I was very caustic in my report and stirred up a bit of a hornet's nest. Then we started to realise how good the Typhoon was at low attack and army support, and how with such a good view it could really be terrific as an army support aircraft more than anything else, as it could carry a big load, so that's what we did.
>
> Dieppe was about our first op. We'd done some sweeps up and down but we were always on the fringe of things. I really had to screw some arms even to be allowed near the Channel – the Spitfires thought they had got a monopoly on war. Finally, after a lot of belly-aching we were allowed to do the odd shipping patrol. We also did one or two semi intruder jobs; in other words when all the German fighters were up we'd try to catch them when they were getting back to base. Whilst this was reasonably successful it was fairly soon decided that the Typhoons were extremely valuable aircraft for special ops, taking out headquarters, etc: anything which required a considerable accuracy and a real big punch.
>
> *Wing Commander D.E. Gillam, Wing Leader, Duxford Wing*

Yet this didn't happen overnight and it was slow progress to get onto real ops. Even the view from the cockpit was slow in changing. In fact the whole concept of the cockpit seems strange, with doors that opened outwards, and side windows that one could wind down with car-door type handles. One pilot described that, as a joke, the pilots used to wind down a window and stick an arm out when taxi-ing and making a turn, just like driving a car!

> The cockpit hood and doors were absolutely appalling. It was objected to in 1941 by Prosser Hanks, Beamont objected to it in

December 1941 and I had objected to it earlier but they went on turning the things out till 1943. They used to rattle like the devil too.

Squadron Leader P.H.M. Richey, OC 609 Squadron

Coffin doors! The jettisoning was an odd operation. You had to cross your hands and grab rails both sides and pull inwards to open, elbows hit the doors and the top went off.

Pilot Officer B.J. Spragg, 257 Squadron

Finally the real ops began.

Then we started operations. First we were sent down to the south coast. There were what was laughingly called 'hit and run' raids going on at that time and they thought that the Typhoon might just be the things to catch Me109s at low altitude and I think they took the squadron down to Tangmere for a week or so but of course nothing happened which was very disappointing. Then they decided to put us onto low level work and by this time we were up at Coltishall. We did a certain number of operations over the North Sea at low level.

Squadron Leader H.S.L. Dundas, OC 56 Squadron

I was leading 609 on a sweep one day, on our own and were sweeping inland over St Omer under 11 Group Control. They were getting 'windy' about us because they were reporting 30 plus bandits between us and England. They went on reporting this in a more and more strained way, then someone called and actually said, 'Be careful!' – somebody I knew, I think it was Johnny Walker actually.* We started diving to come home very fast and they still went on reporting these 30 plus, so I was looking up and ahead where they might be and saw two FW 190s diving towards us on our left side. They flattened out to our left and we could have gone after them but it would have meant turning the whole squadron round with our tails to the other 30 who might be diving down behind these two, so I left them. I've always

---

* Wing Commander P.R. Walker DSO DFC, who had also been with Richey in No 1 Squadron in France.

regretted it! On the other hand I think I was probably right!

There was another op over Cherbourg, covering American Fortresses. We were at nought feet so as to be under the radar and pulled up about half way across, into a steep climb to about 20,000 feet over Cherbourg. We turned round and the idea was to stop the Fortresses being chased back by 190s. 266 Squadron were still down on the water, they stayed down and lost two Typhoons to 190s but we never saw any. The sky is a big place.

Squadron Leader P.H.M. Richey, OC 609 Squadron

Just over a week after the Dieppe show, Flight Lieutenant A.V. Gower DFC of 56 Squadron had a spectacular crash when his engine over-revved. He crash landed in a field just west of the aerodrome, bounced over a hedge and across a road. His starboard wing hit a tree on the way, the engine fell off and he finally stopped 50 yards further on.

During their Channel or North Sea excursions, the Typhoons occasionally found enemy aircraft. On 14th September Flight Lieutenant M.R. Ingle-Finch (R7846 'R') and Pilot Officer W.E. Coombes (Canadian) (R7629 'P'), flying right on the deck under low cloud, found a Ju88. Coombes attacked, followed by Ingle-Finch, who saw pieces fall off the fuselage and right wing and engine. Smoke streamed from the stricken machine which then went into low cloud. As the two Typhoon pilots circled they saw oil on the sea which confirmed 56 Squadron's first Typhoon victory.

Meantime 56's CO and the other leaders at Duxford were rapidly approaching decision time for the Typhoon. Grandy and Gillam tried to present a solid defence of the wing but then Paul Richey was caught on his own by 'higher authority' and he had to be honest and say he thought its present role was wrong and that the Typhoons should not operate as a fighter wing. He felt it should operate at low level where it seemed to be more suited. Dundas too had his views:

I do know that Broadhurst, who was Group Captain Ops at Fighter Command at that time really decided that the Typhoon wasn't going to be any good for fighter ops as such. I was naturally determined to have a fair crack of the whip to try and see how we could get on with the Typhoon. Broadie really wanted to keep us out of all the sweeps and ops over the Channel and I thought this was very disappointing and argued strenuously that we ought to be given a role whereby we could see how we could progress. So I went to Fighter Command for a meeting about it. Sholto Douglas heard me out, and I always recall him saying to Broadie, 'Well Broadie, you've had one or two ideas recently which haven't worked out too well, let's see whether there's anything in what young Dundas says.'

Squadron Leader H.S.L. Dundas, OC 56 Squadron

Finally it was agreed to use the Typhoon in a totally new way. Hopes of its ever being a pure fighter faded and the Duxford Wing was disbanded on 18th September 1942. With increasing pressure for Fighter Command to combat the new threat of the Luftwaffe hit and run raids on the south coast, the low level capabilities of the Typhoon might prove an answer. The three squadrons were sent to different stations: 56 went to Matlaske, 266 to Warmwell and 609 to Biggin Hill.

We had bad luck for about the first month and even after Beamont took over 609 on 19th October it wasn't till December that a standing patrol got a hit and run raider.

Once you get down to standing patrols, of course, you've gone back to the First World War and you may as well throw your radar away; you're back to the days before radar.

Squadron Leader P.H.M. Richey, OC 609 Squadron

Squadron Leader Roland Beamont DFC took command of 609 Squadron in October 1942. He had been a test pilot with Hawkers following his period with 87 Squadron in France and the Battle of Britain and was soon to become as famous as the Typhoon itself.

In the meantime, the Typhoon took over its new role as a low level fighter and later fighter-bomber. Its targets ranged from hit and run raiders to shipping off the coasts of Holland and France. Then it began to raid inland. Aircraft, airfield, trains, troops, road transport, etc, all became prey to the Hawker Typhoon.

Cocky Dundas, like Paul Richey, left the Typhoon scene; Richey to go to the Far East, Dundas to the Middle East, but not before he began operations from Matlaske. On Guy Fawkes' day 1942 he led a four man sortie on a 'Jim Crow' mission and found enemy ships which they attacked.

Squadron Leader H.S.L. Dundas, OC 56 Squadron

I remember I loomed up out of the fog one day and found a lot of ships in front of me and we charged at them. I got a cannon shell through my tail fin which made it extremely difficult to control the aeroplane. There was this great big hole on one side and I had to keep both feet on one rudder. It was quite dicey as a matter of fact, I didn't think I was going to make it. First of all I didn't think I was going to be able to turn the aeroplane around. There was such a terrific pressure on one rudder, I suppose the actual hole was in the rudder and all the wind was getting in one side. We were only about 50 feet above the sea and it was quite a long way back. However, we made it and I just went straight in and put it down without the benefit of undercarriage at Coltishall.

The Typhoon was quite a nice aeroplane to fly, it really was. It wasn't difficult to fly. It was a bit different from the Spitfire to say the least but I couldn't criticize it from a handling point of view.

Johnny Johnson came down to Matlaske; he was marrying a girl from Norwich. His squadron was way up in the north of Scotland in the winter of 1942. I was his best man and we had the most disastrous time really, because practically every motor vehicle in the place got bust up, turned over or terribly pranged and put out of order, during the course of getting Johnson married off, which seemed to take about three days. I was convinced I was going to be court martialled – really it was a very bad moment. The fact was that Johnny, when he couldn't find any other motor car, got into the Camp Commandant's old Bentley, roared down the road, failed to go round a bend and ended up about 40 yards inside a potato field with a rather mangled Bentley. Just at the end of this terrible scene of mayhem, I got a telephone call from John Grandy saying that they were going to form a fighter bomber wing at Duxford and would I agree to go as Wing Commander Flying? So I said, 'For goodness sake, get that settled before they hear what's been going on here, will you?' I think that was in the nick of time for I was sure I was about to be demoted to flight lieutenant. However, a couple of months later I was posted to the Mediterranean.

CHAPTER TWO

Hit and Run Raiders

Bomb-carrying Me109 or FW190 fighter-bombers had become a nuisance to Britain's air defences in 1942-43, with some indiscriminate bombing of south-coast towns. They would either fly in low, avoiding radar, or dive down from a great height from the French to the English coasts in order to make their attacks.

> Not only did the Germans try to get in under our radar when coming in low but they used also to come over having started at anything up to 30,000 feet over the French coast. They would then start diving from there, get up a hell of a speed and come over North Foreland at nought feet going like bats out of hell, and the poor GCI Controller, who had them on radar most of the way across and knew exactly what they were doing, but were getting up such a speed that they couldn't be caught. If you already had Typhoons in the air you could chase them back as they gradually reduced their speed and they could be caught.
>
> *Squadron Leader P.H.M. Richey, OC 609 Squadron*

They usually came in small formations and more often than not they failed to select any particular military target, just lobbed bombs into any small town or installation, and perhaps strafe them too for good measure.

> Soon after I joined the squadron I flew a sector recce and I was on one radio channel when two FW190s did a low level attack on Brighton. My first wife's friend was killed by a bullet while she was lying in bed. When it happened I was just a few miles away and didn't know a thing about it. If I had been on the other channel and heard the warning I might have been able to do something about it.
>
> *Sergeant R.W. Cole, 3 Squadron*

The Typhoon now came on the scene. With its high level effectiveness in doubt, its low level capabilities seemed ideal to try and combat the menace of these raiders. They were still suffering from engine and tail problems but there was a need for them to be pressed into service.

A new Typhoon squadron now arrived on the scene, No 486 (New Zealand) Squadron, New Zealand's second fighter squadron in the UK. It was formed in March 1942 and began to re-equip with Typhoons in July. It was commanded by Squadron Leader C.L.C Roberts RAF.

Two of its pilots were Pilot Officers Allan Smith, a former accountant, and Vaughan Fittall, both from Auckland:

> Allan Smith entered the RNZAF with me in 1941 and we stayed together at Levin, New Plymouth, Canada, and Sutton Bridge, and all the aerodromes with 486 until I left the squadron in 1943. Something of an achievement in service life. Allan later was best man at my wedding and I returned the compliment for him, also in 1944, in Portsmouth.
>
> *Pilot Officer V.C. Fittall, 486 Squadron*

Still friends today in New Zealand, both gave generous contributions to this book. Fittall continues:

> For some months after we equipped with Typhoons and transferred to 11 Group at North Weald, West Malling and finally settling in at Tangmere, our main role was anti-sneak raider patrols. This activity, although a bit of a come down from their efforts during the Battle of Britain, was still a considerable and dangerous nuisance.
>
> We were rostered to have two Typhoons in the air during all daylight hours and a further two on Readiness. The patrol lines were Dover-Dungeness, Dungeness to Eastbourne (flown to Friston), Bognor-Brighton-Beachy Head, and Selsey Bill to St Catherine's Point, sometimes extended to the Needles. When the weather was completely u/s we would sometimes sit in the cockpit on the ground and conduct fake operational conversations with Ops, in the hope that we would bluff the Germans into thinking that we had a patrol up, and so keep them from dropping bombs on the defenceless population. 486 had quite a few successes but I

Pilot Officer V.C. Fittall, 486 Squadron (continued)

personally was never in the right place and the right time, in spite of many hours leading a section on this work.

Our control was from a radar station near Ventnor on the Isle of Wight, code-name 'Blackgang', and they were very, very good. They had me quite excited chasing a plot just south of the Needles one day, and they kept insisting that I was in visual range and I was getting very jumpy because I could see no aircraft and neither could my No 2. I was nearly twisting my head off in case they were behind me. Blackgang was also getting excited saying, 'You must see them, slightly to port and below you!' I was nearly on the water myself and completely puzzled, when I spotted about 50 seagulls 'fishing' in that direction. Obviously they had enough bulk to cause a blip on Blackgang's screen.

Our biggest problem was the weather, often very poor visibility where we were trying to fly and navigate by little black buoys in the water, and radio silence of course. With the Napier engine at the time still unreliable it was quite nerve-racking flying for hours at low level with no height for escape from engine failure. Pilot Officer Les Weir lost his life in this fashion and Sergeant Leo Walker had to force-land near Bognor and never really regained his confidence again for low flying.

One of the good memories is flying the squadron Tiger Moth across to the Isle of Wight, landing in the tiny field alongside the radar station to have a chat with the boys who were doing such a good job for us, locked in a poky room, spending hours gazing at a radar screen.

Flying Officer A.H. Smith, 486 Squadron

While based at West Malling our patrol line ranged between North Foreland and Beachy Head. For most of the distance the French coast was very close and it was very difficult to make an interception unless you were right above the target area where the German aircraft make their 'hit and run' attack. Initially we flew at 500 feet. This gave us a chance to speed up an interception by increasing our speed in a shallow dive. We had no luck while stationed at West Malling but I am sure our presence acted as a deterrent and the sight of us flying above them must have improved the morale of the people in the south coast towns.

Top: 486 (New Zealand) Squadron 1943 (l to r): P/O R. H. Fitzgibbon (KIA 6/9/43), P/O Faircloth, F/L I. D. Waddy (PoW 25/8/44), F/O H. N. Thomas IO, S/L D. J. Scott DFC, F/L A. H. Smith DFC, P/O F. Murphy, F/O N. Gall, F/O J. R. Cullen (later shot down 16 V1s and was OC 183 Sqn 1945), P/O L. Appleton, 'Doc' Jones MO, P/O N. Preston (KIA). Kneeling: F/O R. Dall and P/O A. N. Sames.

Left: Roland Beamont DFC, OC 609 Squadron after Richey.

Above: F/Sgt Frank Murphy and F/O Allan Smith, 486 Squadron, Tangmere, 1943.

Flying Officer A.H. Smith, 486 Squadron (continued)

During October, several sections were detached to Tangmere where they patrolled the area from Beachy Head to Selsey Bill and on 30th October, 486 moved to Tangmere where we were to stay until January 1944.

Patrols continued through November until March 1943 with each pilot flying one or two patrols a day. The normal procedure was for two aircraft to take off and stay on the deck right from take-off. No R/T was used unless there was an emergency. We flew about ten feet above the water and moved some ten to twenty miles out to see where we would be picked up on the radar by Blackgang. We flew as low as we could so that we would not be picked up by the German radar which was much further away, with the No 2 flying line abreast so that we could cover each other's tail. We tended to keep the same pilots flying together and most of my patrols through this period were with Frank Murphy as my No 2. With the constant flying together we reached a stage where we were almost able to read each other's thoughts.

We flew backwards and forwards on the patrol line using lean mixture and low revs to conserve fuel so that we would have maximum reserves in the event of combat. We developed skills at flying low above the water, bad weather flying and an uncanny ability to hit the right landfall when returning to base. Each section leader developed leadership qualities and learnt to make decisions in emergencies. These skills were all to stand us in good stead at a later date.

Apart from keeping a watch out for enemy aircraft we had to keep a close watch out fc⸱ british aircraft returning from missions over France. In bad visibility we could easily be mistaken for 190s. We were also shot at from time to time by anti-aircraft batteries stationed on the south coast.

We flew in all kinds of weather. Those pilots who had been with 486 Squadron since its formation had operated as night-fighters on Hurricanes and could handle very marginal conditions. The 'hit and run' raiders were most likely to come across in bad weather and the basic rule was that we would take off if we could see the other side of the aerodrome.

On one occasion (19th January 1943) Tangmere was closed in fog and every other aerodrome on the south coast was also closed. Enemy aircraft were plotted in the Channel and my section was the one due on patrol as soon as the weather cleared. I was watching

Flying Officer A.H. Smith, 486 Squadron (continued)

conditions closely so that we could get into the air as soon as possible. At that stage we could see about half way across the 'drome but from time to time it clamped right down.

We took off in formation but when we got halfway down the runway instead of being able to see the far boundary, we ran into a solid wall of fog and I had to convert from visual to instruments right at the point of take-off. With my night flying experience this should have been no problem. I was flying on the instruments and starting what I thought was a steady climb away from the runway and increasing speed as our undercarts came up. Some instinct made me do something which is normally fatal under these conditions – I took my eyes off the instruments and looked ahead – a fraction of a second later we would have hit some trees. I pulled the stick back hard and went straight upwards, bursting out of cloud and fog at 700 feet and to his everlasting credit my No 2 stayed in formation with me. We gained control of our aircraft before we stalled and spun and headed out to sea after the bandits but they turned and ran before we could make an interception.

The next problem was how to get down again. By this time all aerodromes within range were closed with very little prospect of their opening. The fog and cloud stopped a couple of miles south of the coast and the best advice Ground Control could give me was to conserve our fuel by getting onto the most economical mixture and rev setting and just hope the fog would lift somewhere. When we ran out of fuel we were to bale out over the sea. I made a couple of attempts to fly into Tangmere by coming in at sea level, crossing the coast at roof top level with the gasometer at Bognor about 50 feet above me. We probed into the murk towards Tangmere but had to give up for fear of flying into the South Downs behind the aerodrome.

Back we went out to sea and waited. Somebody must have been looking after us because as we flew backwards and forwards I saw the fog start to roll back from the coast near Ford aerodrome. I called my No 2 and we made a shallow dive towards where Ford should be, dropping our undercart on the way down. For a matter of seconds the end of the runway became visible and we dropped onto it in formation. We had barely settled on the runway and were still rolling when the fog closed in again and stayed that way for the rest of the day. The flight had lasted one hour 25 minutes and we were close to the end of our endurance.

Flying Officer A.H. Smith, 486 Squadron (continued)

The strategy behind the patrols was that the Blackgang Controller would plot the enemy aircraft approaching the south coast and would give us vectors to position us between the enemy aircraft and France and would then give us further vectors to close the gap and make the interception. They were outstanding controllers at Blackgang and 486 had reasonable success, shooting down approximately 25 aircraft during this period. Personally I did not have too much luck on these patrols, only encountering enemy aircraft on three occasions.

On 18th February 1943, Frank Murphy and I were on patrol on a line between Selsey and St Catherine's. There was a thick murky haze low on the water and visibility was particularly bad, especially when looking into the sun. Blackgang picked up some enemy aircraft and vectored us south west towards Cherbourg. We had covered about two-thirds of the distance and were starting to get close to the French coast when we saw two Me109s coming at us on the deck from 10 o'clock. Visibility was still very bad and they were almost on top of us before we saw them. We turned hard port to get at them and they also turned hard port, presumably to return to France. It was a bad interception particularly in the bad weather conditions.

In my port turn I pulled back hard enough to black out which is not the smartest thing to do when flying about ten feet above the water. When I had completed the turn I peered round in the haze and saw two aircraft heading south into the sun for France and went after them. I thought it was the two 109s but in fact it was one of the 109s followed by Frank Murphy. Frank saw me coming up behind him and in the haze thought it was the second 109. He turned port to defend himself and it took one circuit for us to identify each other. Meantime the 109 Frank had been following disappeared into the haze and where the second 109 went after the initial encounter we will never know. We returned home very disappointed.

I was 'scrambled' from Tangmere on 29th April, with Frank Murphy. We headed straight out to sea keeping low on the water and awaiting instructions from Blackgang. They had plotted bandits approaching from the south and their first vector was to position us between the bandits and the French coast. The bandits kept on coming and the trap was set. We were given further vectors which positioned us behind the bandits and were then given the message 'Buster' which meant open the throttle and increase speed, so that we could close the gap.

Flying Officer A.H. Smith, 486 Squadron (continued)

Shortly afterwards I saw two aircraft low on the water and called 'Tally Ho' to Blackgang. At about the same time the bandits either saw us or received a message from their base that they were being intercepted and decided to handle the situation by making a run for France at full throttle. Their turn towards France gave us the chance to close the gap further and I identified them as Me109s. We tucked in behind them and it must have been very difficult for them to know just where we were because they were not flying far enough apart to cover each other's tail effectively.

We were flying about ten feet above the water and as we moved into firing range I told Frank to attack the second aircraft which was lagging a bit behind while I kept an eye on the leader. I did not know it at the time but Frank was having trouble with his reflector sight and had to use the splashes of the cannon shells on the water to direct his guns onto the target aircraft. There were a number of strikes on the wings and fuselage and the 109 started to move to port and eventually flew between my 'plane and the 109 I was following. As it came into my sights I gave it a couple of short bursts, getting strikes on the fuselage and tail and shortly afterwards it crashed into the sea.

I then closed in on the leader and gave him several bursts from dead astern. There were strikes all over the aircraft, pieces started to come off and it burst into flames. I moved off to port to avoid the debris and as the 109 lost airspeed I finished up in close formation about twenty feet to the left of it. At this stage the pilot turned and looked at me – it was my first 'face to face' meeting with a German and I will remember that face until the day I die.

I suddenly realised that if I were in his position I would have turned hard port and rammed the Typhoon – he took no such action – perhaps his controls were damaged. I pulled away and shortly afterwards he hit the sea. I called Blackgang to advise them that the bandits were destroyed and we headed for home. I felt no elation – rather a fear that God would strike me from the sky for taking a human life or perhaps that some of the German's fellow pilots were on their way from France (we were very close to the French coast by this time) to exact revenge. We were pleased to see the English coast but had to land at Ford where we stayed overnight.

Leaving the normal sections of 486 on Readiness at Tangmere, our new CO, Des Scott, the A Flight Commander, Spike Umbers and myself flew along to Friston aerodrome on 25th May to see if it

Flying Officer A.H. Smith, 486 Squadron (continued)
would be suitable to detach a section there. Friston was a small grass
'drome right on the top of Beachy Head and it was quite difficult to
land a Typhoon there particularly when there was no wind. Take-off
was interesting – you simply opened the throttle and ran straight for
the edge of the cliff with a drop of hundreds of feet to the sea.

We had just checked out the 'drome and decided it would be
acceptable for experienced Typhoon pilots when the operations
people at Friston told us that Brighton, right next door, was being
bombed. We jumped into our cockpits and took off over the cliff
edge. We could see the bomb smoke and fires at Brighton, and
heading out to sea into the sun were about eighteen Focke Wulf
190s.

We dived down to sea level and started to pull in behind them.
One of the 190s was lagging behind and Scottie pulled in behind it
and shot it down. While he was doing this I noticed some Typhoons
coming behind us at about 4 o'clock and starting to cross behind. I
figured correctly that these were the Readiness sections of 486 who
had been scrambled from Tangmere.

Looking back down sun they were quite easy for us to see and
identify but they were looking straight into sun and they must have
decided we were the last three stragglers of the 190s. The next thing
to happen was that cannon shells hit the water all round me and I
pulled hard port and a Typhoon followed me round in a tight turn
on the deck. Luckily I was the more experienced pilot and every
time he looked ready to fire I pulled the circle a little tighter. This
went on until he had fired all his ammunition. I then escorted him
back to Tangmere and told him what I thought of him with a few
well chosen words (he was killed shortly afterwards in a shipping
attack). It was a tragic mistake for we should have shot down half of
the 190s.

Routine patrols continued through April into May and there were
some in June, but patrols were eventually replaced by a pattern
which had pilots moving through three stages. 1) 15 minutes'
readiness for one hour, 2) dispersal readiness with parachute in
cockpit for one hour, 3) cockpit readiness. Under conditions of
cockpit readiness the pilots were strapped in the cockpit, the engine
was kept warm and everything was switched on ready for immediate
starting up and take-off. When the Tannoy loudspeaker system
called for that section to scramble the pilot simply pressed the
buttons to activate the Coffman starter and opened up the throttle,

Flying Officer A.H. Smith, 486 Squadron (continued)

taking-off across the grass and runways in the direction the aircraft was pointing. At the same time red Very lights were fired from the dispersal hut and the control tower to warn other aircraft that a section was scrambling. It was a matter of squadron pride to be airborne within seconds and there were some dramatic take-offs. One of the most interesting I saw was the pilot who had unknowingly selected 'flaps down'. His flaps were coming down as he raced across the 'drome and he finally took off with full flap! He worked out what had happened shortly afterwards, pulled up too quickly and almost squashed into the ground. The readiness programme was carried out between offensive operations later on, by all pilots and when the squadron was away on a mission, by the pilots who were not on that particular operation.

*

Another of the early Typhoon squadrons was No 257, who also swopped its Hurricanes for Typhoons in July 1942. Once operational it too helped to counter the sneak raiders from further along the south coast, Exeter and Warmwell in 12 Group. Flight Sergeant Henry 'Poppa' Ambrose had joined 257 Squadron the previous year to begin an association with it for three years and the Typhoon for four years:

> We spent a large part of our lives in the cockpit at the end of the runway, waiting for something to happen, with one section out in the middle of the Channel flying up and down trying to be ready for low level attacks by FW190s which were being a bit of a nuisance. We'd find ourselves sitting for an hour and a half on stand-by, as they called it, at the end of the runway or airfield, and then you'd go out and fly an hour and a half patrol. With this the hours of duty were quite extensive and you were pretty tired out at the end of the day. It wasn't much fun either flying up and down the Channel on a summer's day, with windows that you couldn't open and with no ventilation system. If you opened the windows, you couldn't hear the R/T so you had to keep them shut. We were screaming for port-holes and ventilation – they sent us heating! These were the frustrations of the Typhoon in the early days.
>
> In the normal course of events you hardly saw anything at all and you were lucky if you shot down a German fighter because it

Flight Sergeant H. Ambrose, 257 Squadron (continued)

wasn't very often that you were either scrambled in time or happened to come your way. Once we caught up with some getting back to Jersey, and caught some off the Isle of Wight on another occasion. Peter Steib clobbered one of the 109s which attacked the aircrew hotel at Bournemouth, where the aircrew coming from Canada were billeted before going onto OTU. We in turn retaliated by attacking the Luftwaffe rest centre on the French coast.

A chap named Brian Calnan (Flight Sergeant B.C.J. Calnan) and I were cycling down from the mess one day (2nd December 1943) as we were due on Readiness at 10.30 am. The rockets went up so the section on stand-by scrambled and then the section at Readiness were scrambled. Brian and I rushed into the crew-room, put on our parachutes etc, and out to the aircraft. The ground crew had got my Typhoon in a bay and the sun had come down on one wing and melted the ice and snow but had not touched the other wing. I jumped into the cockpit and took off from the dispersal, across the airfield, which was quite a short run. I took off with the stick in the far right hand corner and with full rudder on, sweating like hell! The sergeant in the hangar later said my wheels missed the hangar roof by about an inch. The ice on the wing, which really wasn't extensive, was enough to disturb the airflow to such an extent I only just managed to get off. It taught me a lesson about ice on the wings for the rest of my life. It wasn't until I reached 500 feet that I was able to bring the stick back to normal and flew off to the Isle of Wight [where they shot down a FW190].

Another 190 Brian and I shared we knocked down off Jersey. We scrambled from Warmwell and went out on a course and the interception point was Jersey.

It wasn't much fun flying down to the Bay of Biscay with long range tanks at nought feet, on a winter's day, above the wavetops, knowing full well that if the engine coughed or hiccoughed you didn't stand much chance. We still had problems with the engines so if it hesitated or coughed it was quite frightening. So we always flew with our tail trim just slightly nose upwards, so if anything untoward happened and you had to fiddle in the cockpit and relax the stick, the aeroplane went up and didn't go down. It gave you a chance to sort things out before you went into the 'oggin'.

CHAPTER THREE

On the Offensive

With some squadrons continuing to combat the Luftwaffe's hit and run raiders along the south coast, others began to use the proven low level capability to take their war across the Channel into France. Others were reaching further – into Holland and the Dutch Islands. These operations involved a long flight across the North Sea before ranging across the waterways that comprised the Dutch islands and into Holland itself. It was low level all the way, needing good navigation. These operations began in 1943, many in direct support of Allied bombing raids into Germany. The task was to keep German fighters occupied while also attacking their airfields. As these operations progressed, some of the Typhoons began to carry bombs with which to attack a whole variety of targets which presented themselves, road transport, shipping and waterway traffic on Dutch canals.

Some of these operations were carried out by 3, 198 and 609 Squadrons and we shall look at them through the eyes of three pilots. Vaughen Fittall had left 486 (New Zealand) Squadron to become a flight commander with 198 Squadron. In 3 Squadron were two recently arrived sergeant pilots, R.W. Pottinger and R.W. Cole.

Vaughan Fittall's CO in 198 Squadron was Squadron Leader Mike Bryan DFC, while the other flight commander was Flight Lieutenant V. Smith DFC. The squadron had gone over to Typhoons in December 1942 but it was not until 27th July 1943 that it scored its first success over the Luftwaffe when Flying Officer A.R.F. Jonas probably destroyed a Me109 and damaged another during a Rhubarb sortie. 198 was commanded by a Czech pilot, Squadron Leader J. Manak, but he was lost just a month later, on 28th August.

On this date four Typhoons led by Manak flew a diversionary

sweep to Ramrod S.10 – an attack by rocket-armed Hurricane IVs on the lock-gates at Welmeldinghe. The Typhoons flew parallel to the Belgium coast, attracting heavy AA fire from Ostende, Blankenberge and Zeebrugge. The four Typhoons then turned east to cross the coast at Knokke but the CO's Typhoon (JP516 'N') was seen to stream black smoke which turned to white. At the same time the leader of the Hurricanes radioed that because of the weather they were abandoning the raid. Manak called over the R/T: 'We are going out again,' and the flight turned over the coast. Manak's machine was still streaming white smoke and he climbed to 800 feet and jettisoned his hood before beginning to glide towards the sea. Despite a strong wind, Manak made a good belly landing two or three miles off Knokke; however, his machine was seen to nose forward, plunge into a welter of foam and disappear. A second Typhoon flown by Flight Lieutenant L.S.B. Scott DFC (JP613 'O') was also lost, being seen to fly inland. Scott had only recently joined 198 from 1 Squadron.

These two leaders were replaced by Mike Bryan, in from 137 Squadron and Smith, in from 3 Squadron, at the end of August. Vaughan Fittall arrived the following month:

> The Dutch Islands were 198's happy hunting grounds. As far as the long sea crossing from Manston was concerned, I was used to the trip from Tangmere to Cherbourg and Le Havre, so I thought nothing of it by the time I got to Manston, where the distance was less anyway. On the way out – trying to keep one's slip stream just ruffling the waves to stay below radar height – one was highly concentrated and excited, so the time soon passed. Coming back it was normally with a sense of satisfaction, and if we were all still together, quite pleasant. Different of course, on the occasion I was by myself, with no radio, a smell of burning, a numb arm and not knowing how bad it was, expecting blood to start dripping at any time, it was a long way. Luckily the compass was unharmed and I made a good landfall.
>
> Mike Bryan I can only describe as a good bloke and if you know anything about New Zealanders, you will know that it's high praise. I arrived at Manston to take command of my first flight rather apprehensive, not the least at leaving a 100% NZ squadron to join a mixed squadron where I was the only N.Zedder. Mike made it easy for me and we became good friends.

He was what we called a press-on type, very good in war time, and he inspired confidence. The squadron I found, was very inexperienced, mostly Canadians with some English, and most of whom were still to become operational. It took me a little while to realise that Mike and I and Smithy were veterans in their eyes and I then began to feel confident that I could do my job.

Too soon, Mike Bryan went on rest, but we got a top man to replace him. Johnny Baldwin, as his future career illustrates, was an above average human being. Perhaps not so easy to get close to as Mike, but a CO who soon gained our respect also, and even more of a press-on type than Mike.

Flight Lieutenant V.C. Fittall, 198 Squadron

September was only two days old when a repeat of the attempt to rocket the Welmeldinghe lock gates was made. Again the weather defeated the efforts of 198, 184, 164, 137 and 3 Squadrons but Red Section of 198 went looking for trouble and found some shipping. They damaged a small launch, hit two tugs, a barge and a 400 ton coaster. Flight Sergeant E.L. 'Ted' Osborne (Australian) broke away from his second attack, flicked over and crashed into the sea (JP591 'R').

They tried yet again on the 23rd, 3 Squadron trying to bomb the gates but although hits were scored they were not destroyed. Again 198 went off to find targets and found a large tug towing barges along the Mastgat and left it smoking. Quite a bit of flak came up from some nearby launches and Bryan's Typhoon was hit and badly damaged. Meanwhile, Smithy, Fittall and Flight Sergeant B.F. Gilland (Canadian) were after bigger game. Smithy attacked a coaster, Gilland a barge at the mouth of a canal and Fittall attacked a passenger cargo vessel of 1,800 tons, causing a great deal of smoke to pour from it.

Inland river craft became eager targets for the Typhoon pilots, anything that would slow down supplies for the Germans in Holland was fair game.

Nos 3 and 198 Squadrons were often tasked together at this time and they were out again on Monday 27th. 3 Squadron were carrying bombs, usually two 500 lb bombs, one under each wing. 198 used their 20 mm cannon. Squadron Leader Bryan led them out, but the two units split up when they crossed the Dutch coast, 3 Squadron going for the Westerschelde, 198 to the Oosterschelde. 198 found tugs and barges, escorted by three 800-ton naval auxiliaries.

Red and Blue Sections attacked in turn, each scoring hits but the Naval vessels formed a protective screen and filled the sky with bursting flak. So effective was it that two Typhoons were shot down (JP837 and JP840), Flight Sergeant Gilland and fellow Canadian Sergeant J.A. Colvin both baling out over Schouwen. Bryan was again hit, this time in the outer starboard ammunition pan by a 20 mm shell which exploded the remaining ammo., blowing a hole two feet across in the mainplane. This caused such a loss of lift that Bryan had to use both arms and one leg to keep the stick hard over in order to fly back to base. Here again his troubles were not over for his right wing dropped suddenly as he came in, causing the Typhoon to twist over to the right in mid-air. The right wheel banged down hard and the whole aircraft swung so much that he changed his direction to run through 40 degrees to the right and covered quite a distance before it rolled to a halt.

Thursday 7th October was a milestone for 198 – the day it scored its first confirmed victory over a German aeroplane. A dawn Roadstead had been laid on with 198 going out with a squadron of Hurricanes. Rendezvous was made off the Dutch islands but when south of Blankenberge, flying on the deck, Mike Bryan spotted three FW 190s approaching from behind, at the same height and a mile away.

The 190s seemed to see the Typhoons at the same moment they were seen and two turned to the right and made for the coast while 198 pulled round after them. The third 190 made a quick pass on the three rearmost Typhoons but then rapidly climbed away into cloud at 500 feet. Vaughan Fittall recalls:

We were always very disappointed that on our many sorties to France, Belgium and Holland from Manston, and particularly the Dutch islands, the Luftwaffe seldom had a go at us. So sometimes we used to cross the sea with flaps lowered and throttled back in the hope that we would appear on the German radar as slower flying Hurricanes and tempt the 190s to have a go. On this day, as soon as we saw the 190s it was a matter of full throttle and after them, because we expected them to head for the clouds. However, two chose to hug the ground and gradually Mike and I drew ahead of the rest of the squadron, and once in range, fired alternative bursts until one went down. Out on our port side, Jonas got a few strikes on his fellow before he finally found some cloud.

Mike Bryan and I shared the destruction of one, Jonas damaged the other and on the way out we attacked a train to use up our remaining ammunition.

The 190 crashed into a field south-west of Tielt and spread itself over a wide area. Flying Officer Jonas ran out of ammo when he reached Beruwelz. His gunsight had worked loose and was useless. It was only towards the end of the chase that he realised this and he adopted a system of gentle rotational hose-piping to obtain some strikes on the 190's wing roots.

Two days later Fittall recorded in his diary:

9th October. Up at dawn for Roadstead. Made landfall at Domburg but visibility very poor so we crossed coast and climbed to 1,000 feet. The CO made attack on ship just off coast and the flak that came up was something terrific. I was circling for position for a dive attack when there was the devil of a clang and the cockpit filled with smoke. I nearly died of fright and for a moment didn't notice I had been hit in the right arm. Turned inland looking for a place to put down, but realised the engine and gauges were normal (found later it was a hit behind the cockpit and the radio was causing the smoke) so headed for home, by this time slightly worried about the arm but could see no blood. Landed normally and then did a vicious ground loop – tyre had been pierced by shell.

During November, 198 Squadron, flying from both Manston and Tangmere, flew almost daily with sweeps over both France and Holland. They also began experimenting with rocket projectiles as they had seen used by the Hurricane IV squadrons.

They lost Flying Officer Jonas on 25th November during an escort to 3 Squadron over Cherbourg. Flak had been heavy but they got back across the Channel safely. Then off the Isle of Wight, Jonas' Typhoon (JP509 'A') dived steeply without warning, hit the sea and broke up. All the circling pilots could see was some disturbed water, oil and one long range fuel tank floating on the water. 'Cary' Jonas had been the first pilot to join 198 in December '42 and had been deputy A Flight commander.

It was still with cannon that 198 scored a remarkable success on

Left: Flight Lieutenant Vaughan Fittall DFC, 198 Squadron – after a narrow escape over Domburg, Walcheron, Dutch islands, 9 October 1943.

Below: Flight Lieutenant V. Smith, A Flight Commander, 198 Squadron. Lost on operations 20 December 1943.

Bottom: Squadron Leader Johnny Baldwin DFC, OC 198 Squadron, showing 13 and one shared victories (as at 30/1/44). He ended the war with 16 victories, all on Typhoons, with DSO & Bar, DFC & Bar.

the last day of November. It was also to be the last operation for Mike Bryan who was going on rest. A long range sweep was arranged, a support for American B17s making a deep penetration raid into Germany. The Typhoons would range over Luftwaffe bases in Holland hoping to catch German fighters either landing or taking off. They had been trying to set up such an operation for some time. The Typhoons carried long range fuel tanks.

Crossing into Holland at Domburg they made for Gilze-Rijen but found no sign of enemy aircraft. The new CO designate, Johnny Baldwin DFC, flying as Red Two, was then forced to return home with a rough engine. Pilot Officer Max Lamon (Australian) went with him and took his anger out on a tug he spotted on a canal.

The others flew to Deelan, sweeping round to approach the airfield from the north at 200 feet. Suddenly when just a mile from the base a lone Ju188 appeared right ahead of them at their own height. After a brilliant piece of shooting by Flight Lieutenant Smith, one of the German's engines caught fire and the Junkers side-slipped into a field. As Smithy and his section swooped over the burning wreckage they could see 'a philosophic audience of Hollanders' watching the Junkers burn itself out.

Only moments later the squadron spotted several FW190s, all about to land on the airfield. The Typhoon pilots were quickly amongst them and within four minutes, four had been destroyed and one damaged by Bryan, Fittall, Flying Officer C. Abbott and Flying Officer J.F. Williams, with Flying Officer J.A. Macdonald claiming the damaged one. Fittall's diary records:

> Long range fighter sweep to Gilze-Deelan, designed to coincide with the return of Flying Fortresses and so catch Hun fighters landing. We came across a Ju188 cruising at low level and this was destroyed by F/Lt Smith and as we flew back towards Deelan we found four FW190s in the circuit and shot them all down. I got one, pilot baled out and was duly photographed. Others to Mike, Abbott and Williams and we damaged another on the ground.

No 198 went home jubilant, taking time to shoot up some shipping in the Volkerak for good measure. The next day they tried a similar op, finding three FW190s as they approached Harskamp. One was landing and taxiing, one was entering the left-hand circuit while the third was making an approach from the south-east. In the low level scuffle that followed, some of the Typhoon pilots had trouble with their long range tanks; Johnny Baldwin, leading 198 for the first time, shot down one 190 while Sergeant A. Stanley (Australian) probably destroyed a second which had managed to turn onto Smithy's tail as he struggled to drop his jet tanks. This was all the more commendable as Stanley too was having a problem trying to get rid of his own tanks.

Baldwin led 198 on another fighter sweep on 4th December, yet again as a support for a deep penetration raid by the American 8th Air Force. They flew in company with 609 Squadron.

They swept along the Oosterschelde, then on eastwards passing south of Roosendaal and Gilze-Rijen. At the latter base, 609 reported two aircraft on the aerodrome and some others were seen in a distant haze. Then three more were seen and 609 went down to investigate. After recent successes, the Typhoon pilots were highly excited but they had little idea how successful they were about to become.

As 609 went down, 198 spotted more aircraft 2,000 feet below. They appeared to be four Dornier 217s but Baldwin wanted to make sure they were not American B25 Mitchells. Partly to gain a tactical advantage, Baldwin led his men round in a circle into the sun, where they dropped their jet tanks. Leaving Blue Section above as top cover, Red and Yellow Sections went down after the Dorniers.

All heads swivelling and suddenly I saw below us, heading across our course, four twin engine aeroplanes in loose formation. It must be a mirage! or it is a trap. I reached for the R/T button to call Johnny but he beat me to it. While he is talking I search above for the 190s which must be there waiting to pounce but can't see them. Johnny orders the attack. I led Yellow Section into a climbing circle, watching 24 silver tanks dropping away, then saw Johnny firing at what we could now see were Dorniers. The front one dived away trailing smoke and I saw strikes on the one behind. Still nothing in sight above us. I turned in and down towards two Dorniers I saw ahead of me. I headed for the leading one and gave him a three second burst from the starboard quarter with what I hoped was the right deflection. I could see the flashes of cannon shells hitting the cockpit cover and wing roots. Another burst and pieces fell from the aircraft – no, they were

Top: 198 Squadron 1943-44. Johnny Baldwin is 9th from the left.

Bottom: Successful pilots of 198 Squadron after shooting down four Dorniers on 4 December 1943. From the left, J. F. Williams, Ken Bowman, C. Abbott, Johnny Baldwin and Vaughan Fittall.

bodies, two, three, four parachutes, then the Dornier dived away out of control.

Flight Lieutenant V.C. Fittall, 198 Squadron

All four Dorniers were shot down (Baldwin one, Fittall and Abbott one, Williams and Flying Officer K. Bowman one, Flying Officer H. Freeman and Macdonald the fourth). In addition, 609 also found Dorniers and shot down seven. Squadron Leader Pat Thornton-Brown got one and shared another with Flying Officer A.S. Ross (American) who also got one on his own, and shared a third with Sergeant L.L. Henrion (Belgium). Two of the other Belgian pilots in 609 scored, Pilot Officer Charles Detal got two. Flying Officer Manu Geerts one. Another Dornier was seen to force-land in a field from fright but was not claimed.

Unhappily, Pat Thornton-Brown DFC (R8845) and Flying Officer C.W. Miller were shot down by American Thunderbolts on 21st December in yet another mistake. The Typhoons had been escorting American Marauders and the Thunderbolt pilots thought they were FW190s.

Vaughan Fittall became tour-expired and left 198 Squadron on 13th December. He was posted to Napiers at Luton for engine development testing. Fittall had flown 70 missions, destroyed one enemy aircraft and shared two more, left eight trains in various states of disrepair, sunk seven ships and damaged 30 more. His DFC was announced a few days later, the first for 198 Squadron. His place at the head of B Flight was taken by Flight Lieutenant Robert 'Bluey' Dall – an Australian who had joined the RNZAF. Like Fittall, he too had been with 486 Squadron.

Flight Lieutenant V. Smith, 198's A Flight Commander, was lost on the 20th, on a long range fighter sweep in support of Ramrod 374. The squadron crossed the hostile coast north of Walcheren between 5,000 and 10,000 feet. There was no flak but Smithy's Typhoon was seen to emit a small amount of blue smoke and drop back. It was taken as a temporary engine problem and nobody paid too much attention. However, a pilot in 609 Squadron happened to look back and saw the Typhoon crash vertically into the River Waal near Leeuwen.

While squadrons like 198 and 609 were ranging fairly freely over occupied France, Belgium and Holland, and being highly successful with their low level fighter tactics, other squadrons were developing other ways of using the Typhoon.

No 3 Squadron, who had often been escorted by 198 over and around the Dutch Islands, had been carrying two 500 lb bombs. The squadron had re-equipped with Typhoons in 1943 and had continued its anti-shipping role that it had been carrying out with its earlier Hurricanes.

R.W. Cole and R.W. Pottinger both joined 3 Squadron in the summer of 1943. Bob Cole, who had an older brother in the army in North Africa, had had the good fortune to receive his pilot training in the warm and sunny skies of California. Ron Pottinger had been in the army but when returning from leave had found all his pals had volunteered to join the RAF. Not wanting to be left out he joined too. In the event, he was the only one of them to succeed in becoming a pilot.

During a raid on Poix aerodrome in May 1943, five of the squadron's eight attacking Typhoons were shot down. Bob and Ron, who became and were to remain good friends, were both sergeant replacements following this disaster. As Ron recalls:

> Everyone was a bit sick about this loss, because a new aeroplane like that was supposed to be the 'bee's knees'. Everyone was quite subdued when we got to the squadron.

Their CO was a Belgian, Squadron Leader F. de Soomer. Bob Cole didn't endear himself to his new CO when he flew a training sortie soon after arriving on the squadron:

> I couldn't get the wheels down. In these circumstances there was a mechanical way of releasing the wheels; it was a small prong you'd kick that released the wheels with a locking mechanism. Then they'd fall free and then you'd shake the aircraft and throw it out beyond 180° and they should lock. I did this and the lights indicated that they were down and locked so I flew over flying control and they said they looked all right.
>
> I came into land and I didn't know what went wrong, whether I let it swing or what, but it ran quite a way before it went. One wheel went, the wing stuck into the ground and it swung round. The undercart collapsed and dug the engine in. Luckily all I got

was a skinned ankle.

I did a couple of things that I shouldn't have done. You opened the radiator on a Typhoon when you came in and slowed down. It was a piece at the back which dropped down to increase the airflow through the radiator. I'd got the flaps down; there was enough hydraulics to get them down but not the undercart. But I came in too fast, about 120 mph actually.

Putting the flaps down at 200 mph is an interesting experience!! You used to put the wheels down at 200, bring the speed down to 145 or so, then put the flaps down. I did the reverse and it stopped dead. I was glad I was strapped in; it certainly slowed it down at a great rate of knots!

Ron Pottinger and Bob Cole flew a good many Typhoon operations throughout the summer and autumn of 1943. Their recollections stand on their own as fairly typical of Typhoon fighter-bomber ops during this period:

Sergeant R.W. Pottinger, 3 Squadron

The first operation I ever did was an operation over the Dutch islands led by the CO. He took us out late one evening and we were supposed to knockout some lock-gates and he steered us, at low level over the sea, straight into the entrance of Ostende. Of course, all sorts of filth came up from all directions. When you first see all that ack-ack coming it's really quite frightening. These pretty lights sort of come sweeping out to you so slowly, then at the last moment they go by like angry bees. The last few hundred yards you could swear every one of them was going to come through the wind-screen. It was so hot that we had to break off and turn back.

I remember it because coming back to Manston there was low cloud and we couldn't see the strip. This was before they had runways there; it was just grass, and the way we were landing was down the steep hill down to the cross-road, then up the other side. They had this flarepath laid out and the two lights at the head of it were not level across the airfield. I think most of us made two or even three attempts at getting down. I made three attempts to get in but by that time it was just about dark. Of course, what we were all trying to do was line up between those lights and there was the runway going off at some wierd angle. It was quite dodgy really because the Typhoon wasn't a good aircraft to be out in on a black night. All right on moonlit nights but they were not really the sort of thing you wanted to be up in pitch black unless you had to.

A lot of our work in the early days was against railways and boats; a lot of it was around the Dutch islands. We used to go out and beat up refineries and other targets of this sort but I'd say the bulk of work was around the coast with boats. We did a lot of sweeps where we'd just go out on a set route and see what we could find; perhaps follow a railway or something and whatever turned up we'd have a go at. Airfields too, of course, we attacked. We also used to send out two aircraft on moonlit nights – Rhubarbs. I did a couple of these but don't recall much success.

Sergeant R.W. Cole, 3 Squadron

On some of our ops we were only in the air 35 minutes. Take off, scoot across the water, climb up over the coast, bomb, dive back out to sea and home.

Once we dive-bombed Moorslede aerodrome – two 500 lb bombs. I fired at a balloon over the French coast – that was frustrating. I fired cannon shells into it and it still looked the same, didn't sink, didn't do anything. It was a bloody great thing, couldn't miss it, but I thought I was firing blanks.

The night Rhubarbs were pretty hazardous operations for a Typhoon pilot. Very few liked flying the Typhoon at night. The squadron flew nine night ops. on the night of 16/17 August 1943, each carrying 2 x 250 lb bombs. Flying Officer J. de Callatay (Belgium) (JP585) bombed some railway sidings near Hazebrouck then went in with cannon. Flying Officer R. Schwarz (R8977) dropped one bomb on Abbeville aerodrome, the other on a railway bridge at Amiens. Flight Lieutenant J.R. Collins DFC (JP514) bombed the airfield at Laon. Flying Officer Jean de Selys DFC who had gained fame with 609 Squadron when he shot up the Gestapo HQ in Brussels in January 1943, was also out that night but died when he crashed back at base (EJ950 'X'):

De Selys tossed up with Lefty Whitman, who would fly the night intruder and he won. We think he was hit in the tail for as he came in his tail came off on the final approach. His aircraft hit the runway, right on the threshold. The tail fell into a field behind him.

Sergeant R.W. Cole, 3 Squadron

The Belgian, De Callatay, was lost on an aborted op in September 1943, flying Typhoon JP926:

De Callatay used to get into some drunken parties and then egg everybody on to 'do up' the place! One time in particular, in a pub in Margate, we had this party upstairs and we had jug upon jug of beer brought up and we were playing the stupid, Cardinal Puff type games. It got a bit noisy and a bit rowdy and the publican asked them to be quiet but of course they wouldn't. So eventually he called in the police to escort us from the premises. This little Belgian was running around behind everybody, trying to egg everyone else on to throw the police out!

Sergeant R.W. Pottinger, 3 Squadron

De Callatay just disappeared. We never knew what happened to him – disappeared in daylight! Squadron did a show, he went on it and just vanished. He was a very small chap. One of the first ops I ever did I flew as No 2 to him. We got half way across the Channel, having taken off late, went belting out and met up with another squadron of Typhoons who were flying up and down. Instead of flying on we just formed up with them. I kept calling him to say they're not our squadron, but finally gave it up and stayed with them.

Sergeant R.W. Cole, 3 Squadron

The tactics at first for dive-bombing were to go in from low level and just let the bombs go. After some time, tactics changed but under its early CO's, 3 Squadron went in low and dropped from low level. Apart from the danger from flak, the pilots had also to face the possibility of damage from exploding bombs, either their own or one dropped by the aircraft ahead of them.

After Squadron Leader de Soomer left – tour-expired and with the DFC – the next two CO's fully advocated low level bombing. Unhappily, Squadron Leaders S.R. Thomas DFC AFC and P.

Above: Flight Sergeant R. W. Pottinger, 3 Squadron, 1943.

Right: F/Os Bob Cole and Ron Pottinger of 3 Squadron. In the centre is Joy, Ron's wife to be.

Hawkins MC AFC, did not last long. On one of Thomas's few ops as CO, Bob Cole was in his section:

> On one occasion we went from Dieppe to Boulogne with Thomas leading. There were twelve of us, three lines of four, and I was in the four against the coast. The Germans fired at us all the way along to Boulogne and I watched the flak coming up. If you got tracer coming from one direction you could avoid it.
>
> We compared notes afterwards and found we had all been doing the same thing. If the flak was low, we climbed like hell; if it was high we dived underneath it – the stuff was everywhere and Thomas, when we got back said, it must have cost the Germans more for flak than us for petrol! On that basis, he thought, we'd come out on top. But he was about a mile ahead of us at the back, nowhere near the flak at all, it was all coming at us behind. We never lost anyone but it was pure luck.

Squadron Leader Thomas was shot down on 5th September 1943 and Bob Cole was again flying with him:

> We were attacking shipping in the Dutch islands and Thomas bombed one ship in a bay. We were running over the coast and he saw this boat in the harbour and he dropped his two 250 lb bombs. Whether the bombs blew up instantaneously – they usually had a seven-second delay – or the delay didn't function, or something hit him, nobody really knew but he pranged on the beach among the islands and was taken prisoner. I heard him shouting on the R/T, excited as hell, and the next minute I think he said 'forced landing!' – and that was it. There was some flak from one ship but that's all there was.

Thomas was flying Typhoon JP585 and some of the others saw the machine hit by debris from the ship he had bombed, then stagger away streaming glycol.

Eight days later nine Typhoons – or 'Bomphoons' as they were beginning to be called, led by the new CO, Squadron Leader Hawkins, again went looking for shipping among the Dutch islands. They found plenty and sank two coasters and a barge, then damaged a pile-driver, a dredger, a coaster, ten tugs, three barges and a launch, but it was not all one way. Flight Sergeant C. Crisford

(DN623 'U') was last seen heading inland to crash-land, while Flying Officer Downes (Canadian) had to bale out of his Typhoon (EJ989 'S') twenty miles north-east of Ostende. Later, patrols were flown out to locate him but it was thought he'd been picked up by fishing boats.

Flight Lieutenant Collins and Sergeant 'Lefty' Whitman were one pair out looking for him. Whitman (JP594) an American who had joined the RCAF, had engine trouble and had to ditch fifteen miles off Zeebrugge, but was rescued by ASR Walrus.

Two Bomphoons piloted by Flying Officer J.L. Foster (JP857) and Flight Sergeant S.B. Feldman (American) flew out to attack transport in the Ghent area on the morning of 5th October. They found a Ju88 which appeared to have force-landed in a field. It was surrounded by service personnel who waved cheerfully to the two RAF flyers as they circled. They rapidly changed their minds when the two Tiffies dived and opened up with their cannons. The Junkers was hit and left a blazing wreck but shortly afterwards a flight of FW190s turned up. Both Typhoon men headed into cloud and Johnny Foster was heard over the R/T a few minutes later but then failed to return home.

That same afternoon, Hawkins led eight Bomphoons, together with eight from 198 Squadron, to attack the St Clair Petroleum Refinery at Bruges with a low level bombing attack. The plant was hit and considerable damage caused but it cost 3 Squadron two pilots, Hawkins and Warrant Officer LaRocque (JP926), a French Canadian, who crashed from a slow spin from 3,000 feet. Ron Pottinger remembers:

> I was Hawkins' No 2 when he was shot down. We were attacking an oil refinery and the other two of our section of four turned back, which just left the CO and I leading the show. We were flying a circuitous route to the target and came in from the back, across a canal. As we came in and turned, we left the other section of four quite a bit behind, so it left the CO and myself attacking by ourselves and all hell let loose. The Germans had got some railway wagons with guns on them, outside the refinery and I remember it as a carpet of twinkling lights. We were flying at low level and I pulled away to fly to one side of the chimneys while the CO went the other side. As I straightened out I first of all saw the refinery collapsing like a pack of cards and then looking across at

the CO, saw him still turning as he banked away from the chimneys, with smoke streaming from underneath. He went down in a long shallow dive and ended up in a small copse. There was a great smack of flame and smoke etc, and he'd obviously bought it.

He had, of course, got back at least once before and I had the unpleasant job of trying to convince his wife that he really had bought it this time. I have to admit it was one of the least pleasant things I had to do during the war. She just wouldn't believe that he wasn't going to get back this time. He used to have all sorts of things in his pockets, it was just like a workman's overalls – he had pockets sewn everywhere with bits and pieces tucked into his uniform.

Bob Cole also recalls Squadron Leader Hawkins:

Hawkins had got back from an earlier raid on the Kiel canal and walked through Germany, France and Spain to Gibraltar; then he was brought back to England. He used to fly with everything in his kit – he had enough escape kit to keep him going for weeks. But he was killed which was a great pity. Low level bombing would have finished us all off actually, but then Dredge came along and he went in for dive-bombing. Low-level bombing was all right; it's reasonably accurate and it may be getting stuck into the war, but it killed a lot of people on Typhoons.

The new CO was Squadron Leader A.S. Dredge AFC. He quickly put the squadron into dive-bombing from high level rather than from very low. It proved far better although quite a stomach-turning operation. Bob Cole continues:

Orders would come down from Group; they'd give you a target and the CO decided what to do about it. Group wouldn't tell him how to attack it, just that he had to. We had briefings but on some things we didn't have to be briefed if it was a run-of-the-mill-thing.

Everybody went to a briefing but if you were not responsible for navigating it, or whatever, one might go off in a dream and not take it seriously if you were just an ordinary pilot on the squadron. At twenty years old you're not perfect. If something was

Sergeant R.W. Cole, 3 Squadron (continued)

doing and people were older than you, you'd just let them get on with it when you first joined the squadron. You'd take off, do what you had to do, and when we dive-bombed, we'd just forge ahead. I'd map read – I always map read myself, and knew where I was going but I didn't actually have to take everyone to the target.

Over the target you'd stay in the formation and then just move into echelon, the leader would roll over and bomb, and we all followed. That's how it worked.

We usually rolled in at 10,000 feet and pulled out at 6,000 so as to beat the flak. Occasionally we'd roll higher than that, but the Germans usually put up a curtain of flak at 6,000 feet so if you'd messed up your run-in you had to go into it but otherwise you dropped your bombs.

In echelon we usually slowed it up to 230 mph on the clock, pull it up at the last minute, and in the Typhoon 230 is slow; it only cruised at 280, so it was sluggish at 230. Then, as the Typhoon ahead of you went over, you just rolled and kept the nose up till your speed had dropped a lot, because if you went in at speed you'd pull your wings off, as by then you'd be going straight down, and it got up one hell of a lick! It was not like a small aircraft that might reach 150 mph – it went down like a brick, and in the dive you had to line up on the target.

You put your gun-sight on and you'd pull your vertical line on the sight through the target, and as it disappeared under the nose, just drop your bombs. That's as accurate as you could get, taking no account of wind but making sure the target was far enough under your nose. I'd say it was pretty accurate and you'd probably hit the target. A ship was a different matter. You might hit a big ship, but would probably miss a small ship. We dive-bombed shipping three times off Den Helder at one time and I don't think we damaged anything at all, to be truthful. We just bombed and got the hell out of it. We lined up on a ship, anything that was around, and I think there were about fifteen to twenty ships there. I rolled over, saw a ship, lined up on it, dropped my bombs and was away. We had flak to contend with but we didn't lose anybody on any of these three raids.

I think we'd have been decimated if we stayed on low level bombing and with dive-bombing we did just as much damage.

Certainly it seemed it was just a matter of time before we got shot down anyway, but at low level it made the odds considerably shorter.

Ron Pottinger says of this period:

Squadron Leader Dredge came and put things on an even keel really, because I think he had been in a fire and was quite stressful on the horrors of getting burnt. He made everyone wear gloves and boots, where before nobody used to bother. We'd fly in shirt-sleeves with no collars etc; but he really stopped us doing all this low level stuff with 250 lb bombs. We seemed to lose more pilots than it was ever worth and what damage we did was debatable. It wasn't worth the rate of aircraft we were losing at that time. He started us on dive-bombing with 500 lb bombs and we did that from then on and it was really quite successful.

Both Bob and Ron were involved in one semi-amusing episode which both men remember well. Bob Cole:

We dive-bombed a place near Le Touquet. We were playing invasions a year before the real invasion and eight of us attacked this gun point. There was supposed to be a gun at the edge of a wood but we never saw one. We found where a road went into the trees, and as the gun was supposed to be just where the road and the wood met, we bombed there.

As we formed up over the Channel afterwards, someone said one of my bombs was still on. I couldn't get rid of the thing. I put the fuse on, fuse off, select and unselect, putting the Typhoon in a dive – nothing! Then the thing fell off on the runway, and there it was bouncing along but luckily, and it was pure luck, I'd left it 'fused off'. After all my attempts it just dropped when I was about 100 feet up and I knew it had gone when the aircraft suddenly became flyable. With the amount of leverage needed when an extra 500 pounds is dragging the aeroplane off its centre of gravity, it had been quite a job to fly. It also pulled the wing down and I had to keep the speed up or it would stall. When you've got that weight on just one side, and you slowed down, you'd lose control, so I was coming in at quite a rate – I reckoned 220 mph.

Anything slower and the wing would have hit the ground before the undercart.

Ron Pottinger viewed the episode from another angle:

It was a funny day. Manston had a lot of bomb craters on it, so it was a terribly rough airfield. We were at one end of the north-south runway and that used to go down a hill, bump over a metalled road, and then up the other side. It was steep enough down this hill for the aircraft to vanish from sight, then reappear coming up the other side.

On this day, somebody had landed ahead of me and he'd had both tyres burst on one of the brick filled-in bomb holes. The Typhoon was 'brilliant' in that you could only get under the jack-points if its tyres were inflated. So whenever anyone had a puncture, you had to have about 30 'erks' out to help lift it off the flat tyres. Therefore, we had an aircraft well down the runway with about 30 bods underneath it, all lifting with their backs, trying to get the jacks under, and when I came in I had one leg of my undercarriage folded as I touched down. So there we were, me sitting drunkenly to one side and this other lot down the runway, when Bob came in. He'd been told to stay over the sea until he'd got rid of his bomb, but he was getting worried about his petrol and their was a lot of frantic shouting over the R/T, then Bob called, 'I'm coming in!'

He came in and as he touched the bomb came free. He shot past me with the bomb following close behind, and then it rolled off to the side, rolling straight towards this other aircraft, so suddenly there were about 30 chaps running pell-mell across the airfield with this bomb coming at them, some going one way, some another, down this hill. It was quite funny too, because I was blamed for my rough landing which broke the under-carriage leg and they said that when they lifted the 'plane, the leg fell down and locked into position. The CO was quite scathing and sent me across to see the thing towed into the hangar. So they got it to the side of the runway and went to tow it across the airfield. It had got a steel bar about an inch in diameter, with a hook at either end, between the two legs of the undercarriage; it had to be pulled across the metal perimeter track and as soon as it bounced off the track onto the grass, the bar broke and it all just folded up again! I walked off delighted, of course!!

On 10th November, 3 Squadron lost another pilot, Flying Officer R.M. Walmsley, during an attack on a 'special' target in the Cap Gris Nez area. These special targets would soon become well known to Typhoon pilots.

> Walmsley was hit in a dive-bombing show over Gris Nez when we were attacking a 'doodle-bug' site. He was hit by one of those phosphorous shells and I remember I was escorting the CO at the time. Looking back over my shoulder I saw this great white flash, then this aircraft going over and over, tumbling down, a flaming mass. I was tucked in with the CO and just dived down and away.

That was what Ron remembered; Bob Cole recalls:

> Bob Walmsley had just been left £10,000 in a will, which was a fortune in those days; an aunt had died. He was very pleased with life, bought a sports car and had a girlfriend. Then he was hit by heavy flak, a direct hit, and went straight in.

Long range tanks, as already related, caused problems in the early days. Ron and Bob both recall these problems. Bob Cole:

> We occasionally used long range tanks, but the trouble with those was that the cock in the cockpit was almost impossible to turn. It wasn't a lever it was just a small wavy edged wheel. I didn't take off once because when I tried it, I could turn it on, but couldn't turn it off.
>
>   In the air, if you turned your main tanks on, instead of going into the engine, the fuel drained down into the drop tanks if you couldn't close off the drop tanks, and of course the engine stopped. That's how we lost a couple of chaps. We were coming back from bombing once, going in and out of cloud, and Johnny Earl never came out.
>
>   We did, of course, use the drop tanks first and if you could then turn the cock off, the gravity feed was safe, but if you couldn't the fuel went from the gravity feed and your wing tanks and drained straight back into the drop tanks instead of going to the engine. As long as you turned the cock off if the engine stopped, and you'd got altitude you were all right; the gravity feed would get

the fuel back to the engine. But if you couldn't turn it off then that was it. You wouldn't drop the tanks unless you had to, it was quite expensive to keep dropping them. They held a fair amount of petrol too. When you knew you were getting low, you'd switch over, and get your gravity and wing tanks on. The drop tanks drained equally, of course.

Ron Pottinger states:

I'd never flown with long range tanks before we were sent up to Swanton Morley, in order to escort Beaufighters across the North Sea to attack shipping off the Frisian Islands. We had to fly just above the stall to stay back with them and of course, we were right on the deck, which meant we had no leeway at all. The LRTs had no gauges so you didn't know how full or empty they were and all you could really do was to run for a certain time, then switch tanks. As we were operating near the limit one had to leave it fairly close to empty before the switch, but the trouble was, if you were too late and the LRT ran out, then you couldn't get sufficient height, when at low level, to switch over and get the engine going on the main tanks. We lost several pilots from this.

We never saw much with these Beaufighter trips until one day we saw a convoy of small ships with E-Boats escorting them. Panic set in and it looked as if the Beaus would crash into each other in their haste to avoid this gaggle of boats – there was quite a row about it. Our CO refused to escort them again, and so for a while we went out by ourselves with half the Typhoons carrying LRTs, escorting the other half of the squadron who had bombs. We were on just about our limit of endurance with our LRTs. We did several trips to an island named Texel and to the steel works at Ijmuiden, which we used to dive-bomb. The idea was that if we were ever attacked, then the Typhoons with the LRTs would jettison them and immediately give fighter cover.

Flying in formation is all right for the leader of the formation because he sets his throttle and leaves it there, but the poor bods trying to formate on him, move their throttles all the time and they're using more petrol. Like a car, every time you press the throttle pedal, a great spurt of petrol goes in. So sometimes you could fly out with a leader and come back with considerably less petrol than him.

When I first joined the squadron the Typhoon I normally flew – 'R' – was one of the oldest and that used to get through far more petrol then other people. If I was out with the squadron and if I was No 2 to the second of the two pairs of a flight, I'd sometimes be almost out of petrol by the time we got back to the squadron.

The squadron scored its first air combat victory on 24th February 1944. Both Ron and Bob were involved. Bob Cole:

We flew a sweep to the other side of Brussels. Two or three aircraft had turned back and there were only five of us left. We were in line abreast and then this thing came floundering along right across our nose. Dryland,* Potty and myself – the CO and the flight commander got cut out, and they never got a look-in before we'd shot it down. It turned right across our noses and I dropped my long range tanks, turned and opened fire. So did Potty and Dryland. It went straight in a field and we blew it up and left it. I remember thinking that it would be one less bomber to drop bombs on England but didn't even know what it was. Only the fact that it was over there, had two engines and crosses on it, though I didn't see the crosses until I was about 50 yards away. Also, it didn't look like one of ours!

In fact it was not a bomber but a Leo 45, one of a number of this French type taken over by the Luftwaffe as a light communications and training aircraft which were quite often surprised by roaming Allied aircraft in the mid-war years. Even Ron Pottinger didn't know what it was:

We were doing a sweep over a set route and suddenly, coming across from our starboard side was this cabin aircraft. Immediately someone called on the R/T but I think we'd all seen it by then and we all had a go at it. We were so excited for it was, for us, such a rare event to see an enemy aircraft in those days that I think everyone just piled in and had a good hammer at it. The thing hit the ground and blew up and I think we were still shooting into it after it hit.

* Pilot Officer R. Dryland JR314, F/Sgt Cole JP534, F/Sgt Pottinger JP857.

Bob and Ron stayed with the squadron to the end of 1944, by which time both had been commissioned and Cole decorated with the DFC. 3 Squadron had converted to Tempests by this time and both men flew against the V1s in the summer of '44. Bob shot down 22 of these, Ron six. Cole also shot down a Me262 jet. Both were eventually shot down by flak when flying in Holland, and both became guests of the Germans till the end of the war.

'Poppa' Ambrose recalls an operation 257 Squadron was involved in on 24th October 1943. In his log-book he later wrote by this operation – 'Innocents' Day':

There was a ship in Cherbourg Harbour, carrying Wolfram (tungsten ore). Our intelligence people said it had got through from Japan and had to be hit at all costs.

We went out with Reggie Baker's 263 Whirlwind Squadron with bombs, while we and 183 Squadron were flying with cannon. We were 24 aircraft. When we went for briefing, they said we were going out at nought feet. We said, don't be silly, only idiots go into Cherbourg Harbour at nought feet – we should dive down, and even that was considered to be virtual suicide.

Reggie Baker rang up the Group Captain Ops at Box, Ludlow Manor, and said, 'What's all this nonsense?' but was told that that was the order – nought feet. Anyway, out of 24 aircraft we lost ten and eight pilots, two pilots being rescued from the Channel.

We came back to the Mess and normally most of us remained sensible and drank beer, not spirits, but I remember that afternoon we opened the bar at four o'clock; we were all hacked off. Gus Gower, the CO of 183, had been lost.[1]

Reg Baker went in with the Whirlwinds and we went in before there was any actual flak from the ship. I remember one chap who actually got a German's head between the cannons on his Typhoon wing and when he got home it was still there.

After the war I met the Group Captain Ops – I had not met him before – and I said, 'You were the bloke who sent us into Cherbourg Harbour at nought feet'. He said yes, but said it had been on Churchill's instructions. Churchill had laid down the

---

[1] Squadron Leader A.V. Gower DFC had been with 56 Squadron – see Chapter One.

tactics – we were to go in 'on the deck' as he put it. Anyway, we blew up the ship!

*

Flight Lieutenant F.W.M. Jensen, 195 Squadron
The Typhoon also did a good deal of night intruder/rhubarbs into Northern France with bombs. I was a flight commander in 195 Squadron and used to deploy down to Manston for these ops. The tactics were simply to go low level across the Channel and into the target area, looking for aircraft railway and industrial targets on which to unload the bombs. Bearing in mind the Typhoon's night flying characteristics and the lack of homing aids they were somewhat uncomfortable and nerve-racking ops.

CHAPTER FOUR

Operations 1944

By early 1944, Wing Commander Denys Gillam was commanding 146 Wing and starting his fifth year of war flying. The 12th January was far from an auspicious start to the year:

> We flew an intruder operation in support of a main armada over France and I think we had long range tanks at the time. We went off to catch German fighters around Paris. It was very misty at low level, very misty indeed. We set a course, our object being to get in under the radar over the coast and went in at a fairly flak-free area at deck level, and went straight for Paris.
>
> We really wanted to get to the aerodrome south of Paris but navigation was pretty accurate for we finished up at the base of the Eiffel Tower! The top was completely invisible but it suddenly loomed out of the murk, so we quickly whipped south from there and we had a quick go at one or two stationary aircraft on the ground on some aerodromes, then headed for home. We encountered some flak and my aircraft caught some of it.
>
> The squadron was reformed in two sections of four and were flying at about 200 feet when I saw some FW190s above and following us. They were, of course, appreciably faster than we were. As they overhauled us I kept a straight course and gave the boys a running commentary on the radio of the Germans' progress. As the 190s started their dive I waited until they had fully committed themselves into the attack and just before they started firing, I gave the order: 'Break!' This should have resulted in the two flights of four turning inwards, crossing over, then going round to try and get behind the 190s. Unfortunately my radio, unknown to me, had been shot out by the flak over the aerodromes. The squadron went sailing on oblivious to the danger and I did my turn – alone – to meet about twenty 190s head-on!

I then had about five or six minutes' dog-fighting with them at deck level until they started to get spread out and shaken off, then I ducked down a valley, really low, right between some trees, past some farm houses, over a small river – flew up this river and shook the rest off.

I was now getting low on fuel, because it takes a lot of fuel dog-fighting at low level, but I set course back to Tangmere and landed there with the minimum amount of fuel left.

Wing Commander D.E. Gillam, OC 146 Wing

Wing Commander Charles Green, who had previously commanded 266 (Rhodesia) Squadron in Gillam's Duxford Wing, was now commanding a wing of his own – 121. On 14th February 1944 he led a long range sweep around Tours with two Typhoons each from 247 and 182 Squadrons, and eight from 174 Squadron, which proved a disaster.

They crossed the hostile coast at 8,000 feet, then dropped to 6,000, then finally on the deck as they approached Vendôme. After flying for one hour, five minutes, long range tanks were jettisoned, which was when the trouble began. Almost immediately, Flying Officer B.F. Proddow was in trouble when his engine failed and he had to force-land. The Typhoons flew on south of Tours, then on to Laval. Meantime, the Wing Commander himself was in trouble. Petrol was leaking from his overload tank cock and he could do nothing about it. He took his section out across the coast at 8,000 feet, leaving Squadron Leader W.W. McConnell DFC and bar, OC of 174 Squadron, and one section of 182, to continue the sweep towards Avranches before turning to come out of France east of Ste Mère-Eglise. As they reached the French coast, McConnell reported he was short of fuel and turned inland.

So problems with long range tanks had cost the wing two aircraft, two pilots – one a squadron commander – for no return, and nearly cost them a Wing Leader. McConnell was reported a prisoner in April.

*

More and more squadrons were converting from Hurricanes to Typhoons. Flight Lieutenant R.E.G. Sheward – known as 'Bentos' to some of his friends (he came from Argentina) – was in one such

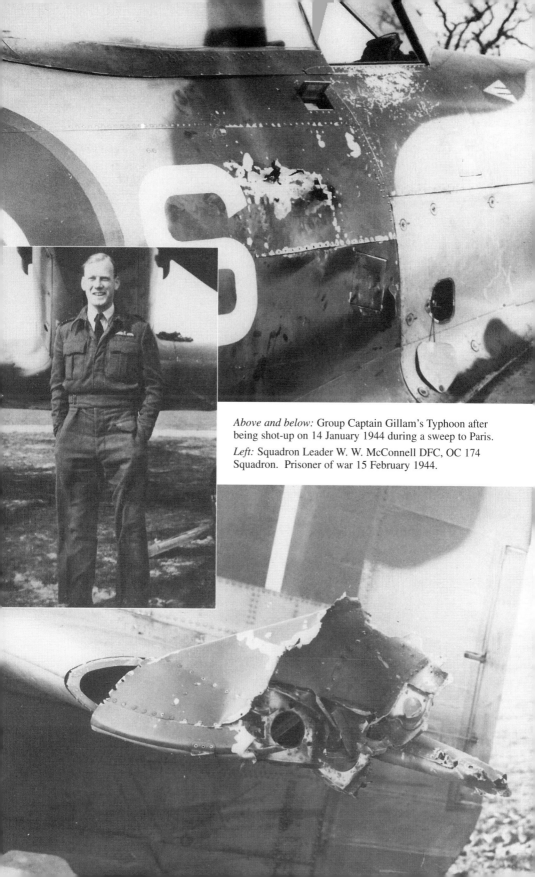

Above and below: Group Captain Gillam's Typhoon after being shot-up on 14 January 1944 during a sweep to Paris.

Left: Squadron Leader W. W. McConnell DFC, OC 174 Squadron. Prisoner of war 15 February 1944.

Hurricane squadron, and had been flying ops using rockets:

> By December 1943 I was with 164 Squadron at Fairlop and on the
> 23rd I was posted to 137 Squadron as Flight Commander A
> Flight. The Ramrods we did were dive-rocketing V1 sites in the
> Pas de Calais area. Before I left 164, I asked Squadron Leader
> D.M. 'Butch' Taylor DFC, if I could borrow one of his Typhoons
> and I got twenty minutes' flying as 'Experience on Type'.
>   We moved to Colerne in January 1944 and 137 Squadron
> converted to Typhoons. Going back to Lympne on 4th February
> and back on ops but this time as escort to the other poor sods in
> Hurricanes who were still Ramroding targets of V1 sites in
> France.
>
> *Flight Lieutenant R.E.G. Sheward, 137 Squadron*

No 263 Squadron began to receive Typhoons in December 1943 in
place of their twin-engined Whirlwinds. On Christmas Eve, Flying
Officer Funnell, while flying a practice dog-fight at 12,000 feet, went
into a spiral dive, then a spin to crash fatally. He managed to bale
out at 100 feet but was killed moments later.

Two days later, flying in overcast and poor visibility, Flight
Sergeant W.S. Handley and Flying Officer Mogg flew into low
cloud. Handley pulled up and was vectored back to base but Mogg
failed to get home. His body was later found, still in his cockpit,
having crashed into high ground near Melbray.

Although not an auspicious start, 263 later flew its first operation
in February 1944, flying long range sorties over Cherbourg and the
western approaches. Almost immediately they lost Flying Officer
Blacklong when he attacked shipping off Cap de la Hague at night (in
JR251). He radioed the signal 'Apples are Red', which meant he was
attacking a target. Nothing else was heard except an uncertain call,
'I am going into ...'

Things looked up on the 12th when the CO, Squadron Leader
G.B. Warnes DSO DFC (JR440), led a sortie which ran into a Dornier
217 near Gael. The bomber was at zero feet and Warnes chased it.
over tree tops until it pulled up, then Warnes got it. Six parachutes
came from the Dornier before it crashed and exploded. The
following day Warnes shot down a Me109F over Chartres airfield
during Rodeo 82, while Flight Lieutenant G.G. Racine destroyed
three 109s he found on the airfield. The flak, however, was intense.

Flight Sergeant G. Williams (JR215) was shot down, Pilot Officer W.E. Watkins (JR309) baled out, his parachute opening at 500 feet.

Long range tanks caused 263 Squadron serious problems on 22nd February during a planned sweep over Kerlin Bastard aerodrome. Finding 10/10ths cloud over the French coast, Warnes began a shipping recco instead, over the Channel Islands. Ten miles off the west coast of Guernsey, Warnes said he was ditching. Flight Lieutenant Racine and Flying Officer R.B. Tough saw him in the water apparently swimming towards a dinghy pack. Flying Officer Hunter (JR304) also failed to return and Racine also reported trouble with his petrol feed when changing tanks. He eventually got back, to force-land at Roborough.

At the end of March '44, Racine himself was reported missing, on Rodeo 108. The operation was mounted to catch long range Ju88 fighters off Vannes and Kerlin Bastard at last light. The Typhoons flew into the Ile de Groix from the sea at zero feet and began to search, but thick cloud began to hinder them. The cloud probably caused Racine mistakenly to lead the formation into the hottest flak area. The Typhoons evaded the gunfire but Racine was seen to turn back into the flak. Radar thought they saw his Typhoon struggle out to sea again but then his plot failed. Just over two weeks later, Gerry Racine was back. He had in fact been attacked by a Messerschmitt 410 but Racine had got on its tail and shot it down but then found his controls jammed and had to bale out. He evaded capture and eventually escaped to Spain, Gibraltar, then England.

Also at the beginning of 1944 the first Canadian wing was formed under the command of Wing Commander Frank Hillock, the Wing Leader being Wing Commander R.T.P. Davidson DFC, from Vancouver. The wing comprised 438, 439 and 440 RCAF Squadrons. They flew their first op on 20th March, when 438 Squadron strafed troops in the Cherbourg area.

During this early part of the year, 198 and 609 Squadrons continued to fly long range sweeps over both Holland and France, and continued to get among German aircraft and canal shipping.

Flight Lieutenant J. Niblett and Flying Officer B. Roper of 198 shot down a Ju188 near St Quentin early in January, while Johnny Baldwin led four Typhoons later the same day – 6th January – to the west of Paris. They shot up some Me110s and Me210s they found parked in a wood and then surprised a school of Bü131 training aircraft practising aerobatics south of the Eiffel Tower. Bluey Dall and Flight Lieutenant J. Scrambler (Canadian) shot down one, Dall damaging another, while Baldwin shot down a FW190 on the way home, and then shot up a train.

The two squadrons got another good result at about this time when they flew a sweep to Gilze-Rijen, 609 turning north to run into a batch of Dornier 217s. Flight Lieutenant Ian Davies DFC (JR379) spotted an aircraft flying low and when going for it saw others in the airfield's circuit. The first Dornier raced right across the airfield followed by Davies who ignored the defensive flak. He opened fire at 300 yards and the 217 crashed in the north-east corner of the airfield. Flying Officer W.F. Watts (JR312) flew right up the runway at 100 feet and met a Dornier coming the other way at 1,500 feet. Watts pulled up and fired, seeing hits on its tail before the bomber crashed. Squadron Leader Johnny Wells DFC (JR364) was about to attack this aircraft when Watts beat him to it. Another Dornier was attacked and chased by Manu Geerts (JR429) and Flight Sergeant L.W.F. 'Pinky' Stark (JP659). Stark caught a 40 mm shell in his jet tank but both pilots dropped their tanks to chase the German. Setting it on fire, four parachutes appeared before the 217 crashed south of the airfield. Charles Detal knocked down a fourth as three of its crew also parachuted to safety.

Meanwhile, Pilot Officer J.G. McLaughlin (JP792) dived down and destroyed two Do217s on the ground and strafed a Ju88C, as it taxied (being guided by a number of ground crewmen) and set it on fire. 609's only casualty was Flying Officer G.J.C. Daix (Belgian) (JR374) whose engine failed over the sea on the way home, being lost when he ditched.

While this was happening, 198 had flown south, found no Germans, so shot up some tugs and barges on their way out. Sergeant Fraser Petherbridge, however, had been forced to leave the main formation with a rough engine and he ran into a lone Dornier which flew right across in front of him, with wheels lowered preparatory to landing at a nearby airfield. Despite the uncertainty of his engine, Petherbridge went after the Dornier and shot it down in flames.

Mike Bryan visited his old squadron on 13th January and grabbed himself a place on a Ranger Op, led by Johnny Baldwin. The six Typhoons took advantage of the poor weather to sweep the airfields in the Montdidier, Juvincourt and Laon areas. In the circuit at Poix, Bryan shot down a Caudron Goland, Baldwin shooting down another. Shortly afterwards, light flak came up and hit Flying Officer Max Laman's Typhoon (JR435), the Australian failing to return.

The Typhoons evened the score when they then ran into two Me109Es near Rosiers. Flight Lieutenant Niblett shot down one, Mike Bryan and Flying Officer Freeman getting the second.

Meanwhile, four more Typhoons had set out on another Ranger led by Bluey Dall. They found a Ju88 which Dall shot down, then Flying Officer Macdonald destroyed another and Flying Officer Plamondon a third. A little later these three, together with Warrant Officer J. Allan (Canadian) shared the destruction of an Arado 96B which crash-landed and caught fire at St Cyr-en-Arthies, an island in the Seine. They then had to dog-fight their way out of trouble with five Me109s, but all came home safely.

These growing traditions of 198's excursions were continued on 24th January. 198 and 609 flew to RAF Coltishall at first light but a rendezvous with 3 Squadron failed. It had been planned to escort Beaufighters to the Frisians but it all failed and the weather beat them. However, Flying Officer W.G. Eagle – a veteran of the air fighting in the Western Desert in 1941 as an NCO pilot where he had scored at least four victories – ran into the enemy.

Having become separated from the others, he was hoping to rejoin when he saw twelve Me109s. By this time he was 30 miles north of Ameland, at zero feet. The 109s were at 300 feet and Bill Eagle could see they carried long range tanks. Being in a good position for a surprise attack, Eagle pulled his Typhoon up and went for the leading Messerschmitt, opening fire at 300 yards. Cannon strikes smashed into the 109's belly drop tank which exploded, enveloping the fighter in burning petrol. As the 109 plunged into the sea, Eagle blazed away at another 109 which began to leave a trail of smoke. It lurched to one side and collided with its neighbour and both crashed into the sea. Bill Eagle broke away and while one 109 tried to attack him, he saw the rest streaking away, black throttle smoke trailing behind them. For this action, Eagle was awarded the DFC.[1]

A good deal happened to 198 during February. On the 10th the veteran Warrant Officer Stanley called up to say he'd been hit by flak

[1] Eagle was killed in a Typhoon flying accident in May 1945 as a test pilot.

Top: Armourers of 182 Squadron 1944. Ken Figg is 3rd from right, back row. Flight Sergeant 'Chiefy' Russell is 5th from right, front row.

Bottom: Flying Officer W. G. Eagle DFC, 198 Squadron. He claimed three Me109s destroyed in a single-handed attack on 24 January 1944.

during an air sea rescue mission to investigate burning wreckage off Dungeness. He was later reported to be a prisoner, and commissioned pilot officer while in captivity.

Cheval Lallemant, whom Paul Richey had persuaded to fly again after his collision in 609 Squadron, was now a flight commander in 198: on 12th February he flew a Ranger sortie to Reims and chased Leo45 but lost it near Laon airfield. Lallemant led the Typhoons against the German base and two aircraft were destroyed on the ground. On the return flight he set fire to a barge, Flying Officer Harry Freeman shot down a Leo45 in flames into Arras town centre, while Pilot Officer Jimmy Allan damaged two barges nearby. Flight Lieutenant John Niblett, who had destroyed one of the aircraft on the airfield, later found yet another Leo45 which he forced to crash-land on fire near Doullens.

On the 26th, Lallemant and Flying Officer Hardy were scrambled towards Dunkirk where they found a Me110 at 1,000 feet, and shot it down in flames. In March the squadron began to attack RDF targets as a prelude to the invasion. These RDF towers could be raised or lowered at will and the squadron flew two-man recce sorties to find a tower in its standing position. On the 16th they found one.

Twelve Typhoons, led by Johnny Baldwin with his Red Section, armed with rockets flew out with Blue and Yellow Sections flying anti-flak. The formation crossed the enemy coast at 8,000 feet directly above the intended target, just like a normal penetration would have been flown. Just inside the coast the squadron wheeled round and Baldwin led his section down, spacing themselves out for attack. Meanwhile the anti-flak men dived down in twos to make shallow dives into the area, firing their cannons. Baldwin came in low and several rockets (R/Ps) hit the tower, then Warrant Officer Mason, Flight Lieutenant Niblett and Flight Lieutenant Plamondon, came in in turn. The tower, however, remained intact.

That afternoon they made a repeat attack despite increased flak which damaged several of the Typhoons; the tower was left broken and badly battered although still upright. Johnny Niblett received the DFC shortly afterwards, then following a short period when Mike Bryan returned after Baldwin left, Niblett took command of 198.

The attack on the RDF tower heralded a new phase in the Typhoon's air war – the build up to the invasion of France.

CHAPTER FIVE

Dive-Bombing, Rockets and Engines

As described in the previous chapters, the early attempts at using the Typhoon for bombing were from a low level approach. Casualties were high and results poor from this method and so tactics were changed to dive-bombing from a much higher level – 10-12,000 feet, releasing around 4-6,000 feet. Not that this was always so simple as Sergeant George Clubley discovered:

> I joined 181 Squadron in August 1943 and did my first op in September. Carrying bombs, we flew in echelon fours and we'd peel off more or less in line astern – about the same as we did with rockets later on – going down as steep as possible. (Though with rockets we started from a bit lower.) But our attacks depended very much on the defences.

George Clubley's very first operation was flown as No 2 to his CO, Squadron Leader Dennis Crowley-Milling DFC. On this attack, Clubley followed his leader down, pulled the bomb release, then climbed away, only to find both 500 lb bombs still under his wings. Back at base he had to circle to let the others land before he was allowed to come in. Armourers later had to take off bombs and racks in order to clear the problem.

Poppa Ambrose was still with 257 Squadron, and began using bombs in early 1944 against 'No Ball' targets – the V1 flying bomb sites:

> We flew dive-bombing ops from Warmwell but only when the No Ball targets came into existence. We didn't actually realise what they were. We used to go and bomb a position on a map and very

often we couldn't see what we were bombing. The bombing technique was hit or miss because although we used our gun-sight to judge where to drop the bombs there was nothing very scientific about it and usually it was a matter of luck whether you hit anything or not.

Another member of 257 Squadron was Brian Spragg, who joined it at Warmwell in September 1943. He had been trained in America – Florida, via Canada. When he was posted to 257 he wasn't even certain of what type of aeroplanes they were flying!

Pilot Officer B.J. Spragg, 257 Squadron
One was so much of a novice in those days you didn't even know what the squadrons were flying. Having arrived at Warmwell I saw these great monsters but I really came to like them and during my whole time, never fell out with the Typhoon at all. I arrived around September, then did a few weeks of general training with the squadron, then went onto operations.

We were bombers then, and our main task seemed to be against the flying bomb sites, which we didn't really know too much about; we merely went by the photographs as to what we were intended to attack. They were very well hidden and there was a good deal of defensive flak around. I suppose we really got into this dive-bombing stuff at about this time. Before that I think the squadron had been doing a few Rhubarbs, low level train hunting, looking for trouble, anything that was going. When we dive-bombed we would break upwards after release, never downwards.

I landed at Tangmere once with a bomb hung-up and it came off just as I touched down. It bounced down with me and just missed the tailplane. We used to try all sorts of things to shake them loose, even firing the cannons, but once they stuck they seemed to stick, but as soon as one 'lightly' touched down, off it would come!

Flight Lieutenant A.G. Todd, 164 Squadron
With bombing we liked to roll over and go down vertical style. You could get a fair old speed up, and one got quite good at it in the end.

Flight Lieutenant R.E.G. Sheward, 137 Squadron

On the early bomb ops, we found we couldn't get into a good vertical dive from just a turn and a wing over, hence the slight pull-up; then as the target passed by, you'd go over onto your back and drop down – then you could get vertical. The G-force when pulling out was terrific and pilots would often black-out but having set the controls to climb, when one regained consciousness, the Typhoon had climbed away out of trouble.

Sergeant A. Shannon, 257 Squadron

You just put the nose on the target and pulled through, and as you pulled through the target you pressed the bomb release – but you shuddered all the way down.

We did low level, delayed action bombing as well – 11 seconds' delay – when we bombed railway tunnels etc. Sometimes the bombs of the chaps in front of you would go up in your face and debris and all kinds of things would come up.

The men on the ground on bomb-carrying Typhoons had their own ways of doing things too. LAC Kenneth Figg had been an armourer with several squadrons at RAF Biggin Hill, including 133 Eagle Squadron and then the 307th American Pursuit Squadron. He then joined 182 Typhoon Squadron with whom he stayed until the end of the war:

When we lifted the bombs up we never used to winch them. We made a stretcher like cradle, put the bomb on it, then four of us used to lift it up. It was so slow winching – especially if we were taking rocket rails off and putting bomb racks on. As you lifted the bombs up it would automatically clip onto the hook on the side of the bomb. Then we had to get an electrician to connect the circuit, so it could take half the night if you used to winch.

There was then a wire that used to hook on under the wing, attached to a small propeller, which when broken on release of the bomb, enabled the propeller to turn and arm the detonator. There were different detonating times, 5 seconds, 10 seconds, 25 seconds, etc, and according to the required delay we would fit in a different detonator fuse, each with a different colour coding.

The bombs had two steadying arms front and back. If you pushed them down too hard, and of course we didn't have any

Top: 182 Squadron armourers at Eindhoven 27 November 1944. Front row (l to r): LACs Hal Swain, Ken Figg, Bryn Thomas; rear: -?-, LACs Tom Casby and Geoff Baker.

Bottom left: LAC D. C. Shepherd, 137 Squadron.

Bottom right: LAC D. N. Macdonald, Fitter IIA 121 Wing, 2nd TAF.

gauge to tell you what was too hard, it would act as a vice so that when the pilot pressed the release button it was so tight, they wouldn't release. Several times when bombs were brought back we found that was the cause – the electrics just weren't powerful enough to open them. Yet we had to clamp them tight or the pilot would complain that they moved about once in the air, and they didn't like that.

Long range fuel tanks too had a similar clip and of course, were fitted in the same positions as the bombs.

LAC K.F. Figg, 182 Squadron

Des Shepherd was an armourer with 137 Squadron and had worked on their Hurricanes and Whirlwinds before the unit re-equipped with Typhoons. As far as bombs went he recalls the bomb trollies:

Among the things I was responsible for were the bomb trollies. They could carry a large weight so they were always needing new tyres. They had hydraulic ramps because you had to lift the bombs. One had to put the bombs on the trolley then pump it up so it was well clear of the ground. These pumps always seemed to be going wrong – so it was quite a full-time job maintaining them.

LAC D.C. Shepherd, 137 Squadron

Jerry Eaton was another pilot who flew with 257 Squadron. He had previously been on Mustangs with 4 Squadron, flying low-level reconnaissance missions. When 4 Squadron's role was going to be changed from low level Tac/R to high level photographic sorties he requested a posting to Typhoons. However, his CO was against it; then one day on a visit to Tangmere, Eaton saw Wing Commander Gillam in the Mess. In conversation with him, he mentioned his desire to fly Typhoons but that his CO was unwilling to forward his request. Gillam said he should leave it to him, and shortly afterwards the posting came through. It was only later Eaton discovered that it was probably due to the high casualty rate on Typhoon squadrons that the posting was expedited!

Flying Officer S.J. Eaton, 257 Squadron
We had three marks on the gunsight. It was fairly accurate but at the same time fairly crude. These marks were intended to give the angle of dive – 60° or 30° I think, and you had to try and line this

Flying Officer S.J. Eaton, 257 Squadron (continued)

mark up when you went down. Sixty degrees felt like almost 90, though I don't think it was very often we did 60. The art came with practice – the same with firing rockets. You had the same set-up on the gunsight and by lining them up you could assess the angle at which you were diving.

When dive-bombing you formed your echelon port or starboard, depending which way you were going, and literally it was a question of peeling over – there was no other accurate way of doing it. It was no use just pushing the nose forward because the Typhoon had a very broad nose and you couldn't see down over it. Inexperienced pilots used to get lost on these sort of things because they hadn't yet learned to keep in line with their leader. Usually rather like a tail chase, one follows straight down and when ground flak starts and the Germans start aiming for the leader and under deflecting because of the angle of the dive etc, it was usually the pilot down the line that got in trouble. On a lot of trips, those who were Nos 3 or 4 of sections were hit more often. I soon found this out from experience of seeing what happened and I always weaved behind until the last moment possible and then straightened up, but never in a dead line with my leader – it was absolutely fatal. This was why it was invariably the newcomers to the squadron who were hit for they were not around long enough to learn to avoid this sort of fire. There were also the chaps who went down too low for example.

We always dropped both bombs, and indeed with the 500 and 1000 lb bombs there would be too much weight under just one wing to do otherwise. I only remember one occasion of a chap who lost a bomb on take-off, at Antwerp, and he struggled round the circuit and could barely keep the 'plane upright it was so heavy. He was ordered to jettison the bomb 'safe' on the airfield but of course it blew up. It just missed the runway but there was an enormous amount of shrapnel flying everywhere.

Flight Lieutenant C.D. North-Lewis, 175 Squadron

My dive-bombing experience was fairly limited but one used to go across at 12,000 feet, something like that, and get the target somewhere over on your left and just wheel over and point the nose down, go down and just aim the aeroplane, release the bombs and pull through. It was an entirely hit or miss affair; you didn't have any bomb sight at all.

One rarely saw any results and who knows how close we got? It was just a question of pointing the aircraft downwards and releasing the bombs when you thought that you were about the right distance down.

'Kit' North-Lewis had been a Blenheim pilot with 13 Squadron but then went onto Mustangs, flying Tac/R sorties with 26 and 231 Squadrons. He was operational from August 1942 till January 1944, winning the DFC. He initially joined 175 Squadron and was to rise rapidly from flight lieutenant to wing commander when he began flying Typhoons. North-Lewis continues:

I went to Typhoons at the end of January 1944 when I was a supernumerary flight lieutenant on 175 Squadron, but only for a month. I then went to 182 Squadron as a flight commander at Merston and then we moved to Hurn. Mike Ingle-Finch was the CO of 175, and Squadron Leader M.E. Read was the squadron commander of 182 Squadron. I was told I could have the next squadron which became vacant and when Jimmy Keep was shot down in May 1944, I took over 181 Squadron. I stayed in command until August when I took over 124 Wing as Wing Leader.

When I originally asked to go onto Typhoons, after the Mustang squadron I was due to take over disbanded, they jumped at it because they were short of pilots.

Another pilot who recalls the Typhoons as a dive-bomber is Jimmy Simpson, who joined 193 Squadron early in 1944:

For dive-bombing, the Tiffie really was quite a respectable animal. Once you had got the technique and were able to hold it in a very steep dive, it was pretty stable and all you had to do was put your gunsight onto the target and at the point of release you pulled through about 20° and then let go. We found bombing could be a bit inaccurate if you had any slip or skid on and it's not very easy to look at your turn and bank indicator and to look through the gunsight and be dead accurate in your flying.

I think it was Dave Ince who was with me towards the end in Holland, who devised a little spirit level thing, which we attached to the bottom of the gunsight. If I remember rightly he nicked these from a collection of aircraft spares which the Germans had left behind. It proved quite useful, because you could see the bubble and keep it absolutely dead central and at the same time look through the gunsight and do all the other things that you had to do, like flying, firing your cannon and pressing the bomb release. I don't think it was ever adopted as a modification but I know several aircraft of 193 Squadron had them installed, including mine.

Pilot Officer J.G. Simpson, 193 Squadron

✤

The new weapon was the rocket projectile, a weapon with which the Typhoon was to become famous and with which its name was to become synonymous.

Rockets had been fitted to the Hawker Hurricane when this aeroplane became redundant as a day fighter in Europe. The Hurricane, like its intended replacement – the Typhoon – was at first made into a fighter-bomber with bombs carried under each wing, and then equipped with rockets. However, the Typhoon was ideal to carry on the rocket saga and take it into history.

Air to ground rockets became formidable weapons in the hands of Typhoon pilots. The initial firing thrust was equal to a ton weight and attained its maximum speed of 1,580 feet per second in just $1\frac{1}{2}$ seconds, which was the length of its burn. A rocket with a 25 lb warhead travelled 500 yards in that time.

The SAP/HE 60 lb head, which contained fourteen pounds of TNT and with a delay fuse, could pass through the side of a merchant ship, travelling between five and fifteen feet before exploding. The 25 lb AP/SAP rocket, was solid, made of steel and used against tanks, trains, etc, and under optimum conditions they could penetrate four inches of armour.

Firing a pair of rockets, or a salvo of all eight, caused no recoil effect on the aeroplane and one advantage over a bomb was that its velocity on impact was far greater.

We went up to Eastchurch, where rocket-firing Hurricanes were going to give us a demonstration. They had been successful in the Middle East against tanks but had not seen a great deal of anti-aircraft opposition. So, their tactics were to attack at low level and they, of course, took great delight in coming just over us to release their rockets. If you've been anywhere near a rocket when it goes off it can be a bit hair-raising. We tried this out but with the Typhoon, up against ground fire, we were a sitting duck – it was just not on. So we tried diving and developed a technique of diving at 30°, and while experimenting, we were taken off ops for two weeks. Then the squadron flew an operation from Chichester. We sent six aircraft, led by Squadron Leader F.W.M. Jensen, and of them only three came back. The target was a power station at Caen and they were slaughtered, just shot out of the sky. In a 30° dive they were just too low – about 2,000 feet, and they clobbered them.

We altered it and started to dive at 60° and this was generally what we aimed for each time. It became very effective.

Sergeant G. Clubley, 181 Squadron

Squadron Leader Frank Jensen DFC AFC, was the CO of 181 Squadron and it fell to him to lead the first Typhoon rocket attack:

The operation on 25th October 1943 in which I was shot down (for the second time: the first was in a Hurricane in the Manston circuit by twelve Me109s) was indeed 181's, and the Typhoon's first use of R/P. It was to have been a curtain raiser, to attack the target in Caen. I took six Typhoons in two flights of three and there were supposed to be three escorting Typhoon Wings, to create bombing and other diversions. Because of my doubts (expressed at the briefing) about the viability of the line of attack – up a straight railway line to Caen – I had put the second flight a good way behind me. Sure enough, as my three aircraft climbed to R/P attacking height we met a barrage of flak, trained on the point where we were bound to appear. My No 2, Hugh Collins, and I were instantly shot down and crash-landed in fields. We were taken prisoner after various vicissitudes. My No 3, Paddy King, was, sadly, killed instantly. The second flight, seeing what had happened, diverted around the target and went safely back to Merston. Happily, I was able to pass a quick R/T message for my wife.

The tactics used for this operation were similar to those we had employed for dive bombing. Very low level across the sea to a point which would give us a quick climb to bombing height just before the target. Then a short, straight and level (if the flak allowed) to position the formation over the target, with a half-roll into the dive. When the bombs had gone we beat it back to base, preferably loosely formed-up, at low level, to avoid interception from above. In the Caen attack we did the low-high bit to be able to identify our run-in to the target, and then went down on the deck again. On the final run-in we were below the level of the railway cuttings and the flak was firing down at us. I imagine, too, that the signalmen were ringing up the line to say that we were coming![1]

Squadron Leader F.W.M. Jensen, OC 181 Squadron

Eventually the Typhoon leaders developed the right tactics and from then on the rocket-firing Typhoon squadrons became one of the most deadly weapons in the Allied armoury.

Not that all Typhoons went over to carrying rockets. Specific targets needed specific treatment. Some Typhoon squadrons remained as Bomphoons right to the end of the war while others used rockets only. Others would use bombs and rockets, much to the consternation of the ground crews who needed to change bomb racks for rocket rails at short notice. Bomb weights changed too; 250 lb, 500 lb, and finally two 1,000 lb bombs being carried.

We were able to carry rockets and switch over to bombs almost at a given moment, it was just a matter of putting bomb racks on instead of rocket rails. Then, of course, we changed to the 1,000 lb bombs later on which was quite a load for the Typhoon. I remember the stick being very very rubbery; you could move it from side to side on take-off and nothing would happen, there being so much weight at low speeds.

Unlike the Spitfire the best thing about the Typhoon from that point of view was that it was a very steady bomb carrier or even rocket firer. The Spitfire would tighten up at high speed, where the Typhoon would stay fairly well under control – fairly light in other words. I didn't fly the Spitfire until after the war and I did some rocket firing from it but on no account was it up to the standard of the Typhoon as a platform.

Flying Officer S.J. Eaton, 257 Squadron

[1] S/Ldr Jensen JP513, 'F' F/O E.H. Collins JP435, F/O W.R. King JP590. 'C'.

Des Shepherd, as an armourer, had to learn the new techniques of arming the Typhoon with rockets. He also recalls how the 20 mm cannons were sighted:

In the early days when there were experiments with rockets they fitted very heavy plates under the wings because it was burning the wings. So the plate that the rails were fitted to was very thick and was such a terrible weight for the aircraft that even when it had fired its rockets it was as though it were still carrying a full load. What they then did was to add something to the cordite to cut down the flame at the back of the rocket. They were then able to give us a very thin gauge plate which cut the weight down considerably.

The four cannons were all set to converge at a point directly in front of the aircraft at a set distance. This varied according to the pilot or even the target. The idea was to set the gunsight against boards we made and erected about 25 yards in front of the aircraft, with coloured discs, worked out mathematically to where the cannon shells would meet at, say 250 yards. Then we took the breech-block back and dropped in a sort of telescope which you'd look through. It had an angle mirror and you could see out along the gun barrel and then one armourer (one would work in pairs normally) would adjust the cannon after releasing the lock nut, then move the cannon, while the other man guided him to which way it should move, so as to pick up the view of the coloured disc on the board.

We would also set the gunsight so that the middle spot showed directly on the centre of the target. Then you had a line which measured the wing span of the aircraft one might shoot at. So if you were setting it all up for 250 yds for a wing span of a Focke Wulf or a Messerschmitt, you would then adjust that line. There was an adjusting point at the bottom of the sight which told you how many feet you set it at, then you'd make certain that it was set correctly against lines on the board.

Later when we had rockets fitted and they were using the same sight, we then had to get the rockets to converge at the distance they were going to strike. So again one would work out where the rockets would converge. As we were one of the first squadrons to have rockets we had to make our own sighting tube. We emptied a tube of cordite and welded a sort of ring and bead sight at either

LAC D.C. Shepherd, 137 Squadron (continued)
end. We then slid that onto each rail and looked through it until we had the sight on the target board, adjusted the rail as necessary, then moved onto the next rail. To speed up the operation we would usually work on two wings at once. The pilot, of course, had to know what his settings were.

Working on the mainplanes of the Typhoons was not easy. It was so high and so steep when the 'plane was sitting on the ground for working on the gun bays, which were covered by two big folding panels which were unscrewed and folded up. This gave you a big opening where the cannons and belt feed ammunition boxes were. But because it was so steep if you didn't have some support, you'd just be hanging on trying to stop yourself sliding off. So we had big wooden platforms made which were cut at the same angle as the wing, so that when you clipped that over the edge of the gun-bay (but in reverse) you were level.

When we were sliding the rockets onto the rails it was important that the two saddles at each end were square and rode well down the rail. When we put them on, we didn't only push the rocket down once, we slid it backwards and forwards a few times so that there would be no kind of stoppage when it was fired. We would clean the rails with a slightly oily rag but that was all that was necessary.

Everything got a slight oiling. All the cannons were cleaned with anti-freeze and this was most important, particularly when flying over the sea, which our squadron was doing continuously till after the Invasion; they were in sea spray all the time. In fact our bomb carriers we used to paint with what we called a Marine Blue, which put a thin film of protective coating over the carriers because they were having so many hang-ups in the early days. Salt water was playing havoc with the carrier mechanism itself.

LAC D.C. Shepherd, 137 Squadron

The rockets themselves had to be plugged into the aircraft's electrical circuit in order to be fired. This caused problems when loading and great care needed to be exercised by both the armourer, the fitter and the pilot.

LAC Figg, 182 Squadron
With the wiring of the rockets we used to have to plug an electric

bulb in first. They used to short circuit a lot so we had to carry a little thing with a bulb attached to test the circuit. If it didn't light up then you could plug the rocket in. This was just before take-off, so if it lit up the rocket stayed unplugged until the problem was sorted out. One of our armourers plugged one in without testing and the rocket blew back into his face. In the back of the rocket there was a bag of silaco jell which was like a crystallized soda which kept the damp out of the cordite. For months afterwards this armourer would scratch his face and pull a bit of this stuff out of his face, just like a splinter. His face did heal and didn't scar badly.

When the actual rocket was fired, the electric wires used to start it burning from just behind the head and work backwards. The cordite would burn right back to the fin. It was very 'Heath Robinson', just like a bit of gutter pipe really with a square metal set of fins. The fins went into slots as you tapped on them and then there was a tiny square cut out which you'd bang over with a screwdriver to secure in position. When the rockets fired, the wires stayed behind, snapped off by the departing rocket. When the aircraft came back they always had the loose bits of wire dangling down. Then we'd unscrew these bits and just throw them away. I think they were made of brass too – it must have cost the RAF a fortune in brass!

I have known aircraft come back with rockets not fired, and were very gingerly looked at in case the cordite was burning. Sometimes, not often, you might have got the plug pulled out. It was a two-pin plug, secured by tightening a small threaded fixing ring. Sometimes it might be a bit cross-threaded in the hurry to get a pilot away, or perhaps the thread was a bit loose.

Flying Officer H. Ambrose, 257 Squadron
The technicalities come to mind more readily, about the Typhoons and how the first rockets just dribbled off the end and didn't go anywhere. In fact in my garden one day – long after the war – was a German who came up to do some rotovating for me. We got talking and he had been in the German Navy and Typhoons had attacked his E-Boat at St Malo with rockets and he said they hadn't worked properly, just dribbled off the end. I recalled a similar incident so we checked with my log-book with

Flying Officer H. Ambrose, 257 Squadron (continued)

his diary to find I actually fired cannons at this guy that day, and here he was now, rotovating my garden. He became a POW when captured from the Channel Islands and later married an English girl.

With rockets you had two selections you could make and only two – you had pairs or salvo. If you fired pairs you did your own rippling by pressing the button four times, each time releasing a pair. There was no automatic rippling, you fired two, then two, then two, then two – which is sensible because you may only need two on a target and go on a few miles before you fired another pair. If it was a formidable target which they wanted knocked out or if you only had time to make one attack, you'd elect to fire a salvo. Some problems used to arise when instructions would come down to attack a certain target and the 'erks', say, in the middle of a terrible winter's night, would put on long range tanks and then suddenly it would all change and they'd be told to take off the tanks and put on bombs. Then no sooner had they taken the tanks off and put bombs on, then some idiot would decide to change that and they'd have to put on tanks again or perhaps rockets. This was the sort of thing that used to drive the poor bloody groundcrew mental. They were supposed to be sleeping but in fact were working all night, obeying altered instructions because people were picking different targets.

Rocket firing became quite an art if you were good and 181 Squadron were good (Ambrose commanded 181 in 1945). Those of us who had fired a number of rockets were quite good really, but at first, rocket fire was very haphazard. It was almost criminal the way it was tackled by the RAF. The training, the practice, was non-existent. I'd never fired a rocket until I went to Bognor, fired some rockets into the Channel twice and then I was back on ops. As you can imagine I wasn't very effective for the first few trips. I was all right with the cannon but rocket firing was a bit of a laugh. Some of the rocket fire was criminal and the people going to France didn't know what was going on.

Flying Officer H.G. 'Pat' Pattison joined 182 Squadron just a month before the invasion of Normandy.

There was a switch in the cockpit labelled 'Pairs' and 'Salvo'. You selected whichever you required and pressed the 'tit' on the throttle lever, once for the whole lot to go or four times to fire the eight rockets two at a time. Our normal attack was from 8,500 feet and in either a 45 or 60 degree dive, with everything shoved forward and during the latter part of the dive you opened up with cannon if there was any ground fire, to keep the ground gunner's heads down. We had the old GM2 gunsight, which was a fixed ring gunsight and we had to make certain settings on that for R/P. We used the centre dot, aiming high to allow for the drop in the trajectory, with the cannon initially, and then towards the end of the dive you took up your aim with the bottom leg of the cross and used that when you were within range of the R/P.

During the firing sequence you obviously had to hold the aircraft fairly steady but then we were getting so low and in fact the pull-out was very close to the ground, most of the time below 500 feet – and if you hit the target absolutely right on, say an ammunition dump, or an oil tank, which would explode, you had to break pretty sharply to avoid both the debris from the rockets and also from whatever was flung up from the explosion.

Normally we only carried eight rockets but a double-tier was developed which housed 16 rockets which again could be selected and fired in salvo or pairs.

Flying Officer H.G. Pattison, 182 Squadron

Incidentally, LAC Ken Figg was later Pattison's armourer in France, and when Ken saw Pat mentioned in my book *The Battle of the Airfields* I was able to put them in touch with each other for the first time since the war.

Squadron Leader G.J. 'Gerry' Gray DFC was Pat's CO from August 1944. He had been on Defiants and Hurricanes since the end of 1940 and had flown night patrols and night intruder ops on both types. His experience of fighter ops stood him in good stead when he began flying Typhoons just about D-Day, though he didn't become operational until July 1944:

Squadron Leader G.J. Gray, OC 182 Squadron
Sixteen rockets were not too successful. The second eight rode in

Top: Squadron Leader G. J. Gray DFC, OC 182 Squadron, 1944-45.

Above: F/O Pat Pattison (182 Squadron) fired his rockets at German MT at Or-Bois on the evening of 25 July 1944. A salvo from a previous Typhoon is going down top left.

Right: Flight Lieutenant S. J. Eaton DFC, 257 Squadron.

tandem under the first, and tended to wobble about a bit when fired and were not that accurate. You could mix the types of warhead, so that a pair could be a fragmentation type and another an armour-piercing. When we fired a salvo it was reckoned to be the equivalent of a cruiser's broadside, which was quite fantastic.

LAC D.C. Shepherd, 137 Squadron

We found in the early days that when the rockets were slid along the rails they had to be stopped from sliding off. You can imagine that without a restraint, when the aircraft took off and started to do a nose-dive, they could easily slide forward. So we had a copper shearing pin which was put into the rail. This would shear when the rocket was fired. Also the early plugs which were left dangling from each wing would wrap themselves round the aileron so later the plugs would pull out and fall away.

The final plug in before take-off was the very last thing we did. Officially it was to be done when the aircraft got onto the end of the runway so that there was no chance of the pilot firing them accidentally while he was taxiing out, but when hundreds of Typhoons were taking off on a wing show, or when we were having to turn them round fast in the beach-head in France, we were not so careful as that. That meant the pilot could be quickly away and not wait for us to plug them in before he could take off.

The rockets were quite heavy, especially the 60 lb head on one end of it. We had to try and balance it as you carried it and it was a two-man, sometimes a three-man, job to put each rocket on. Being a fitter-armourer I didn't often do that, I had the problems when they couldn't get them on. There were two types of rocket head, the semi-armour piercing, non explosive head which would just put a hole in anything. The other was the types with explosives inside. Once they entered, depending on the fuse, they would explode inside. When attacking tanks the heads would have a slight delay as it was better for the rocket to explode inside the tank than for it to go right through it. You needed the explosion to 'brew' it up.

Flight Lieutenant A.G. Todd, 164 Squadron

When one taxied around the track or whatever, the actual plugs to the rockets were not put in. There would be an armourer at the end of the runway who, when you put your hands up to show you weren't doing anything, plugged them in. It happened once when we were at Hurn, somebody did it wrong and these things were going swish across the aerodrome! It was a good angle, as the aircraft was sitting on the ground!

Squadron Leader L.H. Lambert, OC 168 Squadron
The rockets themselves were armed and you had a switch which you were supposed to depress after you had reached the battle zone and not before. This pilot or the armourer had left it on. As he turned onto the runway he must have pressed the firing button on the throttle, which was easily done. Eight rockets immediately went 'whoosh' and hit the corner of a hangar, which was full of people and aeroplanes etc.

*

In the early days of the Typhoons, as we have seen already, the engines were one of the main concerns of both air and ground personnel. Ask any former Typhoon man about the aeroplane in general and he is bound to mention the engine. The main difference in the starting procedure of the Typhoon as compared with, say, the Spitfire or Hurricane, which was started with the aid of a Trolley Acc, was that it was self-starting, the pilot using the Coffman starter.

Flying Officer H.G. Pattison, 182 Squadron
Starting sequence for the engine. You had to use the throttle lever, also a special little lever adjacent to it for setting the position of the throttle in the quadrant. Having selected fuel-on, then you would prime the carburetter with one of the two priming pumps to raise the fuel pressure to between five and six pounds PSI and then according to the temperature of the engine you would prime the cylinder a given number of strokes. In very cold weather when it was literally freezing, there was a special high volatile priming tank which the ground crew could operate, in one of the wheel bays. This put an especially volatile mixture into the cylinders which helped start the engine. For normal

Flying Officer H.G. Pattison, 182 Squadron (continued)

purposes, somewhere between two and eight strokes on the cylinder priming pump were necessary. If the engine was warm or hot, obviously you would use less strokes on the primer – it was a fairly healthy sized pump. If it hadn't been used that day then you would probably need six to eight strokes to prime it.

Having primed you would put the ignition switches on and having set the throttle in the quadrant with the assistance of the start and cut-out lever, you would press the booster coil button and the Coffman starter button to fire the cartridge. (Both buttons were next to each other just to the left, on the forward instrument panel board.) All being well and you'd got the number of primes right, the engine fired and caught first time. However, being a sleeve valve engine which was tremendously critical on lubrication, if you over-primed or it failed to start after two cartridges, the engine had to be blown out by turning the propeller backwards to clear excess fuel from the cylinders. You weren't allowed to fire more than five cartridges, because if you did then the engine had to be stripped and the cylinders primed with oil because of the lack of lubrication and the fact that any oil that had been there had been washed away with the priming. So two cartridges basically were all you were allowed; if you used more then you were in trouble. Once you got to know your aircraft you could set the throttle without using the throttle setting control and knowing the engine and its particular vagaries, the number of primes was just right and it fired first time.

Occasionally the safety disc in the starter, if the engine didn't turn over for some reason or other and the disc blew out, then that had to be replaced which was a fairly lengthy procedure but we found that the disc, which was either copper or steel, was the size of a sixpence which was much harder and much more difficult to blow out, so there were a number of them replaced with sixpenny pieces.

If one over-primed, it might cause a fire in the carburetter and although in the early aircraft the air intake was quite open, because of the fact that they could be subject to intake fires, they put little flap doors on the front. Therefore if a fire occurred the flame would shoot out, opening the doors and then the doors would close and stop any air getting in to help combustion. Of course, every start you had one of the ground crew standing by with a fire extinguisher against that eventuality.

Squadron Leader G.J. Gray, OC 182 Squadron
Starting up the engine by Coffman starter was an absolute trick. It was quite a technique especially on cold starts first thing in the morning. Each Typhoon was different. You'd set the throttle, press the tits for two seconds – then bang, and you'd try to catch it. One got quite good at it in the end.

Flight Lieutenant A.G. Todd, 164 Squadron
In the awful winter at the end of the war if they hadn't had their big covers put on etc, they would not start. Then you had to get this hot air unit to warm them up. I remember once we landed at another airfield after a show and eventually we had to stay the night there. In the morning not one of our Typhoons would start and it took them all the morning to get them going. But flat out the engine worked a treat.

Pilot Officer B.J. Spragg, 257 Squadron
The other thing they had happen was the blower drive used to shear on occasion. They also had a big four-barrel carburetter which if it did go wrong was the devil to cure. I had one aeroplane which I could fly across the airfield and she'd be back-firing all the way and they never did seem to cure it. I think a lot of the older hands used to always hand-turn their props for quite a bit before they tried to start them, and we got to know exactly how much to prime before starting, but lots of pilots just couldn't.

When Flight Lieutenant Vaughan Fittall ended his tour of ops with 198 Squadron in December 1943, he was posted to Napiers at Luton as a test pilot. A few months later Flight Lieutenant A.G. Todd also went to Napiers from 164 Squadron:

I didn't go to France with 164. We were losing so many people they said I had better go away for a rest, but went to Napiers! This was quite interesting really. We had a Typhoon which had been given an engine with a 12 lb boost rather than the normal 7 lb, and we had regularly to fly this to see how long it would last. It lasted about 100 hours. There was no radio in it, they had taken it out. It had a cine-camera in the back with a duplicate set of instruments and we often simulated chasing a flying bomb and took pictures of the instruments. In fact, until the thing blew up – 18th September 1944 – it flew very well indeed.

We had long range tanks on it and if one ran out, as I did on one of the tanks, you'd get an airlock and it wouldn't pick up again. I thought I was going to get into the airfield with the wheels down at one stage, but I thought then that I was going to hit the hedge, so pulled them up again before belly landing in. Napiers were not over pleased about that at all.

Flight Lieutenant A.G. Todd, Napier test pilot

Flight Lieutenant Robert 'Bluey' Dall also arrived at Napiers from 198 squadron in 1944, when his tour with 198 came to an end. He too had been awarded the DFC:

Flight Lieutenant V.C. Fittall, Test Pilot, Napiers

Bluey Dall seemed to follow me around. Like me he was a foundation member of 486 although he actually was an Australian but living in NZ and married a NZ girl so joined the RNZAF when the war started. He took over B Flight of 198 from me, followed me to Luton when his rest period came round and was later repatriated back to NZ. He applied to return to UK and was killed on the Continent. Others who passed through Luton during my time there were Gus Davies, 'Digger' Cotes-Preedy who later commanded 3 Squadron, 'Barney' Wright, a South African, Cheval Lallemant, James Dykes, Jim McCaw DFC, also ex-486 Squadron, and Squadron Leader Phillips who later fractured his spine in a Tempest crash.

Mike Bryan wrote while I was at Luton saying that he had a squadron lined up for me when my rest period was over, but by this time Napiers had already been on to Air Ministry to retain my services in connection with some long running engine tests I was doing where apparently I was a little more conscientious than some of the boys in accurate flying and note-taking. So I ended up staying at Luton for twelve months instead of the usual six weeks or three months. Napiers later realised that they had prevented my promotion to squadron leader (but probably saved my life!) and endeavoured to persuade AM to put this right, but

Top: Test pilots at Napiers, Luton. Operational pilots 'on rest'! F/Lts Vaughan Fittall DFC, A. G. Todd and Robert 'Bluey' Dall DFC.

Bottom: Arthur Todd's wheels-up landing at Luton in R8803, September 1944.

Flight Lieutenant V.C. Fittall, Test Pilot, Napiers (continued)

without success. They gave me the title of Assistant Chief Test pilot to E.W. Bonar, which sounded good but didn't mean much.

'Jock' Bonar had been flying since God was a boy and used to tell us how in barn-storming and joy-riding days they became expert in increasing the throughput of paying passengers. Jock of course was a civilian but so that he could land at RAF bases and compare notes with Typhoon pilots about the Sabre engines, he was made an honorary pilot officer. This would arouse puzzlement and amusement when this grey-headed pilot with the George Cross showed up in a Mess in a PO's uniform. I recall an American pilot once saying to me that he knew the British were conservative but this was too much!

In my time at Luton Jock did not do any routine flying if he could help it, but when we could get him into the mood to put on a show, his low flying aerobatics had to be seen to be believed. I saw him one day dive vertically after a loop – and the Typhoon dropped like a ton of bricks in that attitude – disappear behind the hills on the other side of Luton and while we were waiting for the crash and smoke cloud, he came at us from behind the ground level to barrel roll away. When he landed I suggested he was sticking his neck out a bit but he said, 'Son, I used to be paid to make it look dangerous!'

Norman Wilson, before he became Technical Adjutant at Holmesley South, recalls a story at Milfield:

I remember Batchy Atcherley came to visit us in his own personal aeroplane, while he was AOC 9 Group. He had an American aeroplane and I think there were only about three examples in England, and no spares, except for some he kept in his locker at home base.

At the end of his visit he trundled up to the flight control van, ready to get on the runway but there were some people coming in, and a very sprog Typhoon pilot who was taxiing up behind him. Like many aircraft, the Typhoon was tilted back when on the ground and the pilot would find it difficult to see forward while on the ground, so would zig-zag from side to side to see forward. This pilot must have zigged when he should have zagged, because he just climbed up the back of the AOC's little 'plane, its huge propeller chewing its way up the fuselage towards the AOC's cockpit. Those that saw it said they have never seen an Air Vice-Marshal move so quickly! Then he stood and described the sprog pilot's ancestry, his dubious parentage, etc, in the most wonderful flow of language which didn't stop for a good ten minutes, after which the poor chap was in the guardhouse without his feet touching the ground! It was the end of the AOC's aeroplane; I sent the signal which wrote off the machine officially.

Towards the end of the war, Flight Lieutenant Tom Hall, who had completed a tour with 175 Squadron, was sent to 83 Group Support Unit, which had moved from Redhill, where Pat Pattison had been, to RAF Dunsfold:

My job here was to give operational training to pilots awaiting allocation to squadrons on the Continent and to ferry them in new replacement aircraft as soon as enough aircraft numbers had built up. Pilots would be given about seven hours' operational training and I would lead six or seven to locations in Europe. An Anson would pick me up for the return trip.

Some of the ferry trips were flown in dicey weather and I was never happy in flying through the southern gap into the Channel with cloud on all the Downs at a very low ceiling. I recall one trip when weather was bad in England but better over the Continent. We flew out over the Channel but found cloud over the French coast. Using another radio channel so my pilots could not hear me I asked our intended base – B100 at Goch, Germany, for a course. Changing back to the other channel I told the boys that we were on course and that we would soon go down into the overcast, got them to spread out, warned them to set their gyro compasses, then down we went. We broke cloud at about 900 feet and straight ahead of us was the 'drome. After landing the boys thought that my navigation was superb! I took it in my stride, with fingers of both hands crossed, and never did mention that my own course was about five degrees out, and that I'd been given an ETA based on our airspeed, and told exactly when to begin our descent!

CHAPTER SIX

Build-up to Invasion

The Allied air forces had a number of major tasks set them prior to the invasion of France in June 1944. Softening up the German coastal defences, keeping the Luftwaffe from seeing and endangering the Allied build-up in southern England, attacking the German transport system, were just some of them.

An added problem was the V1 flying bomb sites that were springing up in France, especially in the Calais area. Although few of the pilots knew what they were attacking (the bombs themselves did not begin to be launched against England until June) they knew it was important for them to be destroyed.

Pilot Officer J.G. Simpson, joined 198 Squadron in time to fly against these difficult and often dangerous targets – they were well-protected by flak positions. Jimmy Simpson also records a good description of his first flight in a Typhoon:

> I had spent two years prior to 1944 at the RAF College Cranwell as a flying instructor, so that I arrived at an OTU to learn to fly Hurricanes with over 1,000 hours under my belt; then they first let me loose on a Tiffie. According to my log-book that was 8th March 1944 and what I recall of the occasion is that I was given considerable verbal instruction on how to start the thing, how to get into it, because the one I first flew had something like a greenhouse on the top and not the usual sliding hood we later had. Then there was the problem of trying to start the thing without its catching fire; the snag of not exhausting your supply of starting cartridges, of which there were only five, to get the prop to turn.
>
> By this time I was reasonably experienced on single-seaters, having over 50 hours on Hurricanes and a bit on Spitfires. The real problem was the size of the propeller, and the torque

resulting from opening the throttle, and the fact that she swung like hell to the right as you charged down the runway. As I remember this first flight on this beast of a thing, I got airborne about half way down the runway, with my left leg fully extended, and still took off over the flight dispersal at about 30° off straight! However, after a few hours it seemed quite normal and once you had mastered the problem of not opening the throttle too quickly, it was quite easy to fly and very stable. In fact as an aircraft to go to war in, it was a magnificent gun platform.

I joined 193 early in April and had my first flight with them on the 18th. They were based on a strip just near the Solent at a place called Needs Oak Point, just south of Beaulieu and in fact in nearly every case we took off from the airfield straight over the Solent, about 3-400 yards from the end of the runway. This proximity to the water did in fact present one or two problems as we neared D-Day, because all those damn boats had their balloons flying!

Pilot Officer J.G. Simpson, 193 Squadron

Sergeant A. Shannon, 257 Squadron

I remember the Typhoon as being a hairy machine and the wind was put up you long before you ever met it. People said it had a vicious swing and the engine was quite a huge thing, frightened the life out of me when I just got in and opened the throttle. I felt, after the take-off which didn't disturb me too much, that I was up to 15,000 feet before I knew it – before I started to think! It was frightening and I rather think it flew me rather than I flew it, for a while.

I didn't fly the Typhoon at OTU, not until I was with the squadron which was just a landing strip on metal tracking. I remember taking off over the Solent and didn't remember much about it at all. I managed to get down quite safely. From then on, apart from one or two prangs – OK. I did a rocket course at Fairwood Common but only fired a few at sea targets.

Flight Sergeant R.W. Pottinger, 3 Squadron

We then began two or three trips a day, each perhaps about 35 minutes, going for the V1 sites. We would take off from Manston, fly down the coast, cross out somewhere about Eastbourne, cross over, climbing all the time, do our dive-bombing and come back across the Channel still in a screeching dive, then back to Manston.

Pilot Officer B.J. Spragg, 257 Squadron

Against these No Ball targets we used to fly out at sea level, climb about 10-15 miles off the French coast to about 8,000 feet and go in. It was just about the right height to get all the heavy flak that was going! On 6th April we flew a long range shipping strike. We went off in the dark – it was absolutely black. We were carrying 500 lb bombs under one wing and a long range tank under the other. All we did was fly until we hit the French coast then just followed it just out to sea, for as long as you could without running out of fuel. I don't think we saw anything – it was difficult trying to fly at sea level, in the dark, in a finger-four formation. Very difficult.

One of the nastiest trips I recall doing before D-Day was against some German ships in St Malo Harbour on 29th April. We went down to Harrowbeer to operate from. St Malo was a big harbour, three-sided and fairly well defended; a lot of flak there. We had to go back afterwards to complete the job. There was a destroyer in there, a merchant vessel and a tanker. The only thing in the air I got involved with was when a half a dozen of us were on a low level sweep that same morning, before we went down to Harrowbeer. We only identified it when we got back to base as a Leo45. Three of us got it, Dave Ross and Jock Porteous of 198 Squadron and I claimed a share too. I felt a bit sorry for it afterwards because it really did flame. It was fairly low down on the deck when we saw it and we were right on the deck – just saw it on the skyline. Then there was a rush for it.

LAC Donald Macdonald was a Fitter II and immediately prior to joining 2nd TAF had been working on Mosquitos.

My first impression of Typhoons was how ugly and menacing they looked by comparison. I was allotted to a Repair and Salvage unit at Headcorn near Ashford and became part of a team comprising one sergeant, one corporal, one fitter IIE, one fitter IIA and one ACH (aircrafthand). We had a three ton truck with tools, tent, cooking utensils, rations etc. The object of the exercise was, when one of our kites crashed, provided it was not too badly damaged, we were despatched to pick it up. We would pitch our tent near the crash, usually near an airfield, and once organised, set to work dismantling, ready for transport back to the unit. When all was prepared we sent for a low loader (Queen Mary) and mobile crane.

There was snow on the ground when we moved to Headcorn so went into winter quarters at Biggin Hill, and while there we were doing minor and major repairs and inspections. The inspections took place after a Typhoon had done 30 hours flying time. 30 and 60 hours were minor and 90 hours were major inspections.

When the weather improved in the spring we were posted to Ford where we camped on the other side of the airfield from the main camp (I had been there in 1942 working on Boston Intruders). We seemed to be just ticking over, I suppose waiting for the second front to open.

LAC D.N. Macdonald, R & S Unit

*

As direct support for the coming invasion, one of the Typhoon's other main tasks was to knock out German radar. It was imperative to blind the Germans prior to D-Day but to do it in such a way so as not to give any indication of the likely landing places. Thus radar sites from Ostende to Cherbourg and the Channel Islands were all fair game. Some radar sites of course had to be 'missed' and kept open, especially in the Pas de Calais. The Germans always believed the Allies would land here and of course, it was important to keep them thinking that. The Lancaster bombers of 617 Squadron would fly a special low level op over the Channel off this area so that German radar would pick up a possible 'invasion' fleet. This would help the Germans to think the landings in Normandy were only a diversion.

Group Captain D.E. Gillam, OC 146 Wing
As we came towards D-Day the Typhoons were used almost exclusively for taking out radar establishments and covering the whole coast, with the exception of the one on Gris Nez, which was left particularly for them to pick up a dummy raid. I think we got about 90% of the installations out of action before the invasion started and that was almost entirely due to the Typhoons. Very

expensive casualty rate – very, very high. We took a couple of months working on this, often going back to the same place two or three times; if and when the radar station came on the air again, it was treated again.

Flying Officer S.J. Eaton, 257 Squadron

We did quite a few ops against radar sites on the coast before D-Day but I don't think we lost anybody. I didn't like the targets because it was just like firing at cob-webs – bullets seemed to go straight through the radar screen and didn't seem to have any effect.

Pilot Officer B.J. Spragg, 257 Squadron

Our role changed a little bit during the pre-invasion period to knocking out coastal radar in the Fécamp area and all down that coast. The plan was always to go into one side or other of the target, well to one side. We used to go in in line astern (in fact that was one of the tactics), turn a right angle, so we were all coming down pretty well together to hit the radar in a bit of an echelon and then go straight out to sea.

Squadron Leader C.D. North-Lewis, OC 181 Squadron

We did an R/P attack on a radar station at Auderville, and a cannon attack on the site at Vaudricourt, both on 22nd May. A cannon attack on the radar at Maupertus on the 23rd, a cannon attack on the station at St Peter Port Guernsey on the 27th, an R/P attack on the radar station at Fort St George, Guernsey, on 2nd June and another R/P attack on the site at Caen on the 3rd. We suffered pretty heavy casualties all the time from flak, but virtually didn't lose anything from German aircraft. In fact I personally – and I did quite a lot of sorties – don't remember ever being engaged by a German aircraft.

I remember Guernsey – it was very exciting – because it was fine sunny weather then and we attacked the radar site just by St Peter Port and then went out low level through the harbour. The Germans had flak positions on all the little outlying islands round there and everyone was blasting away full bore.

The Canadian Wing lost its Wingco Flying, Robert Davidson, on 8th May. He led them on a dive bombing mission against the rail yards at Douai. On the return flight Davidson's engine cut out and he had to make a forced landing. Over the R/T he called, 'Tell my wife I'm A.1. Have to go now. Ta Ta!' Luckily Davidson managed to evade capture, joined up with the French Resistance with whom he fought for the next few months, finally returning to England in September. He brought with him 4,000 Francs, having taught the Frenchmen how to play poker! The wing was taken over by Wing Commander M.T. Judd DFC AFC RAF.

Another pilot involved in radar attacks was Arthur Todd. He, like so many other Typhoon pilots, had considerable experience before flying these aircraft: Hurricanes with 245 Squadron, then to the Middle East on HMS *Furious*, 261 Squadron on Malta followed by ferrying Tomahawks. He then went to Freetown with a Hurricane flight where he shot down a Vichy French Maryland on one occasion. Back in England he was an instructor at the OTU at Milfield where he first flew Typhoons:

At Milfield we lost a lot of people on the original Typhoons. They had sleeve wear on the engines and the gearing underneath was so designed that if the wheel that drove the fuel pump was faulty and if anything sheared, it was all stop through lack of fuel. We had quite a few of these; in fact so many that we had a flight lieutenant in charge of funerals.

Then I went to 56 Squadron at Duxford in October 1943, which was let to an American Thunderbolt Wing and we were just a defence flight really. The CO was G.L. Sinclair DFC who I believe was a relation of the Air Minister Sir Archibald Sinclair. Then I went as a flight commander to 164 which was back to Hurricane IVs with eight rockets, and then finally we were re-equipped with Typhoons at Fairlop.

We were quite busy as the invasion was coming up, though of course, we didn't know exactly when it would be. We switched from targets in France etc, to knocking out the radar. They were very difficult to knock out being well protected. It became much safer when we got over the other side after the invasion.

Flight Lieutenant A.G. Todd, 164 Squadron

Toddy's squadron was commanded by Squadron Leader H.A.B. Russell, who had been badly wounded in the Battle of Britain. They flew their first Typhoon op in March 1944 and attacked several radar sites in May.

Todd got into some action on 18th May with the elusive Luftwaffe. Five Typhoons of 164 flew into France – one had aborted with engine trouble – and flew towards Beauvais on the deck. Near Pontoise they saw two Me109Fs at '9 o'clock'. A dog-fight began north of Paris and Toddy and his No 2, Flight Sergeant Les Plows were split up. Todd followed one Messerschmitt as it climbed away and Wing Commander Mike Bryan fired at it from below. Todd then let the 109 fly through his sights as he opened fire. He fired again from 50 yards and as he broke away saw it upside down, diving steeply. Les Plows also fired into the 109, and saw it go down inverted, then hit the ground. Mike Bryan fired at the second 109 and Plows saw it explode.

Toddy remembers:

> I remember that fight around Paris with those two 109s. It was a head-on attack and I could see those cannons winking at me. I broke and spun it about 800 feet and was quite lucky to get out of that. I remember Wing Commander Bryan was hit; we hadn't fired any rockets yet and after the fight one of his rockets was just hanging down all the way back to base.

The next day Russell received the DFC for his recent leadership of the squadron. Five days later he led his squadron against a radar 'chimney' near Boulogne. This type of radar position looked just like a tall factory chimney but from each side of it, and running the whole length of the chimney was the radar grid antenna (as opposed to the more usual circular discs). The Typhoons rocketed the site and provided their own flak suppression. One direct hit and two possible hits were scored and one salvo hit the aerial grid. The success of the attack was due in part to one of the squadron pilots, Flying Officer Peter West, 27. West drew the enemy fire from the flak batteries by attacking them with his cannon having jettisoned his rockets. His Typhoon was hit, however, and he was badly wounded in the left arm, side and leg which became useless. He managed to re-cross the Channel despite his injuries and heavy blood loss, and to force-land near Newchurch. As he said afterwards from his hospital bed, '... by all the rules I should have lost consciousness before I saw land. I pulled on the throttle with my good hand, kicked the flaps down with my right leg and made a landing without

Top: 164 Squadron at Llanbedr just before the invasion. Front row: 3rd from left F/L A. G. Todd; 5th, S/L H. A. B. Russell (PoW 28/5/44); 6th W/Cdr Billy Drake DSO DFC; 7th, F/O P. G. West (who won an immediate DSO 24 May 1944); 8th, F/Sgt G. T. Fowell (KIA 6 July 1944); F/Sgt R. J. M. Wilson.

Bottom: Squadron Leader P. H. Beake DFC, OC 164 Squadron May-August 1944.

the stick.' Then he passed out, West received an Immediate DSO for this exploit – a fairly rare occurrence for a Typhoon pilot despite the hazards they all flew almost daily.

The Canadians lost Flying Officer A.A. Watkins on 22nd May when attacking radar sites between Cap de la Hague and Cap d'Antifer. He managed to bale out five miles off the French coast only to spend the next five and a half days in his dinghy before being rescued by ASR Walrus.

No 164 Squadron attacked another radar site near Fruges on the morning of the 28th, two rocket salvos hitting this Freya position. Squadron Leader Humphrey Russell, however, was hit by flak and had to bale out (JR515 'L'). He called that he was baling out after struggling to pull his damaged machine up to 4,000 feet. In this same attack, Sergeant G.M. Fisher had a shell penetrate his cockpit and explode. It made a pepper-box of the cockpit all round him but he was not touched!

Squadron Leader P.H. Beake took command of 164 two days later.

*

The pre-invasion period was particularly costly for squadron and flight commanders. On 23rd May, 181 lost its CO when attacking two Freya sites near Cherbourg. Nine Typhoons of the squadron, seven from 247 and 14 from No 143 Wing, flew out. Anti-flak Typhoons went in first at zero feet followed by the others. Both Freyas were hit but 181's Boss was hit also. Squadron Leader J.G. Keep had to ditch ten miles off Cherbourg. Jimmy Keep suffered a broken jaw, broken cheek and bruises but was rescued by a Walrus. Kit North-Lewis took over his squadron.

The CO of 198 was lost on 2nd June during an attack on a radar site at Dieppe. Squadron Leader Johnny Niblett DFC led four Typhoons in at low level from the sea while four more dived down from out of the sun. Niblett's machine (MN158 'H') was hit by light flak, burst into flames and crashed into the cliffs. The unit's new CO was Squadron Leader I.J. Davies DFC from 609 Squadron.

The Canadian Typhoons flew to knock out radar on Guernsey again on the 3rd but a recce later showed only three of the four out of action. On the morning of the 5th they went for the fourth one, dive bombing it from 12,000 feet to 4,000 feet. Flight Lieutenant

Johnny Saville, the leader, was hit by flak and went straight into the sea.

With the build-up for the invasion coming to its climax, the Typhoon squadrons were fully prepared to be despatched to France as soon as adequate landing strips could be organised. As these would be very primitive, the pilots and ground crews had to become accustomed to roughing it. Thus from early 1944 the various Typhoon wings had been mostly re-located along the south coast of England – under canvas! The wings were called airfields – for example 146 Wing was known as 146 Airfield. Only after the invasion did they revert to being called wings.

Group Captain D.E. Gillam, OC 146 Wing

The year before the invasion we went through all the motions. The first full Typhoon airfield consisted of three wings which I had, which was a hell of a lot of aeroplanes. Then it was decided that was too cumbersome, one man couldn't cope with that. The following year when the real invasion came, we were down to two wings, 146 and 123 under my control. After the invasion I lost 123 and just took 146 Wing, which nevertheless was a five-squadron wing, and an RAF Regiment squadron – all fully mobile – in other words a couple of hundred lorries or so, so quite a lot of stuff.

It was probably one of the major successes, I don't think it has ever been given the credit that it was really due. The Germans, even up to about a week after the invasion, still couldn't believe it wasn't coming in the Calais area and this was entirely due to the fact that we were blanketing their radar.

Flying Officer S.J. Eaton, 257 Squadron

It's quite incredible to think we had four Typhoon squadrons stuck in this corner of the Solent. No strip at all, just fields running by the side of a small country road. One runway, going straight towards the Solent, where every time you took off with heavy bombs on, you barely made enough height to clear the ship's balloons.

When later we flew from Hurn we carried on one side, a long range tank, and on the other a 500 lb bombs. We went across the Channel and looked around until we found something, then jettisoned the tank, whether it was full or not, before attacking. If you got hit by ground fire you'd be in pretty serious trouble. A later variation was that we carried four rockets and two LRTs.

Flying Officer J.G. Simpson, 193 Squadron

My squadron was a Bomphoon squadron and we were one of the squadrons in 146 Airfield, some of whom had bombs and some rockets. The CO was Squadron Leader Dave Ross, but our acquaintance was not very long because he was lost over the Channel just before D-Day, in fact on 5th June, on a wing operation which we did on a radar station at St Valéry. It had suddenly begun to function again and had to be knocked out in a hurry because D-Day was the next morning. We didn't find him but we knew for sure that it was all going to happen the next day because we could all see the huge amount of shipping flowing down from both east and west of the Channel.

Then on the evening of the 5th, we were all briefed for the great operations the next day but in fact the next day we did 'Fanny Adams'; we weren't scrambled or even airborne at all – it was not until the 7th that anyone from our wing got into the air.

Pilot Officer G. Clubley, 181 Squadron

At Hurn, Kit North-Lewis warned us that when we went to France we were going to use small airstrips so we needed to practise short landings. At Hurn we had a huge long runway and we shared the field with a Mosquito nightfighter wing. Kit had an 800-yard section marked out and we had to land and take off within that distance; we became very good at this. When we got to Normandy our strip was 1,000 yards, and the width was about three times the normal width of a runway which we could use to get a whole squadron airborne. So all our hard training came to nought but it was worth it for we later used some funny strips.

When Pat Pattison eventually got into operations he had over 1,100 flying hours behind him. He had trained in America, flown a twin-engined course at South Cerney and spent fourteen months as a staff pilot at Bobbington flying Ansons, before going to various OTUs on Hurricanes before finally ending up at Milfield and Typhoons, although due to a lack of Sabre engines had to be content just to fly Hurricanes. He volunteered for Typhoons having been impressed by the size, power and purpose of the machines he had seen, and ended up at No 83 GSU at Redhill to convert to them.

On 7th May, as a 21-year-old flying officer, I reported to 83 GSU. On that first day I and a Flight Sergeant Ray Price, were interviewed by the Typhoon flight commander. He was interested to know why we had volunteered for Typhoons since the high 'chop rate' was well known. How does one answer that sort of question? Anyway, he was only too pleased to have volunteers, presented us with a set of Pilot's Notes and sent us down to the flight line for cockpit familiarisation and to learn the emergency drills with the appropriate tradesmen. Having done this, we were all set for flying the next day.

My first flight was an epic. An experienced Typhoon pilot had given us a cockpit check and his last words were, 'She'll swing like a bastard if you let her, so give her plenty of boot while you open up smoothly and steadily.' His advice for landing was, 'Redhill is short, just about 900 yards and you'll need every inch. Fortunately the prevailing wind is westerly and the runway is slightly uphill. Use the brakes but treat them with care.'

So the great moment arrived and I was lined up ready to go. Here I should mention that there was a control tower about three-quarters of the way down the E-W runway to the west of which was a short runway; both strips were grass. So there I was with this monster aeroplane strapped to my backside and some trepidation. Seven tons of aircraft and about 2,500 horsepower to cope with!

Open the throttle and we roll; remember 'bags of left boot' and I pressed the left rudder pedal but obviously not enough. The aircraft started to swing and I thought to myself, 'I've got full left rudder.' The swing took me round the control tower and I was airborne heading north! Surprise gave way to some thought and after pulling up the wheels the brain started to catch up with the aircraft.

This first trip lasted for 50 minutes and took in the local scenery and getting to know the aircraft. The landing proved to be easier than the take-off. It is only after a few hours on a type that one can make an objective assessment of an aeroplane but my initial reaction was:

'Christ, what a piece of machinery.'

Pat stayed at Redhill for nearly three weeks, delivering various aircraft to 2nd TAF squadrons, until he finally received a posting to a squadron. In spite of his impressive total of flying hours he arrived at 182 Squadron with just 15 hours 50 minutes on the Typhoon and very much the new boy. He arrived on 182 on 28th May 1944:

Two formation practices and two R/P firing practices and I was put on my first op – a Channel shipping patrol. The first ops were interesting. Trying to stay with the formation I tended to ignore the small black puffs around me. It was sometime afterwards that I realised it was the enemy actually firing at me! During the few days leading up to the invasion the squadron attacked radar sites in the Channel Isles and I gradually settled down to flying and fighting. Black and white stripes were painted on the aircraft for identification purposes one evening, painted out the following day, then repainted on – three times I think, before they were finally left on and the invasion started.

As time went by, the Tiffie became more and more a part of you and I appreciated the roominess of the cockpit, the sturdy airframe and the monstrous Sabre engine roaring away in front. The engine, when idling on the ground, sounded like a lot of tin cans rattling around but once opened up it was like a sewing machine and, although one was always aware of the things that could go wrong and was prepared for low oil pressure indications which called for immediate landing, confidence in the Napier product grew. The early Typhoons had one major drawback in the car-type doors with winding perspex windows. Although fine for ventilation on a hot day they became very scratched, making clear vision decidedly unclear. Also, the amount of metalwork in the structure did not help lookout, particularly to the rear. We were all delighted when aircraft started arriving with bubble canopies sliding on rails.

With 24 cylinders exhausting vast amounts of carbon monoxide which filled the cockpit, it was *de rigueur* to use oxygen from start-up and it was vital not to forget this. The next development was the introduction of four-bladed propellers which gradually replaced the three-bladers. Oil and fuel pressures were critical on the Sabre. Shortly after the first strips were established in Normandy and we were operating from them during the day and returning to Hurn in the evening, we were just out in the Channel coming home on one occasion when my fuel pressure warning light came on. I returned to B2 as a precaution and spent a very uncomfortable night in a slit trench. It turned out to be a fault indicator but it was better to be safe than sorry.

Flying Officer H.G. Pattison, 182 Squadron

Shortly before D-Day, on 29th May, five pilots joined 175 Squadron at Holmesley South. Of these Pilot Officer T.T. Hall and Warrant Officer W.R. Speedie, both Australians, have made contributions to this book. Bill Speedie's start with the squadron was not auspicious for that very day he made his first flight with the squadron, under the keen eye of his CO – Squadron Leader Mike Ingle-Finch DFC – which ended in disaster:

I was sent to A Flight under the leadership of Flight Lieutenant E.C.H. Vernon-Jarvis. My first flight with the squadron was to be a flight with Flight Lieutenant Jack Frost as leader. We were taking off into wind, with me trying to put up a good show knowing the CO and squadron members would be watching the new chum!

The take-off was proceeding normally, my port wing tucked in close to Jack's starboard wing. We had not reached flying speed when suddenly without any warning my starboard tyre burst. The result meant loss of control of HH-D but fortunately I swung away from the other aircraft and indeed, headed for the control tower.

The next few moments were very hectic from my point of view but fortunately the collapse of the starboard Oleo leg brought HH-D to an abrupt stop with the nose of the aircraft embedded in the turf and the aircraft in an almost perpendicular position. Having extracted myself from a rather mangled Typhoon I observed the CO approaching at high speed in the squadron Jeep. Hell, I thought, guess I'm about to get the order of the boot any time now. He arrived. 'Are you all right, Speedie?' came his first enquiry. 'Yes Sir,' was my rather apprehensive reply, but pointing towards the wrecked aircraft, 'That isn't.' Then came an unexpected response. A pat on the back accompanied with 'Good on you, Speedie, I've been wanting to get rid of that bloody thing for some time now.'

Warrant Officer W.R. Speedie, 175 Squadron

Top left: P/O T. T. Hall, 175 Squadron, Normandy, 1944.

Top right: Squadron Leader M. R. Ingle-Finch DFC, OC 175 Squadron, 1944.

Right: F/O R. J. E. M. van Zinnicq Bergmann, 181 Squadron, 1944.

Oddly enough a photograph of Bill's prang was in the possession of another contributor, Norman Wilson, who at the time was a technical adjutant at Holmesley South. Part of his job was to keep the aircraft flying. In the period just prior to D-Day he had 174, 175 and 245 Typhoon Squadrons at the aerodrome.

> The structure was, we had a Wing Commander Technical Officer who was a Chief Engineer of the Station, and I was his assistant. Then we had normally an engineer officer on the operational side and another one with a junior assistant doing 30-hour inspections. The aircraft had a 30-hour cycle going up to 240 hours before it was given a major overhaul.
>
> My job eventually was a Technical Assistant responsible for keeping the tech. records, reporting specific incidents to Group if we'd got a problem, crash signals which was from a minor collision on the aerodrome, to a write-off. The organisation of repairs on a rota system, watching the state of the operational aircraft that we had, making sure half the aircraft didn't do 29 hours and all go in for maintenance at the same time. If they did, I had to organise with the authorities an extension of perhaps another five hours. This was probably another five trips for many were short range ops of only perhaps an hour or so.
>
> One of the problems we had with the Typhoons was that the ailerons were made of alloy for lightness and control. Just before D-Day Typhoons were flying a lot of low level cross-Channel attacks, especially against radar sites. One of the fitters was doing a routine inspection one morning and put his thumb straight through the control surface. What was happening was that the aircraft were picking up salt water internally and being a highly corrodable alloy, its surfaces were being seriously affected. On closer inspection we found we could push fingers through very many of them. There was tremendous panic then to get repairs done or to replace them. And it had to be done very quickly or it would mean grounding the aircraft with D-Day almost upon us.
>
> *Pilot Officer N.B. Wilson, Technical Adjutant*

Another problem they had at Holmesley South occurred when as D-Day approached the order came to paint the black and white invasion stripes round both wings and fuselage of all the aircraft. There was a slight panic when one of the ground crew asked a very pertinent question – 'What about paint brushes, Sir!' On some squadrons they even resorted to using brooms!

Pilot Officer G. Clubley, 181 Squadron

As the build-up for the invasion came we flew recce ops over France making sure our effort was well spread out so as not to be seen concentrating over Normandy. We generally wandered around looking for targets which was quite good fun. Usually four aeroplanes. It varied, of course; if it was a set target we'd take a few more but normally just four in at low level. Along the English side it was quite dangerous for our ack-ack gunners were a bit trigger happy at the time and we were shot at quite frequently. From Hurn we sometimes flew through the Southampton barrage which was quite exciting. There was a passage through it but it was a bit tricky with the wires either side of you. Then low level to Beachy Head before turning out to sea. A climb to 8,000 feet across the French coast, then drop down to low level the other side. We'd attack anything that moved, flying about 3-4,000 feet, allowing sufficient height for a reasonable dive on a target.

Normally we used a GP warhead on the rockets which had a thick skin and a reasonable amount of explosive – a compromise between the soft-head and the AP head – trying to get the best of both worlds. The GP was rather like a 6″ shell with a rocket on it.

Pilot Officer H.G. Pattison, 182 Squadron

We used to do a dawn patrol and a recce inside Cherbourg Harbour to see what warships were there. Normally we flew a pair, low level across the Channel, whizzed into the harbour, through the opening, and just doing a turn all the way around, try to remember what you'd seen, then get out as fast as we could, and back to Hurn.

Then, quite suddenly, it was D-Day.

CHAPTER SEVEN

Invasion

Flying Officer S.J. Eaton, 257 Squadron

On 6th June we knew the invasion was on. The day before we came back from a dive-bombing trip and later we went out again from Tangmere where we'd landed, to search for Squadron Leader Ross of 193 Squadron who had baled out over the Channel just south of the Isle of Wight. We couldn't find him but we were flying across in a long line, searching the sea, when we suddenly became aware of all these boats, hundreds and hundreds of boats, as far as the eye could see. It was an incredible picture and our Wing Leader, Reg Baker, called up and ordered R/T silence '… not another word until you land.' So when we got back he said, 'Well, obviously you know tomorrow's D-Day' – and that was it.

We were up before dawn and we waited and waited but it was almost dark before we left, early evening anyhow. All we could see was horse-drawn transport, troop carriers etc, and no opposition.

The next time we went out was on the 8th – low level bombing and strafing. There were so many aircraft around, but I shall never forget that first trip on D-Day. The sky over France was just a mass of aeroplanes and you could see fires everywhere from our various attacks. There were Spitfires, Typhoons – the whole lot – an impressive sight.

Brian Spragg, on the same evening flight on 5th June, recalls another sight over the Channel:

Coming back we went over a ship that was keel-up in the water and there were a lot of chaps swimming about in the sea. We were on strict R/T silence and couldn't even call up and tell anybody. It was about 20-30 miles off St Catherine's Point, off the Isle of Wight.

Then on the evening of D-Day when the squadron flew out looking for trouble they spotted something on a road:

Flying Officer B.J. Spragg, 247 Squadron
They were on the road but from height we couldn't really tell exactly. By the time we got down – spraying – we found 'they' were cattle. It was all a bit of an anti-climax for we'd been up since 3.45 am, waiting for something to happen.

Flight Sergeant A. Shannon, 257 Squadron
On D-Day we went to Caen and I clobbered two trucks and one staff car, and got two trucks on the 7th. We were a little over-awed by the occasion, and by the forecast of events. It was rather set by Wing Commander Baker who got us all together on the evening of the 5th and said the possibility is that I won't be with you here tomorrow and many of you may not be here tomorrow – but it's going to be a great day for all of us. Circumstances rather overtook us and we were quiet rather than thrilled or emotionally affected by it, more or less reflective. We went to bed early but we didn't see a lot on D-Day because it was hazy. We saw the lines of ships stretching across the Channel and the movement on the other side, the smoke and haze rising, but we didn't see a lot in the way of action.

Pilot Officer T.T. Hall, 175 Squadron
June 6th was a sight never to be forgotten. The bird's eye view showed thousands of vessels strung out over the Channel for as far as could be seen in any direction. Aircraft were everywhere with all their newly painted black and white identification stripes.

Although it is well known that the Luftwaffe put up a very poor showing on D-Day itself, there were a few German aircraft about inland, as 164 Squadron found. Mike Bryan, now Wing Leader of 136 Airfield, led 164 on a late morning op, strafing trucks and lorries. Late in the afternoon he led 164 to the Bayeux area, finding targets for their rockets – trains, bridges and MT (motor transport). A number of FW190s attempted to bounce the Typhoons and Flying

Top: Typhoons of 174 Squadron taxi out at Holmsley South, June 1944.

Above: Typhoon MR-? flown by S/Ldr J. R. Collins DFC, OC 245 Squadron at Holmsley South, June 1944.

Right: Squadron Leader J. R. Collins DFC, OC 245 Squadron, KIA 11 August 1944.

Officer A.E. Roberts (MN454) an Australian, was shot down. However, Squadron Leader P.H. Beake saw the 190s as he tried to reform his pilots, and in a skirmish that followed, shot one down.

The pilots of 198 Squadron, like all the others, were up early on D-Day. They had been briefed for a dawn attack with R/P on coastal gun positions but it was cancelled and the pilots put on 30-minute readiness. At 8.30 am Wing Commander R.E.P. Booker DFC led twelve aircraft to attack a château at La Meauffe near St Lô, which they did successfully. As they flew out to sea much activity could be seen on the beaches and over the water, and one pilot remarked: 'There were more ships than sea!'

On 8th June, 164 Squadron, led by Mike Bryan (MN415) found Me109s in the air. Arthur Todd (MN130 'Y') was flying cover to Bryan's section which was low on the deck, looking for targets. Suddenly the 109s came down on them and the Typhoons scattered and few managed to link up with each other. Todd flew towards Caen and saw a low-flying Me109. His No 3 – Flight Sergeant R.J.M. Wilson (MN419) – who was nearest to it, got in a burst and scored hits. It began to leave a trail of flame and as it turned to the left across Toddy's aircraft, he opened fire from 300 yards. The 109 dived away inverted and crashed into a wood. Meantime, Mike Bryan scrapped with some 109s and claimed two damaged.

No sooner had the troops pushed ashore and a foothold, however tenuous, had been secured, than the main Allied support operation began. Part of this support was 2nd TAF. As soon as it was practicable the equipment for building landing strips went across to the beach-head. It was not a particularly sophisticated job. The airstrips were little more than bulldozed stretches on fairly flat farm land or countryside. Their main requirement was that they were accessible by road and were not hindered by nearby high ground or trees, although a small wood or orchard proved helpful for hiding tents and equipment from aerial view. The take-off points had to point away from the German lines as pilots would not want to be trying to gain altitude with a fully armed aeroplane just above the heads of the German ground forces.

As soon as these early strips were ready to receive aircraft, a selected number of experienced ground crew personnel were sent to man them. They came from various squadrons and were not there just to service their own squadron aircraft. They would deal with any aircraft from any squadron, turn them round, rearm and refuel them in order to get them back to the battle or back to England each evening.

Des Shepherd and Ken Figg were both sent to France at this early phase:

LAC D.C. Shepherd, 137 Squadron

My squadron – 137 – didn't go to Normandy until August but I had to go in June because they were having so much trouble with the guns through operating in these primitive conditions. I was working with a Servicing Commando Unit who landed on D-Day and was with them for two or three weeks. This was when Typhoons were just landing to rearm etc, and were flying back to England in the evening.

From the time we received a 'plane to rearm and refuel, if we'd got everything to hand, I would say in a real push we could probably do it in a quarter of an hour and get the thing back down the runway. We had the added handicap that we were being shelled all the time. The Germans were using 88s, mortars, moaning-minnies, and we were having to work out on the 'planes with that. Sometimes it made you quicker so you could get back to your slit-trench!

LAC K.F. Figg, 182 Squadron

The squadron used to fly out to France each day. We were at a place near Bayeux and at first we were servicing everything, Spits, Hurricanes, Typhoons etc. This was only a few days after D-Day, and later we moved up to just outside Caen.

The Pioneer Corps had laid Summerfeldt matting as an airstrip. My squadron used to fly over from Hurn and go back at night, but after about two or three weeks the squadron came over permanently and we then moved up to a place near Danville.

It was, however, not until 10th June that the first 'Wheels down' landing in France occurred although the event was different from that actually planned. In 245 Squadron was Flying Officer W. Smith and in June he had a succession of eventful happenings. The day before D-Day, on an attack on a radar site at Auderville led by his CO, Squadron Leader J.R. Collins, Smith's Typhoon was hit by flak. Streaming glycol he managed to get up to 7,000 feet before baling out as his engine failed. He came down in the sea, 30 miles off Cherbourg, got into his dinghy and was later rescued by a Walrus. His flight commander, Flight Lieutenant W.S. Reynolds, stayed with him, orbiting to give a fix and eventually he too had to bale out but was picked up by a second Walrus.

Then on 10th June – D-4 – Smith was one of eight Typhoon pilots briefed for an early rocket attack on a reported HQ of a Panzer Division. They met intense ground fire and his Typhoon was hit. Wing Commander Charles Green instructed Smith to put his damaged aircraft down on one of the new strips – the one at Banville, which he did successfully.

As his Typhoon rolled to a stop he was greeted by a swarm of photographers and high-ranking officers who informed him he was the first RAF pilot to make a landing in France since D-Day. Apparently this honour had been reserved for the AOC of 83 Group, 2nd TAF – Air Vice-Marshal Harry Broadhurst DSO DFC AFC, who arrived some time later in his Spitfire. Flying Officer Smith breakfasted in the nearby French village, collected a German helmet from a dead German soldier and when his Typhoon had been patched up a couple of hours later, he flew home.

Smith's squadron was operating from Holmesley South and when a few days later they moved to France permanently, Smith came back to crash-land with engine trouble despite having two wings full of rockets. He later became a flight commander in 175 Squadron and ended the war as CO of 184 Squadron with the DFC.

Pilot Officer G. Clubley, 181 Squadron

We went over to Normandy a few days after D-Day. The army had bulldozed a strip – B6 it was called – for us and the initial idea was for us to go over first thing in the morning. The army had positioned Jerry cans of petrol for us, and little groups of men who had been trained to turn round aircraft, refuel and rearm us from stock piles of rockets, etc. At night we'd fly back to southern England. It was a nice theory but the timing was a little critical! I remember the first one I did, only four of us; we landed and as we did so the mortars started. The Germans were just over the other side of us and had been waiting to see the dust from our strip start to rise. Fortunately there were slit trenches.

As it got dusk we felt we had to get home, so just took a chance and got the hell out of it, so that scheme was laid off a bit until

Left: F/O W. Smith of 245 Squadron crash-lands at Holmsley South, June 1944.

Right: F/L Cedric Herman and F/O Pat Moran of 175 Squadron with goose on Carpiquet airfield, France, 1944. Both were shot down on 14 August, Herman being captured, Moran killed. The goose was killed near Carpiquet airfield.

Left: Digging in, Normandy, June 1944, 175 Squadron. From left, Ronnie Dale, killed at St. Lô, 9 July; Gordon (Joe) Swift, PoW 24 February 1945, baling out after his Typhoon was hit by debris from an exploding V2 attacked in Dülman railway yards; and Bill Speedie, who survived 105 Typhoon missions.

they got a bit further inland. The army rather liked seeing us for we used to fill up the Typhoon's gun bays with bread and fresh fruit they couldn't get so we were very popular.

Flying Officer S.J. Eaton, 257 Squadron
We moved to a little grass strip near Caen, and then to B3 which was St Croix. My wife and I have been back there since and I couldn't find any sign of that strip at all! The little grass strip had great mounds of freshly turned earth where the army had buried lots of German dead and had just bulldozed and covered them up – it wasn't very pleasant.

We had one nasty experience when our Servicing Commandos were refuelling us on one occasion and to our horror we found all our cockpit hoods had been pulled. We had a jettison handle and they had pulled these instead of turning the Coffman starter which looked very similar. Nobody could put them right so we had to wait for some of our own ground people to be sent out from Hurn to put them on again.

As the beach-head increased (slightly) in size, and the fighter strips became firmly established, so 2nd TAF squadron left their south coast bases one by one and began to move onto the strips in the beach-head. With them went their own ground personnel.

LAC K.F. Figg, 182 Squadron
Initially in France, nine times out of ten refuelling of the Typhoons was done from Jerry cans. We didn't have a bowser at first. We used great big funnels with suede leather covering and we would tip all the petrol through these from the cans and that took us longer than to rearm with either bombs or rockets.

LAC D.N. Macdonald, 121 Wing
We packed our trucks and were moved to a transit camp near Portsmouth. There we had our vehicles water-proofed and then stayed in a large tented site with our trucks still packed. On D+9 we went down to the docks and went aboard an American LST landing near Arromanches after a very rough crossing, on D+10.

We travelled about a couple of miles inland and were told to pitch our tents in a field which contained three large field guns, and told to dig slit-trenches. It got a bit hard going after about six inches, so we got down to a bit of relaxation – it had been a hard day. Suddenly about an hour after dark, all hell broke loose. The big guns in our field began firing, making the ground quake. Shells from the big ships off-shore were passing overhead like express trains, then the Luftwaffe came over. It was just like the 5th of November – searchlights, tracer shells, and AA shells exploding.

The German tanks, which we could see during the day, had moved down under the cover of darkness and were shelling the big guns in our field and the rest of the battery nearby. Not having dug our slit trenches, we took cover under the trucks but some of the brave lads who stayed in their tents were wounded by shrapnel and taken to hospital and never caught up with us again. What relief when we saw the RA boys pack up and leave the next day and you should have seen the lads digging the slit trenches!

It was still a period of high 'chop rate' within the Typhoon squadrons and a number of successful and popular Typhoon leaders were lost in the days following the invasion.

Wing Commander Mike Bryan DFC and bar was shot down by flak on D-Day plus 4, 10th June, (in MN415) – an experienced Typhoon pilot and leader the RAF could ill afford to lose. The wing was taken over by Wing Commander Walter Dring, who had been in 56 Squadron in the early Typhoon days.

Squadron Leader Ronnie Fokes DFC DFM had been an NCO pilot with 92 Squadron during the Battle of Britain where he won his DFM. He came into contact with the Typhoon in 1942 when he too flew with 56 Squadron. By early 1944 he was in command of 257 Squadron and won the DFC. He was a married man and a very popular CO but due for a rest. However, when D-Day arrived he asked to be able to continue to lead his squadron during the period of high activity for which he had for so long trained them. He was given two weeks, then he would be taken off ops. On 12th June he led attacks on MT, a bridge and some railways wagons carrying tanks. Eight miles south of Caen his Typhoon was hit by flak. He baled out but his parachute only just deployed as he hit the ground and was killed.

I was on the show when Ronnie Fokes was shot down. I last saw him as I was pulling away and didn't see him at all afterwards. We were very low and on those sort of occasions it's every man for himself really. There was a lot of stuff on the ground which were shooting up.

Pilot Officer B.J. Spragg, 257 Squadron

Then four days later yet another Wing Leader went down – Reg Baker DFC and bar of 146 Wing.

Reg Baker – that was an incredible show. Again it was a wing show and most unfortunate. One of the squadron commanders had led a raid on the first occasion and it was almost dusk when we went over to Normandy and flak was so intense that the leader turned us back. Of course, Reg Baker was absolutely livid when he heard that the wing had been turned back because of flak and so he said we'd go back the next evening. But it was exactly the same time, exactly the same approach etc, and he led. Of course, we had a repeat flak barrage and he was hit and went straight in. I remember it distinctly. It was far too late, dusk, and the flak, you could see the flashes everywhere, was intense.

Flying Officer S.J. Eaton, 257 Squadron

When the flak started and all the aircraft were thrown out of formation by the exploding shells, Baker was seen to be hit and go down. As they tried to reform, a calm, confident voice was heard over the radio, 'Hello Carefree and Vampire aircraft – Port 180° – Lochinvar – Out.' It was firmly believed that the voice was that of Reg Baker which sent the pilots of 257 and 197 Squadrons out of danger, as he was actually crashing, as one pilot saw a Tiffie diving almost vertically, apparently out of control, just before the order was given. Baker crashed near St Mauvieu and buried by front line troops next to the crash. His DSO came through shortly afterwards.

The wing was taken over by Johnny Baldwin DSO DFC and bar, who had been CO of 198 Squadron.

Also on the 14th, 263 Squadron lost their CO, Squadron Leader H.A.C. Gonay, shot down off Jersey on a shipping strike. 263 Squadron were one of the units flying valuable support sorties for the invasion fleet by stopping German forces interfering with the huge Allied armada, from the western approaches. They flew four sorties on the 14th, and their successes included a 500-ton U-boat,

Top: 257 Squadron two days before D-Day. Kneeling: F/O S. J. Eaton, F/Sgt R. R. Blair (KIA 6 July), F/O Ricky Richardson (KIFA 8 Sept 1944), F/O Cunningham, P/O D. P. Jenkins (later OC 257), F/O D. O. Sennett, F/Sgt W. H. Ewan. Middle row: F/O Whitfield, P/O Warren (Adj), F/L Smith, S/L R. H. Fokes DFC DFM (KIA 12 June), F/L Wistow, F/O Smith, P/O Thomson (MO).

On wing: F/L W. W. Kistler (PoW 17 June), F/Sgt W. B. Whitmore, F/Sgt Jones, F/Sgt A. B. Campbell (KIA 24 Nov 1944), P/O B. J. Spragg, F/Sgt Snell, F/Sgt G. E. Turton (KIA 22 June), and W/O D'Albenais. F/O Carr on propeller.

Bottom: Wing Commander E. R. Baker's grave by the wreckage of his Typhoon. He was shot down by flak on the evening of 16 June 1944.

damaged in St Peter Port. Flight Lieutenant Pinky Stark – ex-609 Squadron – brought his damaged Typhoon back from one of these sorties with several control wires cut and others shredded. Flight Sergeant Ryan's petrol system 'fell to pieces' when he landed his shot-up Tiffie. Gonay was later reported down on Jersey where he had force-landed. His DFC was announced a few days later.

No 438 Canadian Squadron attacked a railway tunnel south-west of Lisieux on the 16th, smashing the entrance and track. Then eight Me109s bounced them and shot down Flying Officer R.C. Getty. However, Ron Getty returned later when Canadian troops over-ran his hiding place. He had gone sixteen days without food.

Then 609 Squadron lost its CO on 22nd June. Shortly after mid-day, Ian Davies (JR197 'T') led his pilots in a close support mission in the Cherbourg area. His Typhoon was hit by flak and his engine stopped. He tried to glide to safety but when only 100 feet above the American lines he baled out but his 'chute had little time to deploy before he hit the ground. He too left a wife and small child.

The invasion of Europe was costing the Typhoons dear both before and during the landings. And soon the squadrons would end their period of operating from the beach-head strips and returning to England each evening. They would shortly move into Normandy permanently.

I know the first week after the invasion started I didn't leave my office and I slept in my chair and they brought meals to me. I did go down to the Mess every so often to get a bath and a clean shirt, but essentially we kept at it. The first few days after D-Day we were operating every hour or two, which meant half a squadron, one or two squadrons, going off in support of the landings, approaching the shortest night and the longest day, the first ones off were airborne at 3 am and the last lot were coming home at 11.30 pm. Then the Mosquitos of 418 Squadron were operating all night on long range intruder ops. So unless there was a ground mist or something like that, we were going like 'ding-bats'. There was always some lame ducks coming in, damaged over the beach-head and so on.

Pilot Officer N.E. Wilson, Tech Adj Holmesley South

The three squadrons at Holmesley South, 174, 175 and 245, moved to France in late June – to B5 (Camilly), having operated to and fro since D-Day. They had previously lost most of their ground crews but were re-united with them in the beach-head.

Our ground crews were moved to their assembly areas prior to embarkation for the Continent. The men who replaced them were from a variety of services including the Fleet Air Arm. Unfortunately they had little knowledge of Typhoons and it was absolutely nerve-racking at start-up time for an op, not knowing whether anyone would get you going if you failed with the cartridge start – as there was no chance of them re-loading the starting cartridges.

After carrying out a number of ops from the south of England we landed in Normandy – B5 – one of the British airstrips which had been bulldozed out of the ripening wheat fields. It was re-assuring to meet up with our own ground crews and have them back on the job.

Pilot Officer T.T. Hall, 175 Squadron

CHAPTER EIGHT

Into Normandy

Poppa Ambrose DFC went to France in a very different capacity from many of his Typhoon colleagues, having been rested following a very long tour with 257 Squadron (1941-44):

> I went on rest as one of those supposedly specially selected pilots to control fighters in the beach-head. The promise was from Batchy Atcherley who briefed us that we were going to be given an Auster and fly out to the wings and brief them on what to do etc. and that we'd be very important chaps. In the event I went over in the invasion commanding 30 Sherman tanks, ten 3-ton lorries and a small RAF convoy of my own in a Control Unit. This was about D + 3 and to my horror I had to inspect the ship's quarters with the Captain on a full bull-shit parade going across the Channel! I was the only RAF officer on board and the Navy chaps plied me with jerseys, duffle coats and a hell of a lot of gin at lunch-time. They put me to bed in the afternoon, saying I'd better sleep and we'll wake you up when we approach the coast. In the morning we did the inspection; it was the craziest thing I'd ever seen, but it was done in full Naval tradition. In the beach-head we found our unit and reported for duty.
>
> *Flight Lieutenant H. Ambrose, RAF Control Unit*

More squadrons began to move into the beach-head in July. 198 Squadron moved to B5 on the 8th, as 257 went to B15 (Ryes). On the 9th 609 Squadron flew into B5, 263 to B15 the following day. Meanwhile the Typhoons were still knocking out radar sites, 183 Squadron losing their CO, Squadron Leader F.H. Scarlett, during an R/P attack on a Giant Würzburg on Cap d'Antifer on the 12th.

The Luftwaffe were still active, Flight Lieutenant J.M.G Plamondon of 198 shooting down one of two Me109s on 11th July.

Johnny Baldwin led a section of 197 out on the 13th and were attacked by 30 Me109s. At the time, Squadron Leader Wally Ahrens, leading his 257 Squadron, was returning from attacking rail yards at Verneuil and saw the battle commence:

We had just finished attacking Verneuil when somebody reported 30 plus Me109s and some FW190s above and to the stern. I turned to look and there were thousands of them! Never seen so many in the sky all at once. Squadron Leader Ahrens said, 'Break, we're being attacked, every man for himself.' The sky was then full of aircraft, Typhoons, 109s and 190s and I was suddenly on my own. I kept looking behind as I'd been trained to do and about 3-400 yards behind me I saw a Me109, yanking round to get on my tail. I pulled round as hard as I could to get onto his tail and he flicked over and headed away from me. I followed him and he went into cloud, quite thick 'cu-nim'. I argued that the sensible thing to do when you get into cloud was to break, but I guessed that this chap wouldn't break because he didn't want to come back into the mêlée and that he was going to go straight down. When I came out of cloud, he was straight in front of me, about 500 yards or so. I was tempted to open fire then but my training which was very good cautioned me. I switched on my reflector sight, switched the guns to 'fire' and waited, as I'd been drilled, till his wings were within the range of my sight, then opened fire.

I must have given him two or three second burst and I saw strikes all over, and saw a glowing on a part of the aircraft, glowing red hot, then the whole thing seemed to be covered in strikes. At that moment I thought, 'I'd better get out of this', because he was looming up so quickly. I had to push the stick foward to the left and dive out of position so I wouldn't crash into him. Having passed him, I turned port and headed back home. Looking over to the starboard quarter I saw the 109 descending on fire and saw the pilot bale out. It was my first and only claim and didn't see any aircraft after that, unless they were on the ground.

Flight Sergeant A. Shannon, 257 Squadron

Flight Sergeant M.E. Marriott and his leader, Flight Lieutenant J.F. Williams (Canadian) each damaged 109s in this fight before Marriott was shot down. He got back on 27th August.

Baldwin also got a 109 destroyed, but 197 Squadron lost Flying Officer Trott – PoW.

Johnny Baldwin, earlier that day, had led an attack on Bernay but the bombing was bad and Baldwin strongly suggested an improvement. Squadron Leader Ahrens led the next sortie on an armed recce looking for MT, but finding none he led another attack on Bernay marshalling yards with excellent results. However, Wally Ahrens, who had previously been a flight commander on 197 Squadron, was lost on the 16th.

He led eight aircraft out that evening and found some MT on a road in the Bois de Cinglais. He let his bombs go but his Typhoon was damaged by the blast. He baled out but his parachute streamed and did not open before he hit the ground. Flight Sergeant W.H. Ewan also baled out when his engine failed south of St Lô. He was seen walking south of the town and eventually he got back on 20th August.

> I was with Jock Ewan and saw him down when he baled out. I told him to jump and watched him land in a field, but obviously, once he was down I didn't hang around so as not to give his position away.
>
> *Pilot Officer B.J. Spragg, 257 Squadron*

> Jock Ewan used to be in the Black Watch and he landed safely. He later told us that he played cards with the French, and with German troops. The French had said he was a cousin and when they spoke to him, he answered in Gaelic and the Germans thought he was speaking Flemish. He had many narrow escapes. He once came over the airfield with two 500 lb bombs hung-up and they fell off as he landed but neither went off – he was lucky.
>
> *Flight Sergeant A. Shannon, 257 Squadron*

Jimmy Simpson and 193 Squadron moved to France on 17th July, to the strip at St Croix – B3:

> We didn't get to France as either a wing or a squadron until 17th July. Prior to that we used a strip at B15 – fly over, do a trip, land on the strip, load up, do another op, then fly home. If I

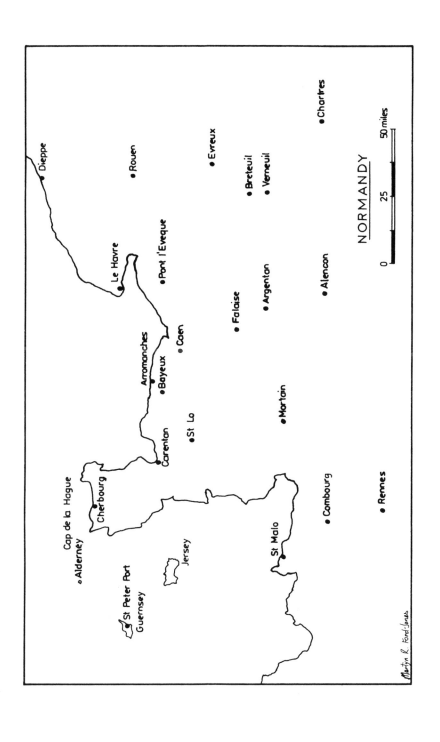

NORMANDY

Dieppe

Rouen

Evreux

Breteuil
Verneuil

Chartres

Le Havre

Pont l'Eveque

Falaise

Argentan

Alencon

Aromanches
Bayeux
• Caen

St Lo

Carentan

Mortain

Cap de la Hague
Cherbourg

Alderney

St Peter Port
Guernsey

Jersey

St Malo

Combourg

Rennes

0   25   50 miles

Martin R. Ford-Jones

remember rightly this strip was really a runway laid across the middle of a valley. If you didn't get off in the first 2-300 yards, you had to thunder down the hill, go up the other side and launch yourself into the bright blue yonder. It was rather hazardous and one or two of us had trouble with catching our props on the ground as we were thundering across the ground with tails up, trying to get airborne. Two 1,000 lb bombs on a short runway which suddenly disappears from view and then presents itself with a hill the next minute is not the best way of getting into the air. But I can confirm that a Typhoon can fly around the circuit with all four tips of its four propeller blades bent inwards and still manage to land again!

Also on the 17th, 197 Squadron received a new CO – Squadron Leader A.H. Smith DFC whom we have already met in Chapter Two.

Another significant event on 17th July was that Field Marshal Erwin Rommel, who commanded the Germans in Normandy, received wounds that effectively put him out of the battle. He had been inspecting front line troops as he expected an Allied offensive. On his return to his HQ his staff car was strafed by Allied fighters. Although one of his officers who was with him thought the aircraft were Spitfires, history records it was Typhoons of 193 Squadron, led by Wing Commander Johnny Baldwin:

> There was a report in July that Johnny Baldwin and seven other Typhoons from 193 Squadron were responsible for shooting-up and putting Rommel out of action. No one has really satisfactorily claimed that they were responsible for the destruction of Rommel's staff car, and certainly I have a cutting from a paper in which all the people are named who took part. There is no doubt that on the 17th we were attacking an HQ and a staff car was shot-up and destroyed and our Intelligence Officer said it had been found that this was Rommel's car.
>
> *Flying Officer J.G. Simpson, 193 Squadron*

The offensive Rommel was expecting was the start of the 'break-out' from the beach-hand. In fact the offensive began on the 18th, General Montgomery's Operation Goodwood. The capture of Caen had been a long and bitter struggle but as it was taken so the British could attempt a full scale break-out. It opened with a dawn bombardment and one thousand RAF bombers dropped their loads on German positions and upon a factory at Colombelles. Lighter aircraft would follow, including the bomb-and rocket-firing Hawker Typhoons.

CHAPTER NINE

The Break-Out

The weather on D-Day was not brilliant and indeed the weather in June and early July 1944 was far from perfect for a major invasion of France. However, it was accomplished.

There was no natural harbour on the part of the Normandy coast chosen for the landing points and there were mammoth amounts of men and supplies to be poured into the bridge-head. So the invasion plan included taking and building a port to the French coast – 'Mulberry'.

Similarly there were no natural airfields for immediate capture and even if there had been they would be ideal targets for German air raids or artillery fire. Thus the planners made provision for a number of airstrips to be bull-dozed at convenient locations.

No former Typhoon pilot who flew and fought in the beach-head will forget the airstrips. They had to contend with German shelling – the strips more often only minutes' flying time away from the front lines – air raids after dark, the primitive conditions – and the dust!

Flying Officer G. Clubley, 181 Squadron
When we went over initially we had a lot of engine trouble with the dust but they did quite a remarkable design and fitted a filter in the air intake in something like ten days. In between time they had to put us back at Hurn, because so many aircraft had suffered engine failure but they fitted these filters and from then on we operated from the beach-head.

Squadron Leader C.D. North-Lewis, OC 181 Squadron
The big problem in Normandy was that the Typhoon had no air filter and when we went over we were just operating off bull-dozed strips with nothing on them at all. As soon as you started up the Typhoons there was something like a major dust

Squadron Leader C.D. North-Lewis, OC 181 Squadron (continued)
storm blowing. In fact it was so bad at times that you couldn't see whether the pair in front of you had taken off, you just had to go when you thought they'd cleared and so if anything had gone wrong in front there was always the danger of bumping into them.

After we'd been over for some days, someone, probably at command HQ, got worried as to whether the dust was causing any wear on the engines, so they did a check and found that an enormous number of engines had excessive wear, so we all flew back to England and all the aircraft were checked and those that had excessive wear had new engines put in. They also rigged up a make-shift air filter, put in a kind of cotton wool effort. It did give you a performance penalty but as we rarely got embroiled with German aircraft it really didn't matter. In a curious way that affected us right till the end of the war, because there was always a shortage of engines. One of the reasons they discovered it, I'm told – and it may have been just a story – is that a command engineer was looking at a piece of sandpaper one day, and printed on the back was, 'Made from the best Normandy sand'!

Flight Lieutenant H. Ambrose, 175 Squadron
The dust in Normandy was also affecting the ammunition belts, which were heavily oiled, and the automatic ejection of the shell cases and clips became clogged with dust as it got up underneath through the ejection chute. So out came a team of boffins from Farnborough to sort this problem and everyone was interested in the time scale. They said they would have the problem conquered in no time at all – two or three months! We all said that was no good to us but Chiefy Schaefer, our flight sergeant armourer on 181 Squadron, solved the problem quite simply. He glued pieces of toilet paper to the chutes so that when a pilot taxied out, dust didn't get in; when you fired your guns in the air, of course, the first shells just tore through the paper. When I later recommended Schaefer for the BEM at the end of the war, I actually put that in his citation.

Pilot Officer T.T. Hall, 175 Squadron
The dust on the airstrips was appalling – every time the aircraft taxied, a huge pall of dust would rise. Within a few minutes of the

dust showing up, the airfield would be shelled. I can still recall every second of laying in the slit trenches with Bill Speedie, near the operations tent as shells whistled over or burst nearby. We were very pleased when after about a week, the shelling stopped as the Army advanced enough to push the German artillery out of range.

Flight Lieutenant G.J. Gray, 181 Squadron

In the beach-head in the early days we had to do all our own maintenance. Apart from three NCO's from the squadron, we only had MU back-up on the airstrips, so when an aircraft went u/s we got another in its place. It made the pilots a sight more conscientious because it was up to them to see the flaps were working all right and check things like the pitot-head cover being taken off, which was vital. So many chaps took off with no airspeed showing and in that event, someone else would have to take off and do a formation landing with them. In the end we tied the cover to the wheel chocks so that when they were removed it had to come off.

The other silly thing was landing with your wheels up. It was so easy to do, especially if you had to go round again, with chaps in a panic, having pulled their wheels back up. If someone did it three times he'd be grounded.

LAC D.C. Shepherd, 137 Squadron

Every Typhoon that had to taxi out onto the runway, with the type of undercarriage system we had then, the pilot couldn't see in front of him – he could only see the wing-tips really. So he had to zig-zag in order to see forward. There were so many accidents with 'planes running into each other etc, that we had to have one of the ground crew sitting astride one of the cannons. The wings were quite high on the Typhoon, so he had to hold on but he was also signalling the pilot, which way to go. We had one or two cases where airmen would slide off the wing and break arms, or fracture skulls. We had to contend with some pretty ropey runways on airfields, great big puddles, holes, dust, etc.

LAC K.F. Figg, 182 Squadron

Once when we were in France, the Germans flew in and bombed us, flying round and round – just nuisance really. They dropped a bomb which hit one of our aircraft which caught fire. There we were trying to get the rockets off and then someone said, 'Oh, what the hell, what's a few rockets – the 'plane's going to go anyway.' The whole lot went up and it fired the rockets but nobody knew where they landed!

Flying Officer S.J. Eaton, 257 Squadron

Whilst we were in the beach-head, it was possible to fly an aircraft back to England. Ted Tennant asked for a slightly extended stay back and when he was due to return it was astonishing to watch his Typhoon for it carried two enormous beer barrels, one under each wing. The barrels had been fitted with a cone-shaped nose point, and helped the airflow. We had the most incredible party as a result.

Flying Officer J.G. Simpson, 193 Squadron

The thing that worried people was the business of starting, particularly on a big wing show when three or four squadrons were operating at once. The sort of sequence of events was that we'd all be briefed, you'd know what the start-up time was – or the 'press-tit' time as we called it. We were suffering a lot in the early days from a mild form of gastro-enteritis or dysentery, so most of us had the 'trots'. Therefore there was a long queue for a quick call to the loo before you went down to dispersal. If we had to hang about, take-off being delayed or something, then you had to have another call to the loo. In fact we had one pilot who had to abort his sortie because he had problems with his trousers whilst in mid-air!

Having got started, we taxied along the perimeter which was tracking, of course; only room for one aircraft – and you lined up at the end of the runway in pairs. If you were the last squadron you'd see the boys taking off – flashing past as you were still on the taxiway as you chugged forward, hopefully not overheating! All the while knowing you'd have to go flat out if the others made too tight a turn round the airfield. At the end of the proceedings there was a real dust haze over the strip and apart from anything else, if you did have a bit of a problem and had to put it down quickly, there was literally nowhere either to drop your bombs, to get rid of them, without hitting something, or anywhere to put the aircraft on the ground unless you could get round and put in

Top: W/Os Jack Henry and Bill Speedie pose in front of a Typhoon, 175 Squadron, Normandy, 1944.

Bottom: 193 Squadron, 1944. From l to r: F/Sgt H. Pratt (KIA 12 Oct), F/Sgt J. Fishwick, F/O A. W. Kilpatrick, W/O Sugden, S/L J. C. Button, F/O J. G. Simpson, F/O D. H. G. Ince, F/O J. Darling, F/L A. W. Switzer. Kilpatrick was shot down on 7 August but evaded capture, while Switzer became a PoW on 15 August.

on the emergency area of the strip. The rest of the territory in the early stages of the beach-head was just full of tanks, lorries, troops, etc, so you'd be bound to hit something.

Pilot Officer N.B. Wilson, Technical Adjutant

By 1944 Spitfires had been 'desertised' and had Fokes air-filters with by-pass flaps on so that you could put air through it or just natural aspiration of the engine. The Typhoon had no such provision. Intended just for concrete runways I guess. So when the Commandos started servicing and re-arming the aircraft in Normandy and when we sent out the squadron's ground crews in Dakotas to establish their units, dust had started to become a problem.

Then one afternoon, by which time Holmesley South had been taken over by a Polish Mustang Wing, we suddenly heard the familiar sound of Typhoons in the circuit and there were our old friends with the HH, MR and XP codes on their sides, staggering in and sounding extremely ropey.

Charles Green had led them back, and he soon told us they'd got problems with their engines and. they suspected it was the dust. We took the cylinder heads off and we could virtually get a whole set of feeler gauges down between the sleeve valve and the cylinder wall and the piston which runs inside the sleeve.

We then had a squadron leader equipment officer sitting on the telephone for three or four days, just ringing round trying to find Sabre engines. We sent WAAF drivers off in pairs in their 3-tonners to go to collect them, and Banner Lane at Coventry was where most of the engines were made. We were working like beavers and it took us about seven days and nights to get all the engines out and new ones in so we could get these boys back to France.

*

The break-out from the beach-head began on 18th July 1944 and the Typhoons of the 2nd TAF were everywhere over and beyond the British front line. With many airstrips within sight of these same lines, the ground crews could often see and hear their own squadron aircraft, climbing up and diving down to bomb, rocket or strafe the German tanks, MT, troops, strongpoints etc. All were vulnerable to the caress of the Typhoons.

Flight Lieutenant G.J. Gray, 181 Squadron

Our forward airfields were literally within a few miles of the front line, all built with metal tracking and just carved out of fields. We would just take off, wind up to 7,000 feet behind the lines and then went down on your target. You could be back and landed in twenty minutes having fired your rockets. We'd then rearm, refuel, and away we went again.

Quite often from these forward airfields the only way to contact HQ was in the air, because there might not be any good communications on the ground. We mostly spoke in clear language, never in code, except when co-operating with the army when you'd have special map squares. Colours of the day changed each day and you wrote these on the back of one's shammy leather gloves – so you'd get through several pairs a week! Even so we tried not to talk at all on the R/T except in an emergency. We used hand signals or waggled our wings. The only times we spoke was when the enemy was sighted or you as leader would say, 'Going down now,' or 'Going down in five seconds – R/Ps on.'

The army would fire red smoke shells, say into a corner of a wood, and that was your signal for attack. If they didn't fire the smoke then we weren't allowed to attack even if we could see the enemy. This was because they were so close to our own lines that we might possibly mistake them, but more often than not all we did was go down and fire our rockets where the red smoke was and have no idea what the results were, for the Germans were very well camouflaged. I was amazed when we did eventually catch up the front lines and saw some of the damage we had done. The fragmentation rockets we had cut soft stuff absolutely to ribbons – little bits, around two to three inches.

There was always a chap in a forward tank who could speak to you in the air and he'd say, 'Red smoke going down now, go to square four, section 6,' or something, wherever they wanted support. We'd be hovering around at about 7-8,000 feet till we got more or less into the area where this chap wanted you and then we'd see the red smoke go down and we'd dive in and bash where the smoke landed. He had a visual siting of the enemy always and could fire his smoke pretty accurately. Sometimes he would say it was a bit short so fire 200 yards in front of the smoke, which was what we did.

Mostly we flew in eights, what we called fluid finger-fours. In theory we'd fly around 7-8,000 feet with the other four stepped up down sun, so if we did get bounced we'd be covered. Or we flew fluid sixes – three pairs with the chaps stepped up down sun. We always attacked down sun too if possible. If we were attacking barges for instance, we always put the sun behind us so as to attack from out of the sun.

Flight Lieutenant G.J. Gray, 181 Squadron

No 182 Squadron lost one of its flight commanders that first July day, Captain G.H. Kaufman, who was a South African like 182's CO, Major D.H. Barlow SAAF. It was 182's second op of the day – an armed recce east of Caen led by 'Dormie' Barlow in the early afternoon. They ran into light ground fire as the Typhoons rocketed and strafed German motor transport. Flight Lieutenant Tony Flood (MN771) called up to say his machine had been hit and he was making for the coast but he failed to make it home. Then Flight Sergeant Price (MN340) saw Kaufman's Typhoon begin to leave a trail of flame and go into a shallow dive, during which time the starboard wheel door flew off. Flames died down momentarily then flared again along the Typhoon's starboard wingroot. The aeroplane banked violently to the left, its nose dropped and then it dived vertically to crash amongst trees at St Jouin. Pat Pattison describes what it was like to see a pal or colleague go down in flames:

It was a horrifying sight. It was something we all dreaded when we were sitting on something like 140 gallons of high octane fuel and the thought that it might go up like a torch was, I suppose, the worst thing that could happen to you. If you were hit by flak and the aircraft was damaged or even if you got a bit of shrapnel or a bullet in you it was something you could expect, but fire I think, is far worse. Single-seaters are not the easiest aircraft to bale out of and if the thing goes up all of a sudden you stood very little chance of getting out alive. So it was very nasty to see Kaufman hit and the flames suddenly spew out and then there was practically nothing.

*

Group Captain Paul Y. Davoud DSO DFC took overall command of

143 Canadian Wing on 15th July. During ops on the 18th one of his pilots, Warrant Officer R.A. Watson had a dramatic escape. Richard Watson had just commenced his dive into a target when his Typhoon was hit and exploded. He was hurled from the cockpit, got his parachute open and landed safely. As he ran from his discarded 'chute, a German shell landed right on it. He found himself in the middle of a barrage, from both sides, so hid in a ditch. Then a German vehicle came right for his trench, collapsing it as he jumped clear. Then he was over-run by forward troops who sent him to the rear in charge of six German prisoners they had with them. Watson later joined up with another two soldiers also taking prisoners back, eventually ending up with 120 between the three of them.

Operation Goodwood failed to reach its objective – Falaise, but it did alarm the Germans, kept them and their Panzers pinned down along the British front as well as inflicting losses on the tanks the Germans could ill-afford. But the struggle went on and finally, by 26th July, the break-out from the beach-head could be said to have been accomplished.

The day before this, the 25th, 182 Squadron was again in the forefront and amongst the casualties once more. The squadron was detailed to send out constant four-man patrols, and in fact sent nine such patrols during the day. Major Dormie Barlow SAAF led the first off at 8.45 am, attacking targets at Breteville-Rabat with R/Ps. As they pulled away Barlow's Typhoon (MN891) was seen to receive a direct hit by flak in its starboard wing, which burst into flames as the petrol tank went up. Barlow baled out and was seen to get down safely but behind the German lines.

Later that morning – 11.45 am – Flying Officer Tony Rutherford (MN575) led four more Typhoons to attack reported tanks. Flying Officer Pat Pattison was with him (in JR220) and Warrant Officer H.C.B. Tallala (JR300).*

The 25th July was a day I won't forget. We were briefed for a close support mission in support of the army. The target was tanks at Fontenay le Marmion and a VCP was to control us near the front line. Diving from 8,500 feet we carried out the attack from south

---

* His elder brother was Flight Lieutenant C.L.F. Tallala DFC & bar, a fighter pilot from 1941-45. Both were from Ceylon.

Right: A 'pair' going down. Rockets being fired at MT in Normandy, 30 July 1944. Photo taken from F/O Pat Pattison's Typhoon, 1245 pm.

Below: Roughing it! Pilots of 146 Wing with their drinking supply at B3, July 1944.

DRINKING WATER

Bottom: 182 Squadron 1944. Front, sitting: W/O N. G. Sievwright DFC (KIA 31 Dec), F/O Dench, W/O H. C. B. Tallala (KIA 25 July). Seated: F/O C. T. G. Shields, F/L W. M. Weeks RCAF (KIA 29 Nov), F/O McBean, F/O N. T. O'Connor RAAF, F/O A. J. Whitamore (PoW 29 Nov), F/Sgt A. Bales, F/O Tatman (adj). Standing: W/O Coburn, F/L P. H. Strong RAAF (KIA 2 Nov), F/L Brough, Maj D. H. Barlow SAAF (PoW 25 July), Capt G. H. Kaufman SAAF DFC (KIA 18 July – the bandaged eye was caused by a playfully thrown apple!), P/O A. Rutherford, F/L A. C. Flood (PoW 18 July). On wing: W/O Henry, F/Sgt R. Price, W/O R. Lockyer, F/O H. G. Pattison, F/O Coxhead (on prop), F/O C. C. Leigh (evaded 19 Aug), F/O W. J. Kasubeck RCAF (KIA 9 Aug), F/Sgt Blue, P/O C. E. Benn RCAF.

Flying Officer H.G. Pattison, 182 Squadron (continued)

to north parallel with the line of advance and broke left at very low level going very fast – something over 400 mph. I think on this occasion I was flying No 2 to 'Toodles' Tallala in the second section.

In these attacks we went in individually; we didn't go on in pairs or as a four. Once the target was sighted and confirmed then we went down at intervals – 1,2,3,4, and once the bloke ahead had broke away, you were concentrating on aiming then didn't see anything of them. It was a question of getting away from the target area and eventually, if you were lucky, joining with the rest to go home.

On the break I felt about five strikes underneath me; not surprising as there was intense heavy and light flak in the target area. Breaking left had put me on the safety course from the target and my immediate reaction was to check the instruments. To my surprise, the oil pressure was falling rapidly, and within five seconds, stopped at zero coincidentally with the propeller coming literally to a shuddering halt as the engine seized. The whole airframe shook but did not fall apart. Then came decision time. To pull up from the deck and bale out or to continue as far as possible with the excess speed and hope to force land behind our lines. I quickly opted for the latter course and kept going. On the way I switched off the fuel and all electrics, then tightened my straps.

Speed was obviously decaying fairly rapidly and at, I suppose, 250 mph I decided to pull up and look for somewhere to put down as all I could see were trees. My lucky star must have been shining brightly as, at about 200 mph, I saw a large clear space ahead. This turned out to be a ploughed field or, at least, it was very rough. Speed dropping to 150 mph I jettisoned the hood, selected flaps down and started pumping like hell. Fortunately they went down and I was committed.

The available space did not look too generous so I had to force the aircraft onto the ground at, I guess, somewhere between 120-140 mph – rather fast! After two or three ricochets it stayed down and we ground to a halt with clods of earth flying everywhere including into the cockpit. Sudden silence while I disembarked and crawled under a wing tip – fortunately there was no fire – then the silence became very noisy. German tanks to the east, British tanks and artillery to the west and me in the middle being fired on by both sides. Needless to say I was somewhat concerned as to what might happen being in such an exposed position. After 30-45 minutes of enormous twitch, the firing stopped and a Canadian Army Captain drove out in a jeep and picked me up. I was debriefed at his HQ and a kindly gentleman instructed a soldier to furnish me with a tumbler of Scotch. It was quite full and only a little was lost due to a trembling hand on its way to my lips.

Flying Officer H.G. Pattison, 182 Squadron

Flight Lieutenant Gerry Gray came from 181 to take command of 182 Squadron following Barlow's loss, while Flight Lieutenant W.J. Johnson of 197 Squadron had filled the gap caused in 257 Squadron when Wally Ahrens had been shot down. Another tragic loss came on 26th July to 257 Squadron. The Canadian Flight Lieutenant J.F. Williams DFC was hit as the squadron attacked the marshalling yards at Bernay. As the attack ended and the Typhoons were climbing away towards cloud east of Caen, heavy AA fire began to explode about them. Almost immediately Williams called to say he'd been hit, wounded and paralysed. He was urged to bale out but moments later his Typhoon half rolled and dived straight into the ground from 3,000 feet and blew up. Williams had won his DFC with 198 Squadron alongside Mike Bryan, Vaughan Fittall and Johnny Baldwin. He had only joined 257 Squadron on 10th July.

When 'Peewee' Williams, our B flight Commander, called to say he'd been hit and was paralysed, we could do nothing but watch him go down – vertically straight down, and go in.

Flying Officer S.J. Eaton, 257 Squadron

As August began so the break-out was consolidated although the Goodwood offensive itself ground to a halt to the east and south of Caen. The Americans had begun their thrust from their defensive positions on 25th July, aided by the fact that the bulk of the German armour was opposite the British front, in anticipation of Montgomery's continuing his attack. The Americans captured Avranches while the British moved on Mont Pincon, which they took on 6th August. At the same time, Canadian, British and Polish troops moved south-west towards Falaise and Trun. Almost every day the Typhoons were out giving support, attacking tanks and strongpoints. The town of Falaise was one major objective which would open the way to Argentan.

The Germans mounted a counter-attack in the area of Mortain in the first week of August but this was thwarted – the Typhoons playing their part in this battle too. As the German Commander, Field Marshal von Kluge later wrote, 'The armoured operation was completely wrecked exclusively by the Allied Air Forces, supported by a highly trained ground wireless organisation. (Von Kluge had succeeded Rommel on 3rd July.)

During the battle of Mortain, Flight Lieutenant R.G.F Lee of 245 Squadron failed to return but he got back on the 15th. He had spent five days in his wrecked and overturned Typhoon after being shot down. In the wreck he had been shot at and wounded in the hand and leg. Fortunately a fire which started in the aircraft went out and he suffered only minor burns.

This same squadron lost its veteran squadron commander on 11th August, Squadron Leader J.R. Collins. On the evening of this day, 245 and 174 Squadrons attacked a strongpoint at Quesnay. While the Typhoons circled, waiting for marker smoke to be fired, Collins' Typhoon was hit by ground fire. Collins baled out of his burning machine but his parachute failed to open.

As this battle raged, the German 7th Army were slowly surrounded. British and Canadian troops pushed south towards Falaise and George Patton's US 3rd Army driving north from Le Mans towards Argentan, trapped the 7th Army between Falaise and Argentan. As von Kluge realised his position he rapidly began to withdraw towards the Seine. The result was that the Allied air effort was unleashed on the Germans, which history records as the battle of Falaise. It was disastrous for the Germans while the Allied aeroplanes, especially the Typhoons, had a field day.

Charles Green was absolutely brilliant about the Falaise Gap. He sorted it all out. He saw what was going on and warned the AOC and the Army that this was a situation that had to be arrested pretty quickly. Some of the German Army did escape, of course, but the Typhoons and some Spitfires, made mincemeat of the German Army at Falaise. They just blocked roads, stopped them moving and just clobbered them. You could smell Falaise from 6,000 feet in the cockpit. The decomposing corpses of horses and flesh – burning flesh, the carnage was terrible. Falaise was the first heyday of the Typhoon.

Flight Lieutenant H. Ambrose, 175 Squadron

Wing Commander Charles Green, during the battle of Mortain just prior to Falaise, had found some 300 tanks. His 184 Squadron destroyed eight and other squadrons followed up to take a heavy toll of this armour.

Flying Officer J.G. Simpson, 193 Squadron
We turned out to stop the German counter-attack at Mortain when the Germans tried to cut off the Americans and we were involved in the destruction of a lot of transport etc, during the Falaise Gap operation.

This involved quite tricky map reading as it was essential to know exactly where you were. The battlefield was pretty fluid and you didn't get a lot of time to identify the tank you were attacking. Being a bomb squadron we did not do so much of this although quite often we bombed a nominated target like the edge of a wood or the end of a village. Then did a range around with our cannon which could do a lot of damage. Our chief problem was that the Germans were pretty good at camouflage – they even re-routed roads so that, sat under the cover of the apple orchards and you thought the roads were empty. Of course, all their tanks were under the trees. It was quite revealing how much of the German Army relied on the old horse rather than the famous Panzer. We chased them all the way across the River Seine; had some fun trying to catch them going over this river.

Flying Officer G. Clubley, 181 Squadron
Then the big push came and we had the Falaise Gap which was absolute murder from the German point of view. I got there at the tail-end as I'd been on leave, but it was dangerous from our point of view because there were so many aircraft trying to get in to have a crack at all these targets. I went down there afterwards, it was quite horrifying.

Flight Lieutenant H. Ambrose, 175 Squadron
As an NCO pilot in the early days – 1941 – I used to sit at readiness on Hurricanes with a flying chap who was an out and out

snob. He really couldn't bring himself to talk to a sergeant pilot. At times things were a little difficult until 'Stapme' Stapleton arrived as CO, and just knocked hell out of this man.*

Stapleton couldn't care less if you were a sergeant or a group captain, he treated you exactly the same. A couple of years later I found myself flying with this chap over Falaise when he was hit. I saw it and saw that he was on fire so I flew alongside him and called, 'You've got to bale out.' He asked if it was that bad and I said yes, get out quick. So he baled out and as he went down he was being shot at in his parachute by ground fire. I'd been hit in the first attack and I was unable to fire any more rockets as I was streaming petrol. All I could do was to dive and fire at the Germans with my cannons, and stay with him until he landed. He later wrote to me a charming letter from POW camp, thanking me for what I'd done, which was ironic after being hardly able to talk to me in earlier days.

Yet another experienced squadron commander was lost on 25th August when Squadron Leader Ian Waddy DFC, CO of 164 Squadron went down. Waddy, a farmer from New Zealand, had been in 486 Squadron where he and Allan Smith had both been flight commanders. When Des Scott left 486, Waddy became CO till January 1944. In August he took over 164 from Beake but only commanded it for a few days. He had been leading an attack on tanks and lorries and met a curtain of flak. His Typhoon (PD457) was hit and he was later reported a prisoner. Two of his men also went down. Flight Sergeant R.A.E. White (MN711 'Z') – in flames – and Flying Officer G.R. Trafford (MN588).

---

* Squadron Leader B.G. Stapleton DFC had flown with 603 Squadron in 1940. He commanded 247 Squadron from August 1944, after service with 257 Squadron.

CHAPTER TEN

Forward into Holland

Flying Officer G. Clubley, 181 Squadron

For the first few weeks after the break-out our problem was to find an airfield far enough forward from which to support the army. We moved to Chartres and landed on this strip which was partially finished and found we still couldn't reach the front line. We had two or three days there, sleeping in a barn, then went to Amiens – a permanent aerodrome. Even there we were too far away for our close support work but we flew some long range ops with long range tanks on and we also caught up some Germans who were retreating. We found them trying to get away in any vehicle they could find; horse and cart, bicycle, the lot. It was mayhem really – we slayed them.

Flying Officer S.J. Eaton, 257 Squadron

We had the 'cab-rank' system when you had a map, and the rank was controlled by either an Army or Air Force chap up at the front in a tank or something, and he'd talk you down. We just flew up and down like a taxi and wait to be called. If we hadn't been called and petrol was running short, we'd call him up and he would send you back, to be replaced by another section of four. I remember one day we wasted several trips trying to knock down a church steeple. I suppose it had a German spotter in it – it was on the Dutch Islands – and we just couldn't get the tower to fall down.

Wing Commander C.D. North-Lewis, Wing Leader 124 Wing

The operations were really divided up, in the pre-D-Day, until we got to Holland, we used to get targets from GCC. They would tell us there was a target at so-and-so and it called for a squadron or whatever, though the number of aircraft was left to the wing. If they wanted a bigger effort, then the wing decided on which squadrons to send. For many of the targets, we were given a pin-point where it was, and told what it was – guns dug-in, or tanks, etc. A lot of the targets, especially the guns that might be dug-in in woods, we never actually saw; we just flew to the pin-point and plastered it with rockets, came back and reported that the rockets went into the target area.

A number of targets were called by the ALO on the ground. They would put coloured smoke down on the target and that's what we went for. These forward controllers might say that there were two tanks at a certain pin-point; then we went in and they often put smoke down to indicate where they were. That was the pattern right up until we got into Holland.

In Normandy we always had a bomb-line, you weren't allowed to do attacks inside the bomb line. If you were given an area where you were allowed to attack anything, you mustn't attack within the bomb line, which allowed our ground forces to be forward of the areas where you thought they were – so there was little chance of attacking our own side.

Flying Officer H.G. Pattison, 182 Squadron

Targets on the ground were small from 8-10,000 feet, but one got a bit used to spotting things on the move and when you were past the bomb-line anything that moved was fair game. Trains, tanks, motor transport and even horse-drawn transport, and so, I regret to say, horses.

On one particular trip, led by Gerry Gray, we went down on four gun positions which were set out in the form of a square. That was one occasion where we had time, with cannon, to aim at one – fire, aim at another – fire, and go right round the whole four. But it was not often that we got four targets so close together. The main object was to squirt with the cannon on the way down, get the rockets on the target, then break off as rapidly as we could. Particularly on defended targets; we were always briefed never to attack twice. If you did have to attack twice, then do it from a different direction each time because if you started to circle with six to eight aircraft, they could wait for you and pick you off as you came back.

Pilot Officer T.T. Hall, 175 Squadron

Direct tactical support was given to the army in rocket and cannon attacks to overcome strongpoints and assist the army advance in any way. This was often directed by a Visual Control Point with the advancing troops. Gridded maps would be used and the controller would indicate where the rockets were to be placed by firing red mortar smoke shells on the target. One of the secrets of making a good attack was to get the squadron into a good position for attacking from out of the sun and taking account of the surface wind and respective location of the troops according to the bomb-line. One had to be wary of the Germans also firing red smoke on our troops to confuse us.

Group Captain D.E. Gillam, OC 146 Wing

If we were supporting the army we'd usually keep a standing patrol of four aircraft up and replace them regularly. The army could then call them up to attack specific targets and we got to the stage where we could operate very close to the front lines. If the army was held up by some specific target they would mark it with smoke. It was fine in a fairly static battle but in a moving battle you could never catch up with it and you had to rely on the army getting their messages back fairly quickly. We had army officers with us who would give detailed briefings – as much as the army knew anyway.

Allan Smith, now a squadron commander in the beach-head, recalls his time in Normandy and also an attack on a railway gun that was causing problems for the invasion forces.

My squadron, 197, were flying from B3, a strip at St Croix-sur-Mer, between Caen and the invasion beaches. We were living in an orchard and were very close to the front line. The guns kept going all night and you could hear shell splinters falling amongst the trees. I used to sleep in a slit-trench dug in the middle of my tent and covered my head with a steel helmet. Food was hard rations. Flies caused a problem and most of the pilots had dysentery. When a flight involved a pull out from a dive we had to select pilots who thought their bowels could stand the strain!

The Mulberry Harbour had, of course, been built off the

Squadron Leader A.H. Smith, OC 197 Squadron (continued)

beaches and ships were unloading supplies constantly. By day they were protected by warships and air cover, but at night the Germans were shelling the harbour with a long range gun and inflicting considerable damage. After some detective work the problem was solved. The Germans were using a railway gun and hiding it during the day in a tunnel near Pont L'Evêque.

On 18th August, 197 Squadron was assigned the job of sealing the gun in the tunnel. Wing Commander Johnny Baldwin decided to lead the attack using eight Typhoons, each carrying two 1,000 lb bombs with eleven seconds delay. The idea was to attack with four aircraft at each end of the tunnel – each pilot flying down the railway line as low as possible and release at the last moment, poking the bombs into the tunnel mouth. Once those four had bombed, the other four would repeat the attack on the other end.

Johnny and I, who were to lead the second four, studied the flak maps; all the flak was positioned to cover an approach from the western end, so I suggested to Johnny that we toss for ends. As was the case in my cricketing days, I lost the toss and finished up with all the flak! I then suggested that seeing I had all the flak, perhaps he would let me attack first, and rather to my surprise he agreed.

Everything went according to plan. I located the tunnel and was able to get a good low run down the railway line and release my bombs into the end of the tunnel. I was so busy lining up that I didn't notice the flak, and when my four had completed the attack, the tunnel mouth was effectively sealed without loss.

Johnny Baldwin then went in to attack the other end. Either the flak map was wrong or my section's attack had stirred up the gunners, for guns opened up from all directions and I could see a number of hits on Johnny's Typhoon as he made his approach towards the tunnel mouth. I took my four down to strafe the gun positions and take some of the fire from Johnny's section. They sealed their end of the tunnel and we headed for home. Happily we didn't have to go far because Johnny's Typhoon was badly damaged, but he just made it and crash landed on B3 without injury. My turn came later in the day when I was hit by flak on another mission.

That was the last of the railway gun. I heard the attack reported on the BBC news at lunchtime and later in the year, at Antwerp, the Intelligence Section had photographs on display which showed the re-opened tunnel and the damage that had been caused by our attack. It made me realise how lethal 1,000 lb bombs are when exploded in a confined space.

Squadron Leader A.H. Smith, OC 197 Squadron

＊

Flying Officer G. Clubley, 181 Squadron
We eventually moved up to Melsbroek, near Brussels. We were the first, or one of the first, RAF units there and we were warned not to touch anything because of booby traps. Yet we lost a few people with bombs in toilets, etc. There was one prize one: a Ju88 in a hangar and with so many cars around, people quickly latched on to draining its petrol tanks. They obviously went under the wing and as the Junkers did not quite fit in the hangar, it stuck out a bit. So they opened the drain tap on the wing which stuck out and as soon as they turned it the whole thing went up.

Pilot Officer T.T. Hall, 175 Squadron
On 28th August we moved to B24 (St André de Leuvre) a French 'drome which had been used by the Germans and often the bomb craters had been filled in. It was great to operate from a good surface again. We then moved onto Beauvais (B42) and we were the first Typhoon squadron to land on an aerodrome over the Seine. On 4th September we moved to Vitry, then to Antwerp on the 17th, then Volkel in Holland on the 30th.

At Antwerp we had some bother, as, after landing, we had to endure endless shelling from across the Albert Canal. My Typhoon HH-T – the first supplied to the squadron with a four bladed propeller, was hit by shellfire and completely destroyed – it had logged $9\frac{3}{4}$ flying hours and was a beautiful machine. I still have the largest piece that was left of it – an exploded 20 mm cannon shellcase as a memento.

LAC D.N. Macdonald, 121 Wing
We were on the move again, trying to keep up with the army who were sweeping through Northern France. The country roads were littered with tanks and vehicles which had been pushed into

ditches on either side to let our convoys through. This was evidence of the destruction meted out by the Rockphoons, on the enemy convoys as they tried to escape complete annihilation which faced them in Normandy.

Our next airfield was just outside Douai, near the Belgian border. There were no facilities to do major repairs so we did little work. We then moved rapidly through Belgium, only a couple of days behind the army, into Brussels which was like 'Mardi Gras' with thousands of people lining the route.

Where were the Luftwaffe? They could have had a hey-day, but of course, we had complete command of the air.

No 257 Squadron had an unfortunate accident on 8th September, operating from Manston. They were at Manston in order to be able to fly across the Channel to attack the Germans who had now been pushed back into Belgium.

Flying Officer S.J. Eaton, 257 Squadron

After we'd been on the Continent for some time we came back to do a rocket course at Fairwood Common. Then after the break-out we moved to Manston. Our airfield had got so far behind the lines that we operated from there. There we lost a couple of chaps – it was quite incredible.

We took eight Typhoons in echelon – pretty late – and Flying Officer Richardson was No 3 in the second section; No 2 was Freddie Broad, Richardson burst a tyre and swung right into him. The two extreme aircraft managed to get by and into the air, but we all landed again with our bombs still on, to find that Richardson had been killed. Broad on the other hand, was found sitting on his parachute pack near his own aircraft at the side of the runway perfectly intact, not a scratch on him.

Flying Officer B.J. Spragg, 257 Squadron

We were taking off from Manston and being a big airfield we were taking off in echelons of four. I went off in the first four, then the second four went off. Ricky Richardson's tyre burst on take off on the inside of the echelon and he went into his No 2. They both slid down the runway – a bit of a flamer. Freddie Broad got out but Richardson didn't – a bit nasty that.

A feature of September 1944 was the famous airborne landings at Arnhem. 2nd TAF Typhoons were not involved initially but became involved in the latter stages. Not that the outcome would have been any different perhaps, but there might just have been a change in emphasis had they been called to help keep the vital supply lines open a little earlier.

Wing Commander Kit North-Lewis led his 124 Wing on an attack against flak positions in the Arnhem area on 17th September as a prelude to the airborne attacks. All four of his squadrons were involved and they achieved some success.

Wing Commander C.D. North-Lewis, 124 Wing

No 83 Group didn't fly in support of Arnhem. All the support was done by units back in the UK. We sat on Eindhoven airfield and only on the last few days of Arnhem did we fly in support of them. And there we were within just a few miles, and if the whole of 83 Group had been thrown into the show I have a pretty shrewd idea that they would have been able to hold it. We had been the first wing to land in Holland and so I was the first pilot to land in Holland. We landed at Eindhoven the day the Germans went out of Brussels and we operated from there for a number of days until we moved after the break-through at Nijmegen. In fact we were over the top when the Guards Armoured Division went across the Albert Canal and the first six British tanks went up in flames as the 88s got them down the road. Then we attacked the Germans.

I led, I think, the last attack in support of the Arnhem people, the night they came out. We went in with the wing at dusk as they evacuated; they were down to a tiny little 'enclave'.

When we got back it was just dusk and a reserve aircraft coming in had crashed in the middle of the runway. There was nowhere else to land and I had three squadrons with me – 24 aircraft. I asked what the form was and was told they would get it off fairly quickly so I decided to wait. We circled round the airfield and none of us had done much night flying since before D-Day. In the end it was pitch dark and too late to divert to Brussels, and there was the possibility of all of us running out of petrol. By some miracle they cleared the runway, put out goose-neck flares and we somehow got 24 Typhoons down. Too dark to taxi so we just left the Typhoons where they stopped.

Harry Broadhurst was calling for my blood, but with all the Typhoons safely down the threats stopped, but goodness knows what would have happened if I'd lost the wing.

Flying Officer G. Clubley, 181 Squadron
We flew some support missions for the Arnhem show, trying to keep the road open for the Guards Division, but our main problem was on daylight ops. We could mount more or less continuous cover, but as soon as night came the Germans moved in. But we were beating up and down there, strafing anything we could find. I remember leading a section and saw some vehicles which we attacked and had just opened fire when it suddenly dawned on me the leading vehicle was an ambulance. I stopped and so did the ambulance and out tumbled a lot of fully armed troops who were using it as cover. We pasted that one.

Group Captain D.E. Gillam, OC 146 Wing
Arnhem, from where we sat, was a tragedy. We were at Antwerp then and were never called in. In fact the secrecy of Arnhem was such that I don't think the Air Force on the Continent really knew anything about it. We really ought to have blanketed the whole area and we could have stopped everything dead in its tracks if we'd been really briefed. When we were brought in it was too late to assist either to pin down German troops and armour, or to protect the route along which the relief forces were proceeding.

Flight Lieutenant H. Ambrose, 175 Squadron
I remember very well the Guards Division going down the road to Nijmegen and eventually to Arnhem had a terrible time with 88s by each side of the road, knocking out their tanks, and it was the Typhoons who came forward and rescued them. We fired off all our rockets and cannon, staying with them for quite a while and making dummy attacks afterwards. We received a very nice signal from the Division, saying thanks for staying with them even though we'd run out of ammunition.

During the period of the Arnhem operation, Poppa Ambrose (MN358) and his section of 175 Squadron were engaged with German fighters. Bill Speedie was one of the pilots in his section (JP753), the others being Lieutenant Capstick-Dale (DN258), Flying

Holland & the Dutch Islands

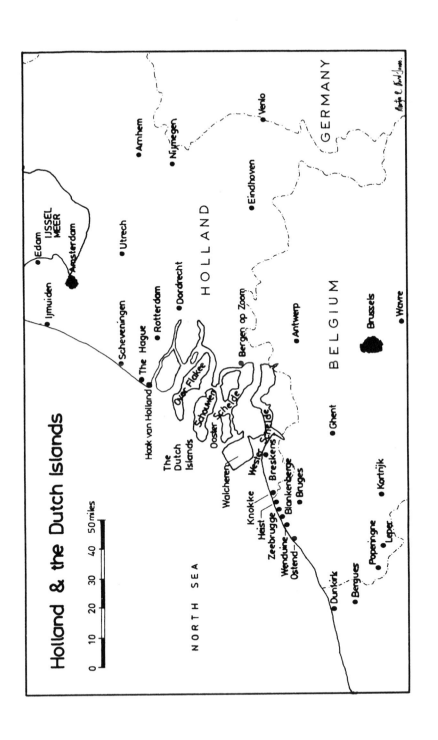

NORTH SEA

0   10   20   30   40   50 miles

The Dutch Islands

Hook van Holland

Over Flakee

Schouwen

Ooster Schelde

Wester Schelde

Breskens Schelde

Walcheren

Knokke
Heist
Zeebrugge
Wendune
Ostend
Blankenberge
Bruges

Dunkirk
Bergues
Poperinge
Leper
Kortrijk

Ghent

Antwerp

Bergen op Zoom

Dordrecht
Rotterdam
The Hague
Scheveningen

IJmuiden
Amsterdam
Edam
IJSSEL MEER
Utrech

Arnhem
Nijmegen

Eindhoven

Venlo

HOLLAND

BELGIUM

Brussels
Wavre

GERMANY

Officer R.W. Clarke (MM966), Captain M.C. Hopkins (MN628), and Flight Sergeant R.W. Hurrell (MN852). It was Hurrell's third operational mission, and armed recce to Arnhem. The date was 26th September.

The Typhoons had just reached Apeldoorn, flying just under the clouds.

Flight Lieutenant H. Ambrose, 175 Squadron

We were jumped by 60 Me109s over the town. I managed to see them in time and I timed the break just right. We broke into them and fired our rockets at them, which broke them up. Then I managed to get two with cannon, then the others were after me. I kicked my Tiffie into a spin into cloud which was quite a brave thing to do because I didn't know what was going to happen when I got into cloud in a spin. Fortunately I came out about 2,000 feet, got it out of the spin but then I was fighting with the 109s again. We really got pranged. One chap landed on an Auster strip – Capstick-Dale, a South African, Ricky Hurrell was shot down and killed but the others managed to get back to Antwerp. Hurrell was lagging behind and was hacked before we had time to break. I landed at another forward airfield, out of fuel.

I remember Hurrell, who was an Australian, coming to see me shortly before this day and saying he was worried in case the other chaps felt he was hanging back. He'd had to turn back from two missions with engine trouble and he thought the others were questioning him. I said, 'Don't worry, fly as my No 2 on the next show.' He did and got badly shot up and he finished upside down on the runway. I recall there was petrol about and some idiot came with a crowbar. Hurrell yelled, 'Christ, don't let him do that!' – one spark and the whole lot would have gone up.

Warrant Officer W.R. Speedie, 175 Squadron

I was Blue Leader with Captain Hopkins SAAF as my No 2. Naturally the Section leaders were looking for targets, whilst their No 2's duties were to watch and report any hostile aircraft. Suddenly 'Hoppy', my No 2, shouted, 'Break port, Quebec!' (our call-sign). I reacted immediately knowing we were in danger by Hoppy's voice. I broke to port and there streaming down from above and behind our formation was a gaggle of 109s. Both members of Yellow Section had already been shot out of the sky. (C-D and Hurrell)

To be caught by surprise left us in a precarious position, Blue Section being immediately separated from Poppa's Red Section. Hoppy came straight on to my tail and we flew straight up through what seemed a never ending stream of 109s. We fired our rockets at the gaggle resulting in apparent panic. 109s were scrambling in all directions to avoid our rockets. We claimed no kills being far too busily engaged to follow the flight of several very shaken German pilots. When fighting our way out of this incredible mêlée, I contacted Poppa who was naturally nowhere in view. He had apparently also fought his way out and said he was all right but he did not return till the next day.

Ambrose landed at Eindhoven. Capstick-Dale tried to evade in cloud but every time he came out he found three or four 109s waiting for him. Eventually he got away (only his No2 was actually shot down) and landed at Leende, which only had a 400 foot runway. When he was later ferried back to home base in an Auster, his pilot lost his way and they strayed a few hundred feet over enemy territory. 'Cap' Dale's first intimation of this was when bullets started hitting the fuselage just behind him. Looking down he saw German soldiers in a farmyard firing up at them, so Dale fired his revolver at them!

In October another Typhoon squadron joined 2nd TAF, 168 Squadron, which had previously been a Mustang squadron. Its acting CO was Flight Lieutenant L.H. Lambert, an ex-soldier who had joined the RAF after seeing action in France before Dunkirk. He had been one of the original members of 168 Squadron when it was formed in 1942. Like Jerry Eaton, Lambert had some exciting moments on Mustangs before flying the Typhoon.

We actually brought our Mustangs back to England and I took my rest, converting onto Typhoons, then converting the squadron. This was the autumn of 1944, having till then had Mustangs in Normandy. When we went back into action with Typhoons, I'd got the most flying hours on the type – ten! They were very good aeroplanes from that point of view. We called it

Flight Lieutenant L.H. Lambert, 168 Squadron (continued)

the 'Club'. That wasn't being rude but it was rather like a club, it had quite a hefty punch and was quite a manoeuvreable weapon as well. That's why we didn't mind having only two weeks or so to convert and get back onto operations.

We were a British squadron in a Canadian Wing, and I think it suited everybody. The Canadians flew squadrons with bombs or rockets. We could operate either independently with our cannons or we'd go with their attack squadrons to do specialised roles such as taking out the small target. Our particular role was low level attack, on trains particularly, where we would try to get the engines, and long range operations trying to attack targets that were beyond the range of other Typhoon aircraft. We were relatively 'clean' with cannon only, and got quite a lot more range in consequence. When flying with the Canadians, we would fly with them and go in fractionally ahead at very low level to silence the flak, because with cannon we could get pin-point accuracy compared to a rocket or a bomb. For example on the attack on the locks on the Dortmund-Ems canal (29th November 1944) the Canadian squadrons actually carried out the attack, with Spitfires overhead to keep any German fighters away or occupied. Our job was to attack ahead of the Canadians who were carrying bombs – eight of them. We had to make sure the eight got in without being knocked down. We picked out individual targets – guns and so on, and as soon as anything opened up, we had to go for it.

We would usually fly eight aircraft, four on each side. We would on these occasions, have seen recce photos so knew where the 88 mm guns were and where the multi-barrelled 40 and 20 mm guns were. Positioned on each side of the attacking squadron, we would in effect lead them in. Because of our earlier low-level Mustang training, we could make quite sure they were properly aligned in their run-in, and each of us would know what particular group of guns we were going for. There was no time for a second choice, of course, and our particular attacks worked quite well, especially against the lock gates. The Germans had taken nearly a year to repair them from an air attack and had just finished them when we made the attack. A total of 72 aircraft were involved, none was lost and it was all over in about 45 seconds.

Flight Lieutenant L.H. Lambert, 168 Squadron

Somehow, higher authority forgot to replace 168's earlier CO when they came back to England, which left Lambert as acting CO. When it was realised he was promoted to squadron leader and given full command of the squadron.

The Canadians lost one of their squadron commanders early in October – Squadron Leader W.H. Pentland DFC, CO of 440 RCAF Squadron. He was hit by flak after releasing his bombs on a target and crashed. He was just three trips short of completing his second tour of ops. It was still a very dangerous business to be on Typhoons.

Despite the comments in Chapter Five about low-level bombing as opposed to dive bombing, there was still a case for low level efforts for specific targets. Allan Smith's 197 Squadron, for instance, had developed a technique in this regard which worked well:

While we were stationed at Antwerp, 146 Wing became involved in a number of 'Cloak and Dagger' operations, which were based on information received from behind enemy lines.

Most of these attacks involved low level bombing which had become a speciality of 197 Squadron. In spite of numerous orders to convert the squadron to rockets, I had always managed to stall off the changeover in the hope that another bombing trip would come along. My luck held good and we had the pick of all the bombing trips because on most occasions we were the only Typhoon squadron available for bombing at short notice.

We had developed a simple but very effective technique for low level bombing. We would obtain stereo pairs of the target photographs taken by the PR boys and once these were fitted into a stereoscope, I could work out the heights of the trees etc, surrounding the target. The object was to work out a low level bombing run into the target, that allowed our Typhoons to fly below the level of the top of the building at the time of release. Our theory was that if we approached below this height and released close enough, the 11-second delay bomb had nowhere to go but into the side of the building before exploding.

Sometimes the run-up was wide enough to take in two aircraft at a time – sometimes we could only take in one and this prolonged the attack. We had to watch that we did not get a 'squash effect' when we pulled up over the building. Nobody ever

Squadron Leader A.H. Smith, OC 197 Squadron (continued)

did fly into the target itself but some of the boys did come back with branches of trees poked down their cannon barrels or in their radiator scoop.

On 23rd October we were advised that there was to be a meeting at the German 15th Army HQ at Dordrecht at 10 a.m. the following morning. Stereo pairs of the target photographs were obtained and I worked out a satisfactory low level run into the target. The attack was planned, and made by 197, 257, 193 266 and 263 Squadrons – a total of 48 Typhoons, timed for 10.10 a.m. on the 24th. The attack was started by a low level attack by 197, the intent being to break the building open with 11-second delay 500 lb bombs, then follow this up by two squadrons dive bombing with 500 lb bombs and two more firing rocket projectiles.

I was leading 197 Squadron and one of the problems of being first in on the low level attack is that firstly you have to do all the navigation and find the target, and secondly everybody in the wing knows how good your bombing is because your bombs are the first to explode.

We had a good run-in and were well below building height when we released – the bombs going straight through the side of the building before exploding. With the delay fuses it took a while to complete our attack but when it was completed, I gathered 197 Squadron together and we climbed above the target to give the other squadrons fighter cover and to draw the flak up at us and away from them.

The dive-bombing and rocket squadrons did a very fine job and subsequently target photos showed just how effective the attack had been. At the time it just seemed like another attack but later we learned that in destroying the building, two generals, 17 staff officers, 55 officers and 200 other ranks had been killed.

Squadron Leader A.H. Smith, OC 197 Squadron

CHAPTER ELEVEN

The Other Ways of Landing

One lasting memory of any former Typhoon pilot is how tough the aeroplane was. Many owe their lives to its ruggedness and its ability not only to absorb punishment but to bring them safely down and allow them to walk away from the wreck.

Flying at low level the Typhoon pilot was almost constantly the target for a whole variety of heavy or light ground fire. Of the men interviewed for this book, most had stories of narrow escapes.

Flying Officer G. Clubley, 181 Squadron
The Typhoon was tremendously strong. There was a flight commander on the squadron named Kenny Gear. On one occasion in Normandy, Kenny got very badly hit, lost a bit of his rudder and quite a lot of one wing. He brought her back in, having tried very gently to see what her stalling speed might be and he found he was going to have to approach at 150 knots – which was a bit fast! He had lost all his hydraulics so it was wheels-up. He touched down and scooted along the runway with bits of aeroplane coming off all over the place, and by the time he stopped, there was Kenny, no wings, no engine, no tail, just the central cockpit section left. He was shaken but only had a slight cut on his nose – that was all! Everything had broken up around him but he was OK. It gave us a tremendous amount of faith in the aircraft.

Squadron Leader G.J. Gray, OC 182 Squadron
The Typhoon was like a very heavy Hurricane. It was a very solid machine in which you felt very safe, with something like five tons of engine in front of you. Chaps were more inclined to crash-land the thing if they were shot-up, than to bale out because you were down pretty low during attacks, so if you did get hit you didn't

Squadron Leader G.J. Gray, OC 182 Squadron (continued)

have much time to think about baling out. The three or four times I crash-landed I felt much safer than actually baling out because you had to jettison the hood, undo the straps, then get the oxygen mask off, and by the time you'd turned it on its back and dropped out, you'd probably hit the ground anyway! So I personally crash-landed. One of these times was just behind the Allied lines at a place called DeRips. I deliberately crash-landed it and just slid to a halt. It was very funny actually, for on that occasion (15th October 1944) my adjutant was having a bath and didn't know I'd been shot down until I got back in an American jeep. He was just getting out of his bath, and in that time, we'd gone out on a sortie, I'd been shot down, crash-landed and got back.

Once, after being hit in the cockpit, I ploughed through a farmhouse when I crash-landed, then through a brick wall and into a field. The whole outside of the cockpit was covered in blood and I thought, Christ – I've bought it this time! I saw all this blood and thought, Hell, I must be ill! I then found I'd gone through a cow! All I had was a twisted knee.

I baled out two or three times in my career and it always seemed as if one had all the time in the world. It was just like a slow motion film – you think you've got days. Then you ask your No 2, and he says, 'You hopped out like lightning. How did you get the straps undone? You got hit in the wing, you turned over twice and then you popped out the top!'

There was a chap in another squadron who had been shot down two or three days running. On one op he was hit in the left wing and he could only fly straight between 280-300 knots. Any other speed it just rolled the whole time. So in fact he rolled all the way back, then over our lines he straightened out, popped out, and landed safely.

Flying Officer S.J. Eaton, 257 Squadron

I was only hit once by flak. We were on our way home from a weather recce and above cloud. Suddenly the cloud broke and I looked down to see we were on the Maas. Just as I was about to call the others, to warn them that we were over a known flak position, it just happened. There were bursts of smoke all round us and I was hit; the smell of cordite was strong and I'd felt the shock but the Typhoon was responding. When I got back I found the underside of both wings were fairly well peppered with little holes.

However, in the leading edge of one wing was the brass fusing ring of the actual AA shell. It had gone through the leading edge and through the self-sealing of the tank and just jammed there!

I'd flown through a lot of flak, of course, even flown through the smoke-ring just after a shell had exploded – an 88 mm – seen the flash ahead of me during a dive, then the smoke ring but by then all the rubbish had gone.

Flight Sergeant A. Shannon, 257 Squadron

My engine stopped once just over the bomb-line. I was with Johnny Baldwin on our way back when it just stopped. We were at 8,000 feet and had enough time to glide over and force-land in a field. I recall much dirt flying up and found myself veering to the right so I put on left rudder! It didn't help, of course, it was just an automatic reflex action.

Flying Officer J.G. Simpson, 193 Squadron

I was clobbered in a dive by a 20 mm in the coolant tank. I had my hood off and my straps undone as it started streaming glycol but I thought I'd give it a go and managed to get back. The Tiffie managed to go on flying with only 18 of its 24 cylinders working.

When you are hit in a dive, doing around 400 mph or so, with two bombs on board – so we were whistling down fairly fast – it's a hell of a thump. What you're really concerned about, of course, is fire. In my case I started leaking glycol which is pretty inflammable stuff, and one should get out pretty quick, but I'm a coward really and didn't fancy baling out. I decided to try and make it and fortunately I did. The airfield was fairly near the bomb-line and I did the whole thing and even landed with the wheels down.

There was an occasion when I had to land wheels-up – not much problem, it's a bloody great engine so unless you make an absolute 'Charlie' of it you don't come to much harm. There were things to remember, however, for on some airfields in France we had up to five squadrons so there wasn't a lot of room. You couldn't put a damaged aircraft down on the runway or the Wingco would have your 'guts for garters' as that would mean ripping up the carefully laid tracking and then nobody could operate. So you had to put it down by the side; you didn't want to go into the nearby fields as the crash wagons couldn't reach you. So we had a spot which was ear-marked for forced-landing which usually ended in a terrific cloud of dust. We had problems with dust in Normandy but at least you could throw it over the aeroplane so it wouldn't catch fire.

Flying Officer H.G. Pattison, 182 Squadron

On 18th August 1944 while attacking some wireless installation east of Vimoutiers I was hit by flak, the apparent result of which was that I lost about a third of my starboard aileron but managed to land back at base – B6. After landing it was found that a flak shell had exploded in the torsion box between the port cannons. Again, luckily, the spar was not damaged and the ammunition did not explode. (MN340)

We went off on an anti-flak patrol on 24th March 1945, along the autobahn east of Wesel. Light flak was certainly there as I sustained three hits in my rudder, tailplane and belly. Fortunately the engine continued to turn very satisfactorily but, on return to B86 I found I had no hydraulics. I was not allowed to land, as a belly landing would have torn up the PSP runway. So I diverted to Eindhoven to land on the grass. Although I could not lower the flaps a copybook landing was made and, after the aircraft had been jacked up and the u/c and tail wheel lowered, the aircraft was towed away with just a bent propeller.

The Typhoon was an incredibly strong aircraft. One of our pilots belly landed and ran into a wood in France. Trees took the wings first, then the fuselage broke off behind the cockpit and he was left driving an engine! Another Canadian pilot was hit by 88 flak and lost virtually the whole of the underside and a lot of the upper surface of one wing together with the aileron. He found it difficult to control below 140 mph but, nevertheless, landed safely, wheels down, but going rather fast! [P/O C.E. Benn RCAF]

Warrant Officer W.B. Speedie, 175 Squadron

On 30th July 1944 I was a member of a formation of eight rocket-firing Typhoons led by Flight Lieutenant Davies, the assignment being an armed recce. We attacked a troop concentration south of Caumont. Still being a new chum on the

Top: Flying Officer H. G. 'Pat' Pattison with his damaged Typhoon (MN340 XM-D) hit by flak 8 August 1944.

Bottom left: Flying Officer B. J. Spragg, 257 Squadron.

Bottom right: Flight Lieutenant J. G. Simpson, 3 Squadron.

squadron, I was arse-end Charlie (No 8) to make my attack. Following a sustained vertical dive with the release of the rockets and the firing of the cannon at the target, heavy flak was experienced. I sustained damage to the constant speed control of my propeller, resulting in excessive revs., and so oil covered all of my windscreen and both sides of the Typhoon. Realising I had no possibility of returning to base, I limped to the nearest available friendly base, A13 – used by the Americans for their Thunderbolts. I elected to attempt an out of wind landing which I was fortunate to manage, and as soon as I landed, my engine cut out.

An American Colonel arrived in a jeep, asked if I was all right and then asked if I realised I'd landed out of wind. 'Yes, Sir,' I replied, 'it was intentional.' Seeing the condition of the aircraft he appeared rather taken aback when I told him the reason was to ensure that their operations would not have been interrupted should I have been unsuccessful!

We made a successful attack on a group of Tiger tanks on 17th September, but whilst leaving the target at a low height, I was hit by light flak. Being obliged to force land my Typhoon as I was too low to bale out, I selected a wheels-up landing in a ploughed field, being continually fired upon during my rapid descent. The deceleration was incredible and I received minor abrasions, a broken nose and the best pair of black-eyes I had ever sported.

Flying Officer T.T. Hall, 175 Squadron

Everybody has their stories of damage to aircraft and how they got back. Because of the use of Typhoons in a close support role and being subjected to continuous light and heavy flak, our share of damage could be expected to be, and actually was, a lot more than usual. I remember Flight Sergeant Ashman (West Indian) having two-thirds of his port aileron blown off after an attack on tanks south of Vimoutiers. The aircraft flew with a 30° list but he got back safely – full marks for the toughness of the good old Tiffie. On November 10th we carried out an armed recce looking for motor transport, but passed up two trucks for the alternative target – a factory at Weeze. I led the squadron and after putting our rockets into the factory, we copped some heavy flak from Goch. An 88 mm shell burst right under me and the aircraft seemed to be thrown about 50 feet up and onto its side. The port

'D'-door was blown off, with some holes in the fuselage and the aircraft flew port wing low. Other than the scary tendency to flick over to port, the hydraulics and undercarriage were undamaged. With a bit more throttle and a bit more nose-up, the Typhoon landed reasonably well.

I had a number of engine cuts on or after take-off, one being on 16th February 1945. I had LR tanks on and the engine cut out on the down-wind leg of the circuit after take-off. As I was still close to the airfield, I dropped the wheels down and stuffed the nose forward and got in just over the fence and cross-wind, after shouting on the R/T to stop anyone else taking off. I was furiously hand-pumping the hydraulics to get a little bit of flap. Just after touch down I jettisoned the LR tanks which bounced along behind me, and was ready to retract the undercarriage if I ran out of runway, but finally stopped in some loose dirt off the end of the runway.

Flying Officer B.J. Spragg, 257 Squadron

I got hit in the engine in a dive on one occasion over a target in the Dutch Islands, and glided over the bomb line. That was on 4th November 1944. We were dive bombing a target at Zanddijk near Goes. Just as I rolled over the old engine sort of whoomped oil all over the place – and smoke. The prop stopped in no time so I just dropped the bombs and pulled away to glide and land near an artillery unit which was using the same target for their guns I discovered.

I was more interested in getting over to our side than baling out as we were fairly close to our own troops. Actually I was a bit lucky; I picked a field and made it, having managed to hand-pump some flap down as well. My radio was still working when I came to a halt so I called Jerry Eaton to say I was OK.

Then about six weeks later I was coming back to base and the engine was faltering a bit, then it packed up not very far from our base at Antwerp. I wasn't quite so fortunate this time, being fairly low by then – about 1,000 feet. I didn't feel like jumping so decided to force-land again and I hit about a dozen trees as I went down, leaving a swath, but this was when I really got to like the Tiffie, because it was built like the proverbial shithouse! I finished up against a ditch with a fairly sudden impact when it stopped, with just engine, cockpit and a little bit of fuselage – the rest was strewn back behind me. I got out with just a slight touch on the lips and nose when I hit the gunsight, that was all.

Flying Officer G. Clubley, 181 Squadron

I once got shot-up in my hydraulics attacking some gun battery or other and had to hand-pump the undercart down. I landed just in time and only just had enough brake pressure to stop. There were holes all over the place but didn't realise how many till I got down, but the engine had kept going. I only once had an engine fail me, taking off on a squadron, and that was quite exciting. It was in August 1944 in Normandy with all the dust. After the first section took off, the rest were virtually taking off on instruments there was so much dust haze. So when my engine packed up I just let the aircraft run as the other machines were coming up behind. I stopped at the far end of the runway with my wheels in a ditch.

And there were some non-operational moments of drama too:

Warrant Officer W.R. Speedie, 175 Squadron

During the later half of November '44, 175 Squadron was taken out of the line for two weeks. We returned to the UK from Holland and set up at Warmwell on a rocket course. On 27th November I took off with the assignment of making a 75° attack on a target placed two miles off Portland Bill. However, whilst still over a built-up area, my throttle quadrant suddenly fell to pieces in my hand. Being left with a mass of different coloured wires to control speed, boost and revs, seemed to be asking a lot of a Typhoon pilot. By means of tentative trial and error I managed to return to Warmwell. I informed them I was going to attempt an emergency landing. A pukka English voice replied, instructing me to land on runway so-and-so. In a heated reply, I informed him to clear the area, and reminded him that I still had eight rockets under my wings, so I would land on any bloody runway I could reach! Fortunately I managed a successful landing, as the likelihood of going round again was impossible.

Flying Officer T.T. Hall, No 83 GSU

I had another engine cut on take-off on 18th May 1945 at Dunsfold. I was testing Typhoon JR531 as it had been reported to be intermittently cutting out. I took off, got the wheels up and held the aircraft down to build up speed. As I pulled up into a climbing turn to port with plenty of speed, the engine cut out. The drill was always to go straight ahead but as there was nothing but pine trees ahead, and due to my initial extra speed, I managed a fairly steep gliding turn back over the 'drome fence with wheels up. I had no worries as the aircraft was so tough I knew that it would hold together and after the initial impact it slithered along in a great cloud of dust.

It was later revealed that the carburettors were empty, which was why the engine kept cutting out, as the petrol tank valves had been put back in an upside-down position. These valves stopped petrol flowing from one wing tank to the other when banking the aircraft. With them upside-down it cut off the supply to the carburettors when the aircraft was banked.

Shortly before 3 Squadron went over to the Hawker Tempest, Ron Pottinger had the experience of having engine trouble just as he took off in a Typhoon from Bradwell Bay, at night, over water, in March 1944:

We were practising taking off at night and getting used to flying at night so that when the invasion came we could be over the beach-head at first light. In the event we were flying Tempests by the time the invasion came.

This particular night the weather had been bad but it cleared sometime in the early hours – we'd been sitting in the dispersal hut for hours. Suddenly I was told, 'Off you go, Ron.' I climbed into the first available Typhoon – it had still got LR tanks on, having been used for trips across to Holland. I took off and had just got airborne, just got the wheels up, when there was this great thud. It really was a hell of a bang and, to be honest, I really thought I'd let it sink and had hit something on the ground. The whole machine began shaking so much I couldn't read any of the instruments at all. I turned to go round the circuit, aiming to get down wind again, but half way round I realised I was too low and if I went back overland I'd hit a tree or a house or something. I'd got my finger on the radio button to tell the ground I was going to ditch the thing because I didn't think I could make it, when it actually hit the water. I didn't do anything clever, like land it on

Flight Sergeant R.W. Pottinger, 3 Squadron (continued)

the water; it just hit it! It skated along on its LR tanks and ended up under the water.

I think I was shocked for an instant but fire broke out on one wing and that made me start clambering out, but I didn't even notice going under the water in the stress of the moment – just didn't notice the water close over me. I remember getting out of the cockpit, having already got rid of the canopy and side panel. I freed the straps and then floated out but was still held by the oxygen and R/T leads. I pulled the R/T out but the oxygen was held by a bayonet-type fixing but I just broke the tube which just shows the strength when one is desperate. It took several kicks to get to the surface and I then forgot all the drill. I just pulled the top off the dinghy pack and masses of rubber came out into my arms. In my hurry I had broken the safety pin but luckily the thing just inflated but the cord which attached the dinghy to my Mae West got wrapped around it so it blew up like a huge figure eight!

It was a pitch black night – couldn't see a thing, but eventually I got it sorted out and clambered into it completely exhausted. It was freezing cold, and I can remember just lying there, my whistle in my mouth, waving the tiny torch attached to my Mae West, but making no attempt to row it. Luckily there was a small Naval boat out and they picked me up within half an hour.

They had been having a lot of trouble with seals on the propellers, the pitch control being operated by engine oil pressure. If the seals went the loss of pressure caused the prop to go fully fine and fantastic revs. If one didn't land quickly, it caught fire and blew up. I got a green endorsement for that ditching. They thought my Typhoon had either had the seals go or perhaps one bank of the valve gear had gone. Another chap had a similar problem but he got round and landed but it burst into flames on the deck it was so hot.

Flight Sergeant R.W. Pottinger, 3 Squadron

The Winter of 1944-45

As the winter approached so the squadrons of 2nd TAF concentrated on captured permanent airfields in Belgium and Holland. There would be no advantage in having aircraft bogged down on airstrips and landing grounds out in the countryside, vulnerable to mud and rain.

Volkel (121 Wing), Eindhoven (124 and 143 Wings), and Antwerp-Deurne (146 Wing) were the homes of the Typhoons during the winter of 44-45 – all with nice, solid, permanent runways and warm accommodation for the men.

Flight Lieutenant J.G. Simpson, 193 Squadron
Antwerp was an interesting station; the Germans were still in one half of the town while we were using the airfield. We later discovered that in the forts and dugouts around the airfield the Germans had a spy system set up with radios, telling someone, without much effect I think, the aircraft movements.

We had splendid accommodation. The town was really worth something after the rather minimum facilities of the Normandy beach-head, and Felix Cryderman, the other flight commander, and myself, occupied a flat in a block of flats which was all very posh. That lasted about a week until the V1s and V2s started coming across in quantity. We were bombed out and went back to some revolting little back to back cottages in the working area at the side of the airfield.

Flying Officer T.T. Hall, 175 Squadron
At Volkel we were attacked by hit-and-run German jet aircraft, Me262s, on a number of occasions. These aircraft would dive on the 'drome, drop their bombs, HE and anti-personnel, and then continue straight on over their own lines. Our billet in a

schoolhouse received a direct hit on one occasion and two pilots were put in hospital with shrapnel wounds.

LAC D.N. Macdonald, 121 Wing

The next airfield we operated from was Antwerp where we had the luxury of sleeping in some civilian buildings on the edge of the airfield. After a few days we started to be shelled from a small island in the estuary which the army had by-passed. Some of our kites beat them into submission and then shortly afterwards we were moved to Volkel where we were to spend the next six months. We had a blister hangar inside the shell of an old German hangar and here we were able to do our repairs and servicing, under cover from the weather which was beginning to get quite wintry.

We had to commute to the village for meals and it was while waiting for transport beside a Typhoon one day, that there was a sudden burst of gunfire. Naturally we all hit the deck, but it seemed to go on for ages and I could feel particles of something hitting me. The chap next to me, an ex-footballer, big and tough, was lying on the ground, screaming, 'Mummy, Daddy, Mummy, Daddy!' and clawing at the ground. Suddenly all was quiet. We looked round and a very sheepish-looking armourer came from beneath the Typhoon. He had accidentally fired off its cannons, the shells hitting the old concrete arch of the German hangar and it was chips off this that had been showering us. Needless to say, our former footballer lost some of his prestige in our eyes.

*

With the net beginning to tighten on the Germans – although they were far from finished and still had a few surprises for the Allies – 2nd TAF Typhoons were able to mount a number of 'special' ops.

German Headquarters were always worthwhile targets but in November 1944, it was a couple of Gestapo HQs that became the targets. The first was the HQ in Amsterdam, planned for 19th November but this was postponed due to bad weather and mounted a week later – the 26th.

It was led by Group Captain Denys Gillam, whose general account of the raid is complemented by three other pilots who were in the attack force, Ronnie Sheward, Brian Spragg and Jerry Eaton. Gillam's task was to mark the target and then oversee and direct the other Typhoons in the attack.

> Depending on the target, I would mark it in different ways. Sometimes I'd just use a pair of rockets, sometimes two pairs, firing one deliberately short, the other deliberately to drop over. Then I'd get back up to 8,000 or 10,000 feet, look at the target then give instructions to the strike force who were coming in at a known time behind me. This is what I did at Amsterdam; told the attack force to line up on the smoke. The rest of the aircraft, the Bomphoons etc, would locate the flak positions – invariably outside the towns, and attack them with bombs and cannon fire – but keeping out of the light flak which was the really dangerous stuff, while the other eight or so rocket Typhoons came in. The bombs in general would be lobbed from a fair height at flak etc, and would be part of the diversionary tactics. It would be the rockets that would go in for the kill.
>
> They just kept on going, flying in very fast, on the deck, then pull up to about 2-300 feet to get their rockets dug in, and dive straight down to roof-top level, then jink away.
>
> *Group Captain D.E. Gillam, OC 146 Wing*

The attack was made at lunchtime and Gillam went in and marked the target building accurately with phosphorus rockets. Following were six squadrons of Typhoons – six sections of eight – two with rocket, two with 500 lb bombs and two with 1,000 lb bombs. Ronnie Sheward was in one of the Typhoons that were coming in low and fast with bombs:

> Squadron Leader Rutter led 266 and I was No 2 to him. Four of us were detailed to go in at low level with 1,000 lb bombs with 11-seconds delay fuses. We found the target straightaway as we'd had a model made of the whole thing, made with the help of the underground. They had told us exactly where the building was; luckily it had an open space lawn in front of it, which gave us a run-in. It had to be done at a certain time because the children in a school at the back would have gone off to have their lunch and the Gestapo people would be having their lunch, and so would be in the target area.

Above: Amsterdam – at centre left the
Gestapo HQ attacked by 146 Wing on
26 November 1944.

Right: Squadron Leader R. E. G. Sheward
DFC.

It was a good day, we went in at nought feet, and Rutter let fly and I was next to him. As far as we could gather from later reports, the bombs went through the front door and front windows. In a short while the whole place went up. There were a whole lot of people supporting us, keeping the guns quiet, and others dive bombed the HQ with incendiaries, rockets, etc. We just belted in as quick as we could for the element of surprise.

Flight Lieutenant R.E.G. Sheward, 266 Squadron

One of the supporters was Brian Spragg:

The attack had been postponed previously because of bad weather and we wanted to be absolutely sure that we hit the right spot. When the day arrived, Denys Gillam led and we got some good pictures, and later heard that the results had been very good. I led a section of four which was supposed to go in on an airfield nearby and keep down any guns we saw firing – you know, give them a hard time. I had a feeling on that occasion there were a couple of German jets bouncing in and just made one quick pass and flew off.

Flying Officer B.J. Spragg, 257 Squadron

Gillam led the raid and went in with a No 2 and fired some phosphorus rockets into the target. As I was Tac/R trained he had me in one day and asked the possibilities of taking one of the cannon out of the port wing of a Typhoon and fitting a camera there. We tried it and it worked. I was by then a flight commander on 257 but occasionally he would ask me to take this aeroplane up and take photographs of the target. I think there were 48 aircraft on this particular raid – the whole wing and I went in after they'd all gone through which was not the best time of course. In my log book I wrote, 'Sweeping over Amsterdam at 3,000 ft, doing 450 mph – bags of light flak.'

This was completely Gillam's idea for the camera. He wanted to know as early as possible what success the Wing had, on what he classed as the important wing shows. The general routine would be that a Tac/R or PRU aircraft would fly out after the raid, return to its own base, the pictures would be processed and then sent to us, which could mean quite a delay. He wanted something immediate and that's why I flew these ops for him. Later there were two of us, David Ince and myself.

Flight Lieutenant S.J. Eaton, 257 Squadron

Three days later the operation was repeated on the Gestapo HQ in Rotterdam with equal success. This time the raid was led by Wing Commander Johnny Wells.

We acted as anti-flak on this show. I led the squadron and made two attacks in the Dock area on barges, rail and gun positions. We were to keep them all busy while others attacked the HQ.

Flight Lieutenant R.E.G. Sheward, 266 Squadron

In 164 Squadron at this time were two brothers, W.K. and N.L. Merrett. The former, as a warrant officer, had been in the squadron since Normandy, his brother, a flight lieutenant DFC, arriving in the autumn.

On 11th November, Warrant Officer Merrett had a lucky escape when attacking a 105 mm gun at Dunkirk. His Typhoon (JP687 'R') was hit and he jettisoned the hood to bale out but managed to reach base and belly land successfully. On 4th December his brother was hit by flak, attacking guns in woods west of Tiel. He continued his attack, his aeroplane streaming glycol, but managed to get back and belly land in a field inside the Allied lines. The Typhoon hit a ditch and turned over but he managed to crawl out. He was recommended for an immediate bar to his DFC.

Then on 11th December both brothers, W.K.M. having just been commissioned, carried out an armed weather recce over the Zuider Zee. On their return they spotted a train west of Utrecht and attacked with R/P and cannon in the face of intense flak. Flight Lieutenant Merrett called up his No 2, saying, 'I have had my time; been hit – going down!' (JR507 'W'). Pilot Officer Merrett circled but did not see anything further of the other Typhoon.

By February 1945 W.K. Merrett, himself a flight commander, was still very much in action. On the 21st he was hit by flak and baled out but he fractured his arm when doing so (PD511). When he got back he was sent on rest.

The next major event in the winter of 44-45 was when the Germans launched their Ardennes offensive – the now famous Battle of the Bulge. This was Hitler's last offensive of the war and planned to thrust deep into the American lines. Field Marshal von Rundstedt's fourteen infantry and ten Panzer divisions opened the attack on 16th December achieving initial success through the woodlands of the Ardennes, the front held by the American 1st Army. The poor weather aided the German ground attacks as for most of the period Allied aircraft were grounded through fog, snow and ice. On 23rd December the weather allowed 2nd TAF to get its aircraft over the battle front where targets were plentiful. The battle raged around Malmédy, Bastogne and St Vith, the latter being eventually the only major road junction through which the Germans could support their offensive.

The Luftwaffe had husbanded its forces in late 1944 and large numbers of fighers were put into the air in support. Although these were supposed to be used to smash American daylight raids on Germany, the offensive changed this plan, and the fighter force was whittled away over the last days of the year.

The weather hindered the Luftwaffe too, but it did make a few large forays during late December, culminating in the famous New Year's Day attack on Allied air bases in Holland, Belgium and France, which proved a final disaster for the German Air Arm.

Squadron Leader G.J. Gray, 182 Squadron
The weather in the Ardennes was not that good, 10/10th cloud much of the time. When we first went down to the American sector, when the Germans broke through, for some extraordinary reason they wouldn't let us take rockets with us. So when we found all these tanks we had to come back, rearm and go down again. Luckily we caught them the second time round, but what made me furious was seeing all those tanks and being able to do nothing about it. But we found them in a pass the second time. Kit was leading and he blocked one end of the pass and I blocked the other and so there was no way out for them – they were just bottled up – an incredible party. That was when the poor old Group Captain went missing – Charles Green. He used to fly all the time. A very sincere man, rigid, very just. He would often take a spare No 2 and just go out and shoot up anything German.

Wing Commander C.D. North-Lewis OC 124 Wing
We were heavily engaged in the Ardennes and attacked a large number of targets down there. We lost a hell of a lot of people

too. In 124 Wing I think we lost three of the four squadron commanders and the Group Captain, Charles Green.

We caught the Germans at their furthest point they had reached with their armour. I led the attack down against it. There was a hill and the Tiger tanks were all over one side and the British armour was on the other. You could see it, just like two armies drawn up at Agincourt, yet they couldn't see each other. We attacked the German armour and they never got farther through the Ardennes. That was the spearhead, and it was on 26th December, at Celle. We claimed four tanks and two half-tracks, 500 yards in front of our own tanks!

We were having a Boxing Day party that evening and of the squadron commanders I think Jerry Gray, Barraclough and myself – wing leader – were the only ones left since the Ardennes started.

Flying Officer G. Clubley, 181 Squadron

When the weather cleared we flew in support. We lost our CO, Shorty Short, who had previously sported an enormous beard. I remember Kit North-Lewis telling him, 'Off! The RAF don't wear beards, you join the Navy for that.' But Shorty managed to persuade the doctor, who was an old drinking friend of his, to give him a chit that he had a skin rash. However, when he was given command of 181, N-L said if you want to be CO you'd have to shave it off.

Squadron Leader H.P. Short DFC, who joined 181 from 137 Squadron early in December, was lost on 27th December. He had been a junior pilot in 181 earlier in the war. On the 27th six aircraft had been out on an armed recce. around Bullange. As Short reduced height to look at some ground transport south-west of St Vith, he collided with another Typhoon of another squadron. His Typhoon exploded. Gerry Gray had a beard at this time too. He had a slight facial infection but very patriotically he would say that he had grown it and would not shave it off until the Allies crossed the Rhine. By March 1945 it was off!

Christmas Day and Boxing Day we did suffer very heavy losses on the Wing, probably the worst we had during the period because

Top: Wing Commander Charles Green DSO DFC (later Group Captain), in his personal Typhoon June 1944. Note WingCo's pennant by cockpit.

Bottom left: Flight Lieutenant George Clubley DFC, 181 and 137 Squadrons.

Bottom right: W/C 'Kit' North-Lewis and G/C E. R. Bitmead DFC, leaders of 124 Wing.

there was a lot of return fire and it was massed due to the bottle-up in the Ardennes.

Flying Officer H.G. Pattison, 182 Squadron

We went up to the Ardennes looking for trouble. It became a bit dicey because we found ourselves messing with Mustangs and Thunderbolts which was all a bit confusing – but we managed to attack the targets. The alarming thing on Christmas Day was a strike on the airfield (Volkel) by the airmen. They were on strike for about an hour in the canteen. One of our technical officers had dropped his pants and broken wind into a microphone and thought it terribly funny. The Group Captain did not and pushed him off the station – hence the strike!

Flight Lieutenant H. Ambrose, 175 Squadron

Gerry Gray's 182 Squadron had flown an armed recce to Malmédy on Christmas Eve and strafed MT and AFVs they found heading west along a road. As was the tactic, they knocked out vehicles at the head and rear of the column, then everyone began to fly up and down the road, firing into the vehicles with 20 mm cannon which destroyed ten and damaged 20 others. Only one Typhoon was damaged by ground fire – Flight Lieutenant Edwards – resulting in a successful crash-landing at base.

The Canadian Wing suffered several casualties on Christmas Eve over the battle front. Flying Officer D.J. Washburn and Warrant Officer R.F. Bean of 438 Squadron failed to return from Malmédy and 439 Squadron lost Flight Sergeant W.A. Wright when attacking MT. Later 439 lost Flight Lieutenant Ken Sage, while Flying Officer F.H. Laurence brought back a badly crippled Typhoon. Wing Commander F.G. Grant and 440 Squadron were attacked by two FW190s but Grant managed to damage one. Flying Officer C.F. Harwood was brought down by flak when ground strafing and to end the day's casualties, 440 lost Flying Officer D.H. Cumming and Flying Officer W.T. Dunkell to a FW190 which was then shot down by a Spitfire.

On Christmas Day, 175 Squadron lost a pilot, Warrant Officer Merlin. Tom Hall tells the story:

Warrant Officer Merlin was originally a Hurricane pilot and had been shot down over France before the invasion. After the invasion he drove up in a German jeep with an Alsatian dog which had belonged to a German major who had been killed by the Resistance – Merlin having been living with the Maquis after being shot down. After seeing the Typhoons he expressed an interest in them and after leave in the UK and converting to the type, he was posted to 175 in October 1944.

On 25th December I was leading the squadron, with Merlin as my No 2, east of Malmédy. We attacked some trucks and there was a lot of light flak. Merlin was hit under the engine and started to stream glycol. I told the rest of the squadron to return home whilst I would cut across with Merlin to the bomb line to get him inside our lines as soon as possible. He kept asking me if we had crossed the bomb line, but I said no and that as flames were now coming from under his engine, he should bale out. He said he would hang on but I told him again to bale out.

He was now losing precious height and had obviously decided to stick with the aircraft. He hit the ground in a good flat position with wheels up and bushes and dirt were thrown into the air as the Typhoon slithered along, then exploded in a large burst of flame. I circled but could see no movement, so climbed, called for a D/F fix, then flew home to report that he had 'bought it'.

At dinner in our mess the next night, who should come in the door but Merlin, his face still black from the smoke of the fire. He had landed about 600 yards from the Germans and as soon as he touched the ground, he undid his straps, and was then thrown out as the port side of the cockpit was ripped away. He landed in an overgrown, unfilled, water channel, his Typhoon exploding some distance from him. As the undergrowth had swallowed him up I obviously could not see him when I had circled. Merlin then heard a noise and a British soldier crawled up to him, motioning him to follow and keep quiet. Bullets were flying everywhere, mostly into the burning aircraft. Merlin was posted on leave, did no more operations and in January 1945 was posted to a non-Germanic theatre of war.

Flying Officer T.T. Hall, 175 Squadron

It was on Boxing Day that Charles Green was shot down. He flew out with Flight Lieutenant John Derry of 182 Squadron, was hit by ground fire and taken prisoner. His place was taken by Group Captain E.R. Bitmead DFC, a former pilot from the Battle of Britain

Top: Rocket-armed Typhoons take off for operations over France.

Bottom: F/O Ross Clarke RCAF and W/O Bill Speedie, 175 Squadron. Clarke was hit by flak on 24 October, baled out and drowned, having landed in the River Maas. Mae Wests had been discarded after the squadrons began operating inland, but after his loss, orders were given to wear them once more.

days, and like many of the fighting group captains, was often in the air, although not officially allowed to fly on operations.

> Bitmead took over from Charles Green, as Group Captain 124 Wing. He used to push off and pretend to do air tests but he had his own war going, firing rockets and cannon at the Germans. He was not allowed to fly with us on ops, as targets were still pretty hot and it was no use sending a Group Captain to do a sergeant's or pilot officer's job. Nevertheless, Bitmead carried on his own war. We used to see him in action. We'd be coming back from ops and see his Typhoon going in to have a shot himself. He never told anyone but we knew what he was doing.
>
> *Flight Lieutenant H. Ambrose, 175 Squadron*

On the 27th, 182 Squadron ran into enemy fighters. Again weather was bad, with frost and mist preventing air operations till mid-afternoon, when Gerry Gray led an armed recce to St Vith. They strafed some MT, Gray and his No 2, Lieutenant J.I.A. 'Buster' Watt SAAF, setting three trucks on fire and damaging three more. It was while looking for further targets that seven FW190s were seen approaching from dead ahead and slightly below. The Typhoons began to climb and the 190s turned to follow but German gunners on the ground opened fire and scared off the Germans. Then Gerry spotted a lone Focke Wulf:

> It was all snow below and we could see this chap just flying along, straight and level at about 2,000 feet – I couldn't believe it. We had got split up but the pairs always stuck together. This chap was either ferrying an aircraft or was as dim as a Toc H lamp.
>
> I attacked and gave him a four second burst and saw him splinter all along his wings, but then Buster Watt screamed, 'Don't, please Boss, I've never shot one down!' So I said OK, and Buster went right up his backside and fired, whereupon the pilot just hopped out and the 190 spiralled in. He had leather flying kit on which I saw quite clearly as he floated down in his parachute.
>
> *Squadron Leader G.J. Gray, OC 182 Squadron*

The Canadians continued with their run of losses on the 27th, losing Flying Officer B.E. Bell, who baled out SW of Aachen while ground strafing. However, Flight Lieutenant D.E. Jenvey of 440 Squadron shot down a Me109 to even the score. Two days later Jenvey crash-landed his shot up Tiffie and was shot by the Germans while trying to evade capture. Also on the 29th, Flying Officer Laurence of 439 saw a Typhoon shot down by a FW190 and then he and his wingman were attacked by ten enemy fighters. They were chased ten miles, but a long-nosed FW190D, who came in too close, tried to follow Laurence in a tight turn and flicked over and hit the ground. Laurence was then attacked by a Me109. He out-turned the German and was about to fire when it too flicked over, hit the ground and blew up.

Miracles continued in 182 Squadron on 31st December, at least for one pilot. The squadron went for tanks at St Vith, despite a frozen runway. They met heavy AA fire, but got one tank 'flamer' two 'smokers', ten trucks destroyed with fifteen more damaged, plus a petrol dump set on fire. Flying Officer N.G. 'Tiny' Sievwright DFC and Flying Officer J.A. Patterson failed to return, and Flight Lieutenant T. Entwhistle had to make a forced landing.

> Tommy Entwhistle got shot down on the wrong side of the lines but he walked through a minefield to get back. He didn't know it of course, and the Americans said it was impossible to walk through anyway! Yet he just walked across it while the American soldiers were waving and shouting at him to stop. He just waved back but was absolutely shattered when he reached them and they told him what he had just done. Being shot down was nothing in comparison, and we had to send him on rest.
>
> *Squadron Leader G.J. Gray, OC 182 Squadron*

Another casualty on the last day of 1944 was Allan Smith DFC, CO of 197 Squadron, who was leading his squadron in company with 193 Squadron, led by Wing Commander Wells. The target was the bridge at Culemberg. He was hit by flak but sucessfully carried out a crash landing and was seen to run from the aircraft. He was later reported a prisoner.

Squadron Leader A.H. Smith, OC 197 Squadron
> I had just come to the end of my second tour of ops, having flown over 400 combat missions. I was feeling a little tired and waiting for a new posting. On 31st December I got out of bed and went

Top: 182 Squadron adopted 'Jane' of the *Daily Mirror* in 1944 and in order to carry her message to the Germans, they would glue her cartoon strip on their drop tanks. Also chalked on this tank is 'Love from Jane's Boys'. Note long-range tanks and just two R/Ps either side for deep penetration raids into Germany.

Bottom: Squadron Leader Allan Smith DFC, OC 197 Squadron in France (B51). The bombing accuracy had fallen off and Smith was telling his pilots that there would be no more leave until it improved. They were back on target the next day!

Squadron Leader A.H. Smith, OC 197 Squadron (continued)

down to the Ops Caravan to see what was scheduled for the day and found the target – a bridge at Culemberg, south-east of Utrecht. This was too good for me to resist.

Bridges were a favourite target for 197 and we had built up a good success record. We had developed a technique of attacking them with 11-second delay 1,000 pounders, going in at low level in a shallow dive of approximately 30° and try to dig the bombs in from four angles where the bridge joins the river bank. If this did not do the job on its own, a follow up attack with dive bombers usually finished the bridge off.

This particular attack was to be made by 193 Squadron led by Wing commander Johnny Wells, with 197 Squadron led by myself, doing the low level attack. If my memory is correct, I think Group Captain Gillam also came along for the ride.

The weather was terrible – very cold – about 9/10ths cloud at 8,000 feet, with the ground covered in snow. As leader of the low level squadron I was doing the navigation which was difficult because we were flying above the cloud to keep out of the light flak and the odd glimpses I could get of the ground were not very helpful because any landmarks were blotted out by the snow.

I flew on a compass course but knew the area very well by then and was able to get a pinpoint as we crossed the River Maas. At this the heavy flak started to work us over and we started to weave and change height to make it harder for them. I felt a crack and then saw white puffs of smoke coming from my exhausts. I figured I had been hit in the glycol and called up on the R/T to say that I had been hit and would be force landing soon. I think I could have made it back to our lines at this stage but I was committed to the attack and decided to press on – I think I was the only person who knew where we were at that stage. The army had assigned this target as a 'destroy at all costs' so knew it to be important.

Shortly afterwards we went down through the cloud and although the flak became more intense I was able to pinpoint myself and navigate accurately right up to the bridge. I knew I was running out of time so my Number Two, 'Cobber' James, an Australian, and I went right into the attack and put our bombs right on target. I had pulled up to about 600 feet when my motor cut. With not enough height to bale out I was forced with a

Squadron Leader A.H. Smith, OC 197 Squadron (continued)

landing so told James I was going down then looked round for a suitable place to land.

It was difficult to make a decision because the ground was all white, and beneath the snow would be canals and irrigation ditches. I didn't have too much time to discuss it with myself because the Typhoon had a fairly steep glide path without an engine.

I decided to land parallel to the irrigation ditches – found a suitable paddock clear of trees and came over the fence at about 150 mph, levelled off (wheels up) about five feet above the ground and then dug the nose in. It couldn't have been better and I was skidding along the surface starting to undo my straps so that I could get out in a hurry, when I realised that I wasn't slowing up – the ground was frozen solid and I was going along like a toboggan!

I saw I was going to hit the far fence so did my straps up again and waited for the impact. The Typhoon hit the fence, went up a bank, knocked down a couple of telegraph poles, skidded across a road, down the far bank and then set off across the next field, which turned out to be a frozen lake! It broke the ice then started to sink.

I scrambled out onto the wing and dived onto the ice before the Typhoon sank and took off at high speed towards the nearest shelter hiding my maps in a frozen potato mound on the way.

I will always be grateful to my No 2 who dived down through the flak to see how I was getting on. He saw me get out of the Tiffie and run away so was able to relay this information to my wife. I was about $\frac{3}{4}$ of the way to some friendly looking woods when bullets started going past my ears and shortly afterwards I was taken prisoner by some Luftwaffe anti-aircraft personnel. The episode ended on a humorous note. We had to walk through a small Dutch village and I was having difficulty walking in my flying boots. The German guards were helping me keep upright but when I saw the villagers, I pushed the guards away, held my head up high and pushed out my chest to let the Dutch know that the Allies would be along soon. I had only taken a few steps when I slipped on the ice, fell on my backside and had to be helped to my feet by smiling Germans. Truly, pride goes before a fall!

Squadron Leader A.H. Smith, OC 197 Squadron

As I have covered the Luftwaffe's attack on 1st January 1945 fully in my book *The Battle of the Airfields* published by Grub Street, London, in 2000, I shall not describe it in detail here, but have chosen one attack in particular, that by 168 Squadron, to represent it in fuller detail.

Squadron Leader Leonard Lambert had led his squadron out to strafe enemy positions around St Vith and was luckily away from his base at Eindhoven when the Germans attacked it. They did however, run into the Luftwaffe soon after hearing over their radios that something was going on in the skies over Holland.

Because of our low level training we had to go to St Vith when the weather in the Ardennes salient improved on 1st January 1945 – and we had to go in under the clouds. Our task was to pick up whatever targets the American Liaison Officer gave to us in that very constrained valley, with cloud on the hilltops. Without bombs or rockets we were able to manoeuvre better and get in much quicker in those weather conditions.

On the way back from St Vith, having been hit by an 88 mm shell, I had a hole in one wing. It was then that we tried to 'rescue' what we thought was a man in a Mustang being chased by a mixed horde of Me109s and FW190s. It turned out to be a German colonel who had been leading the raid on Brussels, flying a captured American Mustang. Because of my damaged Typhoon I was flying with my left foot stuck right out in the corner of the cockpit and my right hand pulling the stick way over to the right so I couldn't do very much except dive through the German fighters who scattered all over the place. The German leader, in the Mustang (I met him after the war and he gave me the whole story) ordered the rearmost Messerschmitts to have a go at us, which they did. What we didn't know was that they were all very short of fuel; they made one pass at us and we were practically out of ammunition anyway, and I'd got less than anyone, on account of the hole in my wing where the ammo ought to be.

After the pass the Germans were called off but this one, solitary Messerschmitt pilot decided he was in a good position to have a go at me and he came round, Flight Lieutenant Joe Stubbs, an Australian, who was a very good friend of mine, and one of my flight commanders, picked him off. I was watching the German in my rear mirror and there was nothing I could do but just keep straight while discussing the situation with Joe and the others. The German thought he had a sitting duck and concentrated on me and Joe just knocked him out of the sky. But Joe was killed the very next day.

Joe Stubbs took off to air test a Typhoon on 2nd January and Lennie Lambert saw him crash and burn to death, unable to do anything about it. Lennie continues:

The armourer who was supposed to screw down the panels on the wing cannon bays forgot. Joe took off to do the air test and I strolled out to our dispersal and watched him go. He got halfway down the runway, then to my horror I saw the wing bays open. I could feel exactly what he was trying to do. He tried to stop but went off the runway, skidded along the frozen, icy ground, went under one of the Typhoons of 247 Squadron that was armed with rockets, and caught fire. Both aircraft were in flames by the time I got there in my jeep, rockets were going off in one direction, cannon shells too. The perspex hood was just melting around Joe's head, then his Typhoon blew up. It is a sight I shall never forget.

Squadron Leader L.H. Lambert, OC 168 Squadron

❋

Lennie Lambert got a Ju188 on 23rd January during an armed recce of Münster-Rheine-Enschede. Flight Lieutenant E.C.H. Vernon-Jarvis (ex-175 Squadron) and Flight Lieutenant J.M. Kay, attacked a train near Münster, then saw some road transport near Nijmegen. Then Lambert saw a rocket aircraft and flew towards it.

We were going after a Messerschmitt 163 over Rheine, chasing it as it came out of cloud just in front of us. We hadn't actually seen one before, we'd only had vague briefings from Intelligence about these rocket aircraft. This thing came rocking out of the sky, going quite slowly – about 300 mph – probably out of fuel. We heard after the war they were supposed to reserve enough fuel for about a 20-second burst in case they had any problems when approaching to land. The pilot must have seen us because he went straight back into cloud in a near vertical climb and I strongly suspect he didn't get out of that because of his limited power which he'd used to get away from us. However, because of what he was doing we knew we were very near his landing point, so we spent the next twenty minutes or so searching around. We found a camouflaged aerodrome at Rheine, where they were operating from. As we were circling round – and there had been no anti-aircraft fire reported in that area at all – it was difficult to see anything. The Germans were being very clever about it – even the runway had been totally camouflaged. But one part of the runway was visible and a Ju188 was just coming into land with a Me109 escort. So we nobbled him just as he was touching down and we think we got one of the 109s as well. But the 188 we got well and truly.

Squadron Leader L.H. Lambert, OC 168 Squadron

The Junkers was shared by Lambert (MN265), Flying Officer J.B.C. Catterns (EK140 'K') and Flying Officer T.B. Noble (RB376).

CHAPTER THIRTEEN

Tactics and Flak

While some tactics had, by necessity, changed since Normandy because the type of land battles had changed, some mentioned in this chapter will complement those recorded in Chapter 10.

Normandy was generally a fluid battle, especially after the break-out from the beach-head. By the winter of 1944-45 the battle front had become static. The Typhoons, based at permanent aerodromes, rather than airstrips, were now ranging deeper into enemy territory and into Germany itself. The Typhoon's war had changed. Although they still supported the army whenever German strongpoints, tanks or guns proved a nuisance, their main job now was one of interdiction. Hitting the enemy's transport and supply lines was the priority. So over the winter of 44-45, whenever weather permitted, the Typhoons would range into German-held territory and into their homeland.

Squadron Leader G.J. Gray, OC 182 Squadron
Long range penetration, armed recces; all around the Osnabrück region, and Hamm or Münster. We used to go about 100 miles into the German lines and just search around, usually in fours, and quite often we'd see a staff car. You knew it was hostile, because it was painted green as a rule!

On one op we got 50 soldiers; we decimated that lot. They were marching along a road and we sneaked up on them and probably wrote them all off. With our fragmentation rockets it splayed outwards, like a bangalore torpedo and just cut things to ribbons – they were really lethal damn things. On our deep penetrations we'd have long range tanks, flying outwards on this fuel then switch when they began to empty. We had 45 gallons in each tank and then stripped them off.

Flying Officer H.G. Pattison, 182 Squadron

First long range op we did, Gerry Gray was leading and we climbed up through cloud and went out on DR over the cloud, and didn't see a thing as I remember. There was, however, an unforecast change in the wind and we penetrated a lot further than we should have done. I seem to recall on plotting out, somebody said we'd ended up about 150 miles from Berlin, which was getting fairly well into enemy territory!

Anyway, we turned round and on the way back we were attacked by 40 or 50 mixed Me109s and FW190s. We were getting rather short of fuel so we just held on course as the Germans climbed up to get a height advantage over us. When they got about 4 or 5,000 feet they released their drop tanks – we could see these silver things just fluttering down – and then we mixed it. There were eight of us against that lot. I don't know if anyone claimed any hits out of it but the mêlée didn't last very long because being on the defensive we had to be fairly aggressive. Although I had a couple of squirts at two of them I missed, but they cleared off fairly quickly and we were left to reform and continue home.

We spread ourselves all over Holland, running out of fuel. I think about half of us got back to base, a couple went into Volkel – I went into Volkel on that occasion, others were at different strips.

That was one of only two occasions during my tour that we encountered enemy aircraft in the air. We were, of course, told not to get into dog-fights. We were supposed to attack the targets briefed, or targets of opportunity, and 109s and 190s were generally superior in the dog-fight to the Typhoon.

Flying Officer G. Clubley, 181 Squadron

Then we settled in for the winter, doing the Münster 'milk-run' as we called it. Every morning we would send a group off as far as Münster, looking at railway lines, etc. We usually attacked trains at 90°, aiming for the engine itself, firing rockets with hopefully sufficient accuracy to knock them out. If we'd run out of rockets we'd use cannon.

We operated in two ways. A short haul – the Münster run, passed the Ruhr which we had to skirt round, carrying full rocket load, or long range patrols with two LR tanks, although this cut us down to four rockets. We'd fly out to full range, drop tanks, and use the rockets on targets on the way back. It wasn't recommended to fire rockets with tanks on.

Targets could he hard to come by; in fact I recall attacking one train and by the time we had finished there were three squadrons having a go at it – ourselves, some Spitfires and then some Tempests.

Flight Lieutenant R.E.G. Sheward, 263 Squadron
We had to fly up to about 4-5,000 feet to be able to see a fair bit. Despite the dangers of flak we used to move it around a bit and never stay too long at the same height so we'd go up to 7-8,000 feet, then come down again, or perhaps even lower. If you got too low everything passed so quickly it didn't give you a chance to get a bead on it. I can remember on one or two occasions seeing transport and being too low and by the time we'd moved round, it had disappeared. But if we were high enough to see it and then go straight onto it, then you'd be able to attack before the target got out of the way. I recall one occasion particularly. I've always been a horse lover since my time in the Argentine, and on this occasion we saw a horse-drawn vehicle which was obviously being used by the Germans. One of the lads spotted it and called, 'Transport down there!', and we moved in to shoot it up. As we went down I couldn't do it, so I called up, 'Moving off!' Then the boys said afterwards, 'What went wrong, Boss?' So I replied, that I was sorry but I love horses too much and to hell with it, I wasn't going to shoot them up.

Ronnie Sheward had left 266 Squadron in November 1944, to take command of B Flight of 263 Squadron. He would return to 266 in March 1945, as Commanding Officer.

The Germans were terrified of the Typhoon. I remember at the Reichswald Forest, and they picked a part of the Forest into which we had to fire rockets if we couldn't find our primary targets. So on the way back, we dumped our rockets into this part of the Forest and later received a signal from the Army, saying that we had actually killed something like 600 German soldiers that were encamped there. We knew they were in there but just couldn't see

Right: 197 Squadron's A Flight, Antwerp. Front (l to r): F/O G. G. Mahaffy, S/L A. H. Smith DFC (PoW 31 Dec) OC, F/L R. C. C. Curwen (DFC). Seated: P/O D. I. McFee (PoW 24 Dec), Matthews, James RAAF, Formiloe, Byrne (on prop), D. Lovell, K. Walsh, J. Ellis. Curwen became OC after Smith was lost.

Left: 263 Squadron, Antwerp, 25 November 1944. Middle four front row, from left: F/O H. M. Proctor DFC, F/L M. T. Rumbold DFC (OC in 1945), S/L R. D. Rutter DFC, F/L R. E. G. Sheward DFC.

Right: 137 Squadron 1945. Middle row: 4th from left F/L G. Clubley DFC, 5th S/L R. G. V. Barraclough, 6th F/L J. Rendall RAAF (DFC and later OC 181 Sqn), 7th F/L R. A. Egley (KIA 24 Mar 1945), 9th F/O Copeman RAAF, 10th Capt J. I. A. Watt SAAF (previously 182 Sqn).

them. And that was just dumping our rockets, which was extraordinary.

Flight Lieutenant H. Ambrose, 175 Squadron

*

On 19th November, 257 Squadron, led by Flight Lieutenant J.D. Howarth, went for a target near Zwolle. The eight Typhoons dive-bombed it, scoring several direct hits. Flying Officer Freddie Broad (Canadian), who had survived the collision on take-off at Manston two months before, was going down and about to release his bombs when his aircraft caught fire. Within seconds it turned sharply to the right and crashed. He stood no chance of getting out as barely five seconds elapsed from him being hit to the impact with the ground. Surprisingly nobody reported seeing any flak on this show.

This same squadron were out again on 5th January 1945, attacking variety of targets. Flight Lieutenant Jerry Eaton and Pilot Officer R.W. Snell attacked a laundry building at Zierikzee where German soldiers were holding up. They dropped bombs with 11-second fuses which were bang on target. This was the day Brian Spragg came back with a ropey engine to force-land (see Chapter 11). Some time earlier

I was the first pilot on our wing to use 1,000 lb bombs on Tiffies. I attacked an observation post on the Breskens peninsula. It was twice as heavy as the previous load but the aeroplane coped with it all right. Then on 8th February 1945, just as our troops were about to go into Germany, we did some high level bombing under radar, which was a bit unusual. We just flew out at a set height and speed, and were directed from so-called accurate radar from nearby, then given a count-down to drop. Apparently the results were relatively good. This was in the Cleve area and what we called 'blind bombing'.

Flying Officer B.J. Spragg, 257 Squadron

During our sojourn at Antwerp the operations changed a bit. We did the Walcheren Islands and Breskens Pocket, and trying to clear the north bank of the River Scheldt, which were all pretty grim operations – weather not very good.

Then in January and February, we were concentrating on the V2 attacks on England. They had their bases in Holland and also brought their supplies up along two or three railway lines. We seemed to spend our time cutting these lines or chasing trains.

Flying Officer J.G. Simpson, 193 Squadron

✳

The Wing Leaders were, of course, not only concerned with tactics but had also to run their wings, which included briefings, interpretation of orders, etc:

Group Captain D.E. Gillam, OC 146 Wing
Every day there was an operational order but it depended. It could be to operate in a certain area of interdiction – stopping road and rail transport over a given area – but it would be left to the Wing CO to operate and how many aircraft, etc. They generally gave some idea of priority, in other words it might be a maximum effort or it might be just a normal show. Maximum effort might need three or four sorties a day depending on distance. If you were not maximum effort but just sustained effort it would be one or two sorties a day, depending also on serviceability.

In the last year of the war I tended to fly the more interesting sorties although I generally flew every other day or something like that – just going out. But anything really interesting I'd certainly fly. I had a Wing Commander Flying as well as myself and we seldom flew as a complete wing. Five squadrons were too many to handle with this type of stuff, so two squadrons were normally about the maximum. So I'd take two squadrons, and he might take two, while the fifth stood down.

Wing Commander C.D. North-Lewis, OC 124 Wing
When we got to Holland for the winter of 44-45, and the ground battle had become static, then we used to get every day from the GCC, an area for the wing to attack, mainly transport, railways, things like that; and anything that moved – at the Wing Leader's discretion.

It was up to the Wing Leader to decide the targets and to detail squadrons, to fly the number of sorties he thought was necessary. Of course, if one of the first squadrons out reported movement in a certain area then you'd send another squadron. So throughout the winter of 44-45 most of the operations were at the Wing Leader's discretion, unless a specific show came up, or unless the 2nd British Army were calling for support.

We flew in eights and then during the winter we flew in sixes – three pairs. I had a theory that for the type of operations we were doing then, when we were going for transport, you needed a very fluid formation with the leader and his No 2 flying in front and two other pairs – one on each side – covering him. They could change over quickly and easily. Until then we had flown two fluid-fours, two sets of fours, eight to a squadron, so a three squadron show would mean 24 aircraft. As Wing Leader, I just used to say, 'Well, I'm going to lead,' and I led whichever squadron was available. I always took as my No 2, someone from that squadron. I didn't have a permanent No 2, which was different sometimes to other wings. I didn't because a No 2 got shot down so often that it was unfair to have a permanent one. The Germans used to shoot at the leader and generally miss him and hit the No 2!

Denys Gillam rarely had a permanent No 2 either – it just wasn't fair on the individual. He too tended to ask one of his squadron commanders to detail someone on each operation.

Flight Lieutenant S.J. Eaton, 257 Squadron
If one talked of speed, then Denys Gillam could show most younger people, and he had a habit, when Group Captain and airfield commander, of just calling up a squadron and saying he wanted an aeroplane and a spare pilot. He'd take the pilot, brief him, then the two of them would shoot off, cross the lines somewhere, attack a target, but almost every No 2 would come back and tell the same story. After the dive they'd pull up and try to keep with him, would black out and when they came round, Gillam would be several thousand feet above. He could obviously keep his senses much more than anybody else. In fact it was said, while at Antwerp, that he flew more as the airfield commander, than the average squadron pilot!

Flight Sergeant A. Shannon, 257 Squadron

I did a trip with Group Captain Gillam once. His fashion was to say to the CO, 'Got someone to fly with me?' – and the CO might say, 'OK, Shannon, you go', and he'd take you up. Just the two of us, leader and wingman to cover him. He went for the fun of it really. If he saw anything moving he'd go down and you'd follow, keeping on his tail and shoot when he shot, pulled up when he pulled up, then come home.

Even at squadron commander level, theirs were heavy responsibilities. Early in 1945, Poppa Ambrose was given command of 181 Squadron, when Gerry Gray went on rest.

Squadron Leader H. Ambrose, OC 181 Squadron

On Typhoons, it was a tremendous responsibility to be given, say, a house 100 miles away from base which might be a Gestapo HQ and told to rocket it. Navigation to get to this house was quite a feat. I think it was a question of practice and the more practice you had the more confidence one got so it became second nature. But at first it was difficult.

One started off with a large map, then worked on a smaller scale one. Then if you were lucky you'd have some reconnaissance photos to use. For the average chap it was often too difficult to find the target, because the target may not be obvious. You might have the right pin-point, the right place on the map, but still couldn't find the target. If they were tanks dug-in it was very difficult actually to locate them and very often I led a squadron down onto a pin-point of a map, knowing full well I was correct on my navigation but I wouldn't pick up the target until I was half way in the dive. There was an awful waste, because unless you actually hit the target, all the preparation, all the fuel, rockets, cannon shells brought over from England etc, etc, – and a result wasn't there. Due perhaps to lack of training, and more and more of the experienced guys becoming casualties the dilution was alarming. Had we all stayed together and nobody was shot down, nobody killed or wounded, or rested, no one would have got experience of leading so there would be a stalemate training new leaders. My experience was that a lot of chaps wouldn't lead because they were too scared to lead. It wasn't just a matter of flying and looking for fighters and then getting stuck in; the responsibility of going to attack a target which may only be 300 yards in front of our own troops or even 200 or even 100 yards, was a tremendous responsibility – and scary in a way. For if you did hit your own troops you wouldn't forgive yourself. So that the leaders of the Typhoon flight, or squadron, were fairly brave chaps in this respect. Not great from a fighter pilot type of courage but brave in that they were undertaking to do something that was extremely difficult unless you'd had lots of experience. And since you couldn't do it without having a lot of practice, you had to grit your teeth when you were first given the opportunity to do it. It was a strange situation.

*

Squadron Leader L.H. Lambert, OC 168 Squadron
The Typhoon was good at low level, for example, FW190s wouldn't follow you at low level because they had no warning of the stall, but the Typhoon had a lot of warning. The stick would shake about but could fly it round in the stall quite happily whereas the 190 simply wouldn't do that, it was too dodgy for them. The Me109 however, at low level, could turn inside us. But somehow, by that time, the 109 was almost entirely engaged in high level operations – fortunately for us.

We used the 'finger-four' formation when going in at low level and I used to try and keep everyone very well up – almost in a straight line. This was for their survival as well as anything else – it was a better formation too. If anyone did drift behind he invariably got hit just because they'd aim at me and get him.

*

By this time of the war, using rocket projectiles, while far from being a science, had become an art. In the early days of R/P, actual training was sparse but by the autumn of 1944, R/P Typhoon squadrons were pulled back from the Continent and given a period at Fairwood Common for R/P training. It also gave the squadron a rest from ops for a week or ten days.

Nevertheless, the 'on-the-job' training was still the main way of learning how to knock out a target with rockets. It was also necessary to know when to use salvo (all eight rockets in one blast), pair (two rockets, one from each wing), or ripple (four separate but consecutive firing of pairs).

There was also the personal way a Typhoon pilot would develop his own attack dive and his cannon gunnery.

Squadron Leader G.J. Gray, OC 182 Squadron

We always fired our cannons on the way down to make the gunners put their heads down. You had your rocket sight on and firing your cannons, they weren't too keen on firing back at you. Then you'd let your rockets go. We used our fixed gun-sight to aim and you would allow for any wind – it became quite easy. One always tried, however, to attack either up or down wind so that the rockets would not deflect sideways.

I'd never fired a rocket in anger in my life – we learnt by trial and error. When I joined 181 Squadron my No 2 would tell me if I was over or undershooting but after about three sorties I could hit a target every time. I'd say by about ten sorties the average pilot could hit a train engine or a tank every time.

Wing Commander C.D. North-Lewis, OC 124 Wing

We used to fire, on the whole, the whole lot together, because we only did one attack. The chances of hitting, if you released all eight, were very much higher than if you just fired a pair. On trains we'd try a pair because you'd then go on and attack another target.

Once we caught some German armour that had broken through the American lines. They were strung out along a road and we went down singly and made four attacks. There was no flak and we went for them in a big way.

Group Captain D.E. Gillam, OC 146 Wing

If you were just attacking trains etc, you'd just select pairs, you wouldn't waste the lot if you got hit first time, unless it was a troop train when you'd obviously work down the train. If it was a German HQ etc, then you only get one shot at it, for after that it's too lethal to mess around. You've got to get the surprise, get the concentration of aircraft over the target all at the same time, then get the hell out of it!

The pilots who went in with reservations and sort of pulled

away or attacked half-heartedly, invariably got clobbered. They seemed always to attract the flak because they'd not pressed on vigorously.

*

As we have already seen, the Typhoon pilots had to contend daily with the very real dangers from ground fire. The German flak gunners were very experienced. Indeed, they had had a vast amount of experience of firing at Allied aircraft since the beginning of the war!

Operating at low level the Typhoon pilots quickly learned how best to avoid the worst of the ground fire. Nevertheless, in the final analysis, they had eventually to dive into it to attack a target, and hope for the best.

Flying Officer G. Clubley, 181 Squadron

The German 88 mm guns were the bane of our lives. In Holland, between the Meuse and the Rhine there were a number of 88 batteries and when flying our patrols there, we always aimed to cross that area at high level – about 8,000 feet – which was about the optimum height for the 88s, or right on the deck, depending where the target was.

They were very accurate guns, and we lost quite a few people while we were in Holland when coming back at the end of a sortie. One would be relaxing a bit and possibly not quite high enough and they'd bracket you very quickly. I used to prefer coming back on the deck, because when coming back from Germany to Holland they had a lot of 20 mm stuff, but they would all be pointing west. So coming from the east, by the time they heard us and had swung their guns, we'd be away.

One of our flight commanders, Ken 'Jonah' Jones, a little Welshman, thought that one way to beat the AA over the French coast earlier in the war was to get over it through cloud. One day four of us flew over, found some cloud over the coast and, tucked in tight, flew through, glued to Jonah's tail. He was so intent he was leaning forward, reading his instruments, but his artificial horizon must have been a little out, for when we came through the cloud, all four of us were flying perfectly but with one wing low. And no sooner did we emerge than AA fire surrounded us. We rapidly broke and seconds later were racing back towards England.

It was not long after that experiment, which was quickly abandoned, that Jonah caught a direct hit from a German 88 shell and simply blew up.

Wing Commander C.D. North-Lewis, OC 124 Wing

The flak that worried one – the stuff that used to shoot one down – was the .5 stuff. The heavier flak one didn't worry about. We used to go in at 12-14,000 feet across the German lines, if the weather was right; obviously we had to go in lower when it was cloudy, to get away from the light stuff. The heavy 88 mm stuff, although uncomfortable, especially when puffs went up beside you, was all right. Then we'd dive down on the target so as to spend the minimum time in the light flak area, then pull up and go out again at whatever height one could get up to.

Flying Officer J.G. Simpson, 193 Squadron

We didn't mind the 88 mm too much because although they were pretty accurate and they would give us a few thumps often when we were forming up to dive onto a target, the thing that worried most of us quite a bit was the fact that the Germans would put up a carpet of 20 and 40 mm stuff. Little white puffs you could get out and walk on. Round about 3-4,000 feet this was and one had to dive through it. You didn't think of the shells that were coming up and had not yet exploded, unless they hit you! It seemed much safer to go through the white puffs rather than fly around and try to screw your courage to dive down through it.

I think on the low level shows you never saw the flak that hit you, and I personally felt very much afraid of flak on a low level op. After an attack and you begin to pull up you are a better target for the light flak and there's no doubt that the German gunners were a pretty brave lot.

Flying Officer H.G. Pattison, 182 Squadron

I'd say 8,500 feet was above the 40 mm flak – the light stuff, and starting to get into the 88 mm range. It wasn't quite so accurate at this lower level, but I suppose around 12,000 feet it could be spot on. But they were lucky if they could get a strike on a fighter aircraft with an 88, when it was weaving at 8,500 feet.

Squadron Leader L.H. Lambert, OC 168 Squadron
The German gunners were generally very courageous; they'd continue firing at you as you were coming straight down at them. You knew you were going to get them and they knew it too, but they'd keep on firing. There is no doubt that the standard of the opposition was very high.

Flying Officer D.G. Evans, 137 Squadron
It was the 88 mm we were concerned about when we were higher up. You could suddenly get a 'boom' – and the first burst was very near you and then you got some flak. That was usually the first intimation the 88s were firing.

In the majority of cases, flak gunners seemed to keep their heads up too, they didn't necessarily put their heads down at the first sign of attack. One would hope that when you were spraying cannon shells around that they'd put their heads down, but often they just kept at it.

Gerry Gray, like the others, had great respect for the German flak gunners, but recalls too the Allied AA gunners they had to fly over when re-crossing the bomb line.

Our army's firing was pretty hopeless; we used to come back from the very accurate 88 mm and just as we were crossing an obvious water line, like the Rhine, almost invariably our army would take up the firing. We soon knew when we were on our side because the firing was so absolutely useless. The Germans, of course, had so much practice. We used to put our wheels and flaps down and fly over our gunners and treat them with derision! My famous story: we had four Canadian Typhoon squadrons and four of our rocket-firing Typhoon squadrons. After we had been at Melsbroeck for a month, an RAF Regiment gunner shot down my No 2. We had been flying in and out all day long and he thought it was a Focke Wulf 190. So we told these chaps never to fire at anything! Luckily my No 2 survived and crash-landed. It was like the time at Tangmere with eight Spitfire squadrons when suddenly a chap blazes away at one Spitfire.

Squadron Leader G.J. Gray, OC 182 Squadron

Jerry Eaton also recalls being fired at by army gunners:

We were near the V1 lane at Antwerp and we had to keep clear of it between Breda and Deurne. The whole area northeast and north of Antwerp was a V2 area and we had a lane which we had to fly out and come back in on, so that the army knew it was an RAF aircraft. We were coming back on one trip, four of us, in this lane when suddenly shots burst all around us and we called up to discover it was the British army firing at us. We called up our GCC and they soon stopped them.

Flying Officer S.J. Eaton, 257 Squadron

CHAPTER FOURTEEN

Trains, Shipping and Bridges

Rail transport was one of Germany's main arteries for supplying men, equipment and ammunition to its front lines, as well as transporting goods and raw materials to and from its factories. They were prime targets for 2nd TAF and especially for Typhoons.

Squadron Leader Lennie Lambert's 168 Squadron spent a good deal of time going after trains. Being a squadron only armed with 20 mm cannon, its tactics for attacking these targets were different from other units. As we will see later, squadrons who carried rockets had their way of doing things.

Squadron Leader L.H. Lambert, OC 168 Squadron

Another thing we used to do with the cannon Typhoons was to go in low and try to catch the trains, particularly if they were carrying the V2 rocket fuel tanks, and also the V2s themselves. One of the particular things, and again, this was where our low level Mustang training came in useful, was to try to find the V2 sites themselves, then try to blow up the fuel tankers. Then take the instance of finding trains in the early morning or late at night, if they'd stayed out a bit late in the morning or had got home early at night – they never used to work in daytime, so that was when we tried to catch them. If we could just get the engine, then either Mosquitos or the Typhoon bomb squadrons would follow on and get the actual trains themselves, as obviously they couldn't move once we'd got the engine. We would radio back and give the exact position. We couldn't wait for them to arrive as it might take anything up to an hour for them to get to the train's position.

Of course, the Germans were quite aware of what was happening and so often the attack squadron came into very heavy opposition until they got the technique sorted out, when they had

Spitfires coming in first to clear the air a bit. Johnny Johnson's wing was generally very good at that. But our job was to stop the engine and very often the train had engines fore and aft, so we'd then have to knock out both. Occasionally they might even put another loco in the middle between flak trucks, all in the hope that if we got one of the engines, then the other one would be able to pull or push the train clear of where it had been located. They knew that if they stayed put another heavier attack would soon follow.

With our roving missions, either at the crack of dawn or last thing at dusk, we were quite successful. We would watch mainly the railway lines coming from the Ruhr, for that was where the fuel generally seemed to come from, or perhaps train loads of tanks for the front line. But if they stayed out too long, or started out too early, we'd have them.

Squadron Leader G.J. Gray, OC 182 Squadron

Attacking trains we always tried to hit the engines, to stop them from working. You could see by the direction the smoke was going which way the wind was blowing, so we always tried to attack up or down wind. Usually these trains were armed with 88mm guns, especially the troop trains, which were pretty lethal and very accurate, so again, you'd try to attack out of the sun, if there was any sun.

We would attack from 7,000 feet, fire our cannons as we went down and ideally let off our rockets at around 1,500 feet. If it was an unarmed train we'd stop the engine with a pair, then fire at the trucks later. With a troop train we'd then go for the troops. If they were pouring out of the carriages you could fly along and cannon them. With my guns, I always had tracer shells for the last 20 rounds, for I hated being without any ammunition, in case we were jumped by fighters on the way back. So when the tracer appeared I'd know I had about 20 rounds left in each gun. I insisted that all my squadron pilots did that in the end.

Flying Officer G. Clubley, 181 Squadron

I recall once being chewed off by Charles Green. We had been on a long range job, two hours, and somewhere south of Hanover we came across a train and we dropped our tanks. I fired my rockets and all four came off as I must have selected salvo instead of pairs. He said, 'You went all the way there and on one trip you fired all your rockets at one target!' 'But I got it,' I replied. 'But you could have got another one!' he insisted. Once we attacked an express train heading towards Hanover. As we attacked it the crew abandoned the engine and the train was still moving. It wasn't far away from the city and still going quite fast, so often I wonder what happened when it reached its destination.

Group Captain D.E. Gillam, OC 146 Wing
Shortly after D-Day we got knowledge that a troop train was coming in on a line from Paris and they believed they would take refuge in a tunnel, which they did. At dawn we went off with bombs and we skidded the bombs, with delayed action fuses, in both ends of the tunnel. In due course it blew up, collapsed the tunnel, leaving the train inside. As we were 30-40 miles behind the front lines there wasn't much flak about so we could do it at fairly low level. The bombs literally bounced off the track and shot into the tunnel.

Flight Sergeant A. Shannon, 257 Squadron
We always attacked a train from line astern, never from the side because if you did the flak concentration could come at you from both sides. If you attacked line astern the flak only came from the back end being unable to traverse from the front.

Flight Lieutenant J.G. Simpson, 193 Squadron
Sometimes the Germans used to have two or three flak guns on their trains, nearly always one at the end, one near the engine and one in the middle. What we used to do if we spotted a train was to bomb the line ahead of it, so that at least stopped the thing and then you'd send in the first two aircraft to go for the engine. We usually came in at something between 90° and 45° and if you were lucky and got strikes on the engine straight away, the driver usually let out all the steam and hopped off damn quick, and you could see him running away to hide in a ditch. After that you could deal with the thing at your leisure. Really, the object was to cut the line and stop it running.

Flying Officer H.G. Pattison, 182 Squadron

Troop trains particularly had flak-waggons front and rear and the aim was primarily to knock out the engine to immobilize the whole unit. Then to take out the flak and then to go for the carriages and trucks.

Normally a section of four would stay with us as top cover while the other four went in and fired off, then they would reverse and the four who had fired would become top cover and the others attack with their rockets. There would be some pundits who would say you start from front to rear, or rear to front and go along the whole lot but you were pulling through all the time which destroys the accuracy of your fire. Particularly with trains, you had to take the engine sideways on with rockets to get a good target, broadside on; it gave you a much better aiming point and allowed for any slight inaccuracy in aiming.

There were schools of thought on this, because if you attack a train lengthways there's a great temptation to start at the beginning and pull right through to the end. Certainly as far as I recall you were taught to concentrate your fire on a particular target rather than spray a whole area, which you would tend to do if you were pulling through.

As far as rockets were concerned there were occasions when you had a lengthways target, say a tank farm or a factory installation which covered an area where you could ripple off and cover a lot of ground with your rockets, but when you are pin-pointing a target like an engine, or a vehicle, then you had to go in to give yourself the best advantage for sighting and accuracy. So with trains it was a broadside attack.

I recall once when there was a train and the railway line was on an embankment which was six to ten feet above the level of the surrounding ground. We came in broadside, right on the deck so this engine was absolutely level with me and was the perfect target, perfect attack and perfect presentation. I put a pair of rockets at the engine, which, having then broken and gone round and looked back, I saw strike the engine between the boiler and the chassis. Then there was the chassis sitting on the line – the boiler and cab had gone completely.

It was amazing the accuracy you could achieve with rockets, when you had a few seconds to settle down and really make an attack a copy-book effort.

Flying Officer D.G. Evans, 137 Squadron
Normally we attacked down the line of the train. I remember one particular flak train; the flak was very heavy down the line of the train. I was relatively inexperienced, but we favoured the line of the train, particularly when strafing. It was very easy to overshoot or undershoot with the cannon, but four cannons did quite a lot of damage to trains or MT etc.

It was the same with a road convoy, one would tend to go down the line of the road rather than from the side, for that same reason, that if you were using cannon as well as rockets, and normally one was using both, and certainly where there was heavy flak, we would use our cannons to keep their heads down. Also if you were at all off line in your attack, you'd probably hit the ditches alongside the tracks where most of the troops or the drivers had jumped into.

So, as we have read, there were personal choices as to method of attacking trains. Some favoured down the line, others preferred to come in from the side. It could depend on any defensive armament the train might have, but in the end it was up to the individual pilot to choose how best he could make his approach and fire.

*

Typhoons, as we saw in earlier chapters, were often used against shipping. By late '44, early '45, 2nd TAF would find shipping on the Scheldt or other waterways in northern Holland. Others would be found and attacked further north, in the Baltic.

Denys Gillam had a wealth of experience in attacking ships when he commanded 615 Squadron in 1941. When leading his Typhoon Wing in Normandy, shipping targets could still be found off the French coast which could sometimes lead to mistakes with so much shipping about.

Group Captain D.E. Gillam, OC 146 Wing
Ordinarily when attacking ships you'd just aim for the middle of it, preferably in the longitudinal way so that under or overshoots would hit. On broadsides, these under or overshoots had a higher error factor. Very often you didn't have time to align yourself up for that, however, if there was a lot of flak about.

Group Captain D.E. Gillam, OC 146 Wing (continued)

We had one very disastrous event operating from B3. I've only seen it referred to once and that was in the magazine *Reveille* of all things. It was very shortly after D-Day when there was a lot of 'twitch' about E-Boats etc, and we were expecting a major naval confrontation at either night or at dawn. The wing scrambled eight aircraft on a report that a couple of German destroyers had left Le Havre heading straight towards the beach-head. There was a lot of cloud around when lo and behold they saw the ships steaming westwards at a very fast rate. They called up for confirmation and clarification that they were hostile and the Navy confirmed them so, and for our aircraft to attack immediately. They went down through cloud and the first two fired their rockets as they broke cloud but then to their horror they saw they were a couple of our frigates. Further attacks were stopped but nevertheless they sank one frigate, no problem at all! There was an enquiry held in the beach-head by the Navy and it appeared that these two ships had got their navigation wrong and sailed too far east, and also that the Navy had got its signals confused.

It just shows the power of those 60 lb rockets, after all they would be coming in from 3-4,000 feet high, packed with explosive bigger than a 12″ shell and a light skinned vessel such as a frigate could be sunk so fast it wasn't true.

Flight Lieutenant S.J. Eaton, 257 Squadron

Once, four of us were flying an armed recce off the Dutch islands and we suddenly found three large ships, absolutely white, red crosses all over them. They were about the size of ferries but each one was being towed by a large tug. We thought, well we couldn't attack them, so called up our GCC and told them what we'd found. They agreed that we shouldn't attack but if we could, sink the tugs! So we attacked and sank two of them, just with cannon fire.

Squadron Leader L.H. Lambert, OC 168 Squadron

Quite often we'd go along the Frisian Islands trying to catch any boats that were about. We attacked one boat once which we damaged – we didn't sink it as we only had cannon, of course. It was going very rapidly north and it must have left very early in the morning, hoping to be well clear. In fact it was just about the end of our range, but we stopped it and got it sunk so it took all our cannon ammunition but we got fires burning.

We often had to go out if there were reports of barges moving – again at the far extreme of our range. Very often they'd pull into the side of canals if aircraft turned up, and they were hard to see, but nevertheless we sank quite a few. A lot of them were carrying heavy goods for the Germans, especially for the build up for the Ardennes offensive – they were using everything, road, rail and canals. With pure anti-shipping our cannons were just not heavy enough, so generally we roved around when the weather was bad, to try and find something and stop it, then call up the other squadrons. Barges of course we could sink.

Flying Officer H.G. Pattison, 182 Squadron

There was an occasion when it was quite frightening to go down and this was towards the time when the Germans were escaping with a load of ships through the Westerscheldte, off Holland. We went over high and dived down to attack the ship and they flung up such a barrage it was difficult to see the targets from the exploding flak and the tracer that was coming up. As far as I can remember on that occasion, there was only one of my particular eight who got a hole through one propeller blade. Quite fantastic considering what was being fired at us. Of the other section, one chap had an overspeed on his propeller and instead of 3,700 revs he suddenly shot up to 5,000 rpm. He did the necessary when faced with overspeed action, pulled up, throttled back and put it into coarse pitch. Fortunately the CSU did its stuff and it came back to the controlled range but it didn't appear to damage the engine at all.

Bridges were always difficult targets. They were usually heavily defended and although static they were very narrow when trying to hit it with a bomb. Rockets were invariably too light to do the sort of damage that was needed to destroy a bridge. It had to be bombs.

One thing that transpired was the ability to hit bridges was really very difficult, and they were almost impossible to destroy or damage even with 1,000 lb bombs. You were very lucky if you got a hit, and so often they glanced off and fell in the river or something like that. Bridges really needed the very big bombs –

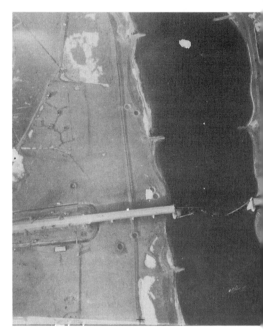

Top: Flight Lieutenant Jimmy Simpson DFC, 193 Squadron, with 20 mm cannon hole, collected from the bridge at Arnhem, 14 February 1945.

Bottom left: The Vianen Bridge, near Utrecht before 193 Squadron dive-bombed it.

Bottom right: The same bridge after the attack on 5 January 1945.

12,000 lb etc, or perhaps 5,000 pounders. We persevered with that for a time but never had much success with bridges.

Group Captain D.E. Gillam, OC 146 Wing

Jimmy Simpson and 193 Squadron, however, had one spectacular success against a bridge, although it took several squadrons several attempts, and several bombs to get it. It was located at Vianen, just south of Utrecht. They finally destroyed it on 5th January 1945.

Each Typhoon carried two 1,000 lb bombs, fused at .25 seconds. Time on target on the 5th, was 11 am with the weather fine and no cloud. The pilots were briefed to dive-bomb from 6-8,000 feet, in two sections. The leading section attacked from south to north, the second from north to south in a 60° dive, releasing their bombs at 3,000 feet.

> Our other speciality was bombing bridges and I suppose the most outstanding effort was the attack on the Vianen Bridge.
>
> I was leading the first four and the angle of the dive was in the region of 50-60° and the bombs were released from slightly less than 3,000 feet. Two direct hits were scored by No 2 aircraft of my section. I didn't hit the bridge but he did. It was remarkable to see. One moment it was there and the next it just disappeared.
>
> *Flight Lieutenant J.G. Simpson, 193 Squadron*

Flak pontoons were also strafed during this attack and two overshoots landed in the flak area. Some trucks crossing the bridge at the time disappeared completely and photos of the bridge taken the next day revealed the bridge completely demolished and resting on the bottom of the river.

CHAPTER FIFTEEN

Operations 1945

Wing Commander C.D. North-Lewis, OC 124 Wing

Charles Appleton who was the Group Captain commanding 124 Wing was responsible for my becoming the Wing Leader. Charles, who only had one leg, the other had been shot off in Malta, after D-Day became the Wing Commander – it had previously been known as 124 Airfield. The leader was then a chap named Erik Haabjoern – a Norwegian, a great character, killed after the war ferrying aircraft from North America to Norway. I took over from Erik. Appleton used to fly with me as my No 2 on occasions. I had to be very careful as he could only fly on one side because he could only keep one rudder on, so you only kept him on one side. Unfortunately I had a bout of gyppy tummy and was laid up for a couple of days and he went out with someone else and was killed. (12 August 1944). Just before this, Haabjoern was rested and Charles went to see Harry Broadhurst and said he wanted me as Wing Leader. He was not happy but Charles insisted, so he said OK. When Charles was killed, Charles Green took over and when he was shot down Eric Bitmead took command.

In 83 Group the Wing Leaders largely ran the show. We had John Derry with us (later the famous test pilot with De Havillands) who was a very good operational pilot and Gerry Gray who was an excellent squadron commander. The only trouble with Derry was that he didn't temper his aggression with discretion at times, especially in the winter of '44-45. He and Flying Officer Van Zinnick Bergmann used to go and attack things like Münster marshalling yards. I really had to lay down the law with him and say, when you're sent with specific instruction not to go to Münster marshalling yards, it's the waste of a good pilot to lose you trying to knock out a train in the middle of this city where there's so much flak about. If you're not going to do what you're told, you'll have to go. Very good chap, John Derry.

Squadron Leader G.J. Gray, OC 182 Squadron

New pilots in my squadron would firstly fly as No 2 to the B Flight Commander, then the A Flight Commander, then he'd fly with me. Then after a few ops we three would have a conference and ask what they thought of this chap and on that we either chucked him out or let him stay. We couldn't afford to do it any other way. If he was no good after three or four sorties then he'd be a menace to everyone else. It was rough justice but it had to be done. Most made it, but some didn't.

Extraordinarily, some wouldn't last more than about seven ops. They just couldn't take it. You'd see a chap going white or not eating and you could see straightaway. Some people, like myself, could just blank off casualties but some couldn't, especially if we'd lost someone from the squadron. You'd see these chaps deteriorate in front of your eyes – or take to drink. They'd try of course, but just couldn't continue.

Others of course, just didn't try, especially some of the training wallahs who used to come out to be a hero for the last month or so of the war. You could sort them out straight away. I had one chap who was a senior flight lieutenant who said, 'Oh, I'm not going to fly on ops' when he came out, so I said you've got 24 hours to think about it! He replied, 'It's all right, I shall be back in England as a squadron leader before you get back.' Harry Broadhurst was my boss and I mentioned this to him and within no time this chap had been reduced to an airman and ended up digging for land mines. It was wonderful justice for this chap had come straight from a desk job and thought we were the stupid ones flying ops. I thought of all the chaps we'd lost and there was this character. We sorted him out!

*

Earlier in the war, 257 Squadron had been 'adopted' by the people of Burma and became known as the 'Burma Squadron'. By 1944 when it was a Typhoon unit, a number of Burmese pilots were in the RAF. Four, not unnaturally, were posted to 257.

Top: Helmond, March 1945. Leaders of 124 Wing. Left to right: S/L R. G. V. Barraclough (137 Squadron), S/L G. J. Gray DFC (182), W/C North-Lewis DSO DFC (OC Wing), S/L H. Ambrose DFC (181), and S/L J. H. Bryant DFC (247).

Right: Escape photos, carried by pilots to use on false French papers if shot down and helped by resistance fighters. One give-away – they were all taken with the same shirt, tie and jacket! Top: F/L John Derry DFC and F/O Robert van Zinnicq Bergmann DFC of 182 Squadron; Bottom: S/L 'Poppa' Ambrose DFC of 181, and S/L D. 'Slug' Murray DFC who commanded 137 in 1945 after flying with 182.

The four Burmese pilots came to us at Exeter and Selwin Khin and Tommy Clift very often flew as my No 2. The other two, Yi and 'Junior' Lao were in the other flight. I saw Yi shot down off the Channel Islands by a FW190. He wasn't really shot down but he got into trouble with his tanks. We had dropped ours and were mixing it with the 190s and I think he was having trouble with his, then his engine cut and he went down. He was a Burmese Prince, whose literal translation of his name was 'Laughing Water' so we called him 'Trickle'. He was a charming young man. Tommy Clift was exceptionally nice and so was Khin and Lao.

We also had a chap in 175 Squadron named Kelsick, who was a very impressive looking man – jet black – came from Montserrat, where his father was a King or something. He was a hard chap, very fine leader of men and a good flight commander and brilliant pilot. He got a DFC later.

Flight Lieutenant H. Ambrose, 175 Squadron

Flight Lieutenant H.O.Y. Lao was lost on 20th January 1945. It wasn't through flak or fighters, but the weather. He wasn't the only casualty:

It was a wing show and very, very cloudy. I think 193 Squadron's CO was leading and as they approached this rather heavy bank of cloud they managed to get above it. 257 Squadron were in the middle, we were flying squadrons line astern, and went straight through it. The third squadron decided not to and stayed below. In no time at all there were emergency calls from 257 Squadron pilots – they were all iced up and three crashed. Lao was killed, 'Ace' Button was killed and Louey Whitmore crashed but returned later.

Flight Lieutenant S.J. Eaton, 257 Squadron

Arthur Todd had left 193 Squadron, with whom he'd been since his return to ops on 21st November 1944. On 1st January, he was given command of 257 Squadron. He too recalls the 20th January.

I always took off with my pitot head heater on and these people didn't. It was a terrible winter; so cold and icy that they iced up as soon as they got into cloud and found they had no airspeed so

Top: 257 Squadron 1944-45. Front row (l to r): F/L T. Clift (Burmese), F/O Sennett, F/O Whitfield, P/O G. B. Jones (KIA 5 Jan 1945), W/O Bellamy, F/O Smith. Middle row seated: W/O K. E. Button (KIA 20 Jan 1945), F/L J. D. Howarth DFC, S/L D. P. Jenkins DFC, F/L S. J. Eaton DFC, F/O Warren (adj), F/O A. W. Horner. Standing: F/O Logan, W/O Deal, P/O A. B. Campbell (KIA 24 Dec 1944), F/L S. Khin (Burmese), P/O Upperton, F/O J. D. Lunn RNZAF (KIA 24 Jan 1945), P/O R. Snell, F/O 'Doc' Thompson (MO), F/O E. A. Tennant DFC, F/L M. Y. Lao (Burmese, KIA 20 Jan 1945), F/O B. J. Spragg DFC, F/O Cullingham.

Bottom: 175 Squadron at Volkel, November 1944. Left to right : S/L R. W. Campbell, F/O T. T. Hall DFC, W/O W. R. Speedie, W/O R. Webb, P/O R. P. 'Rusty' Townsend (PoW 14 Feb 1945), F/O J. Varley. F/O G. Wordsley (leaning on wood), P/O G. B. 'Joe' Swift (PoW 24 Feb 1945), F/O J. Wood, F/L H. Pears.

down they went. It was a real shambles.

Squadron Leader A.G. Todd, OC 257 Squadron

Weather conditions also caused the loss of Flight Sergeant Ashman, a West Indian, of 175 Squadron:

Ashes Ashman was killed on 27th February 1945 as a result of an abortive show which should never have been put on. Because of the weather, no ops were conducted and 175 was just on call. There certainly was a hum when a signal came through for four aircraft to make an effort to see if any targets could be caught moving on the roads in the Steinhuder Lake area. This looked a dicey show from the start and it was decided to draw low cards to make up a section with the CO, Rollo Campbell. I had flown 121 ops by then and Ashes had 103 – normally a tour was completed after 100 ops but as replacement pilots were slow in coming through, we had exceeded our total. The CO said we needn't be in the draw, but we both declined the offer and took part. The three lowest cards were, Pilot Officer Ainsley, and – would you believe it – Ashes and myself.

   Apart from our cannons we had six rockets and two LR tanks. We climbed up through the overcast on instruments and eventually broke cloud at about 6,000 feet, joined up and set course for the target area. When we reached it there was no break in the overcast so after dropping our tanks we dived down into it but as we were still in cloud fairly well down, we climbed again and broke cloud. Above cloud we were scattered and only three in number. It was very touchy getting back through the overcast but the CO and I got into our base, Bob Ainsley overshooting to land at Eindhoven. Some months later, Ashes' aircraft was found crashed on a hill in the area into which we dived.

Flying Officer T.T. Hall, 175 Squadron

Wing Commander Walter Dring DSO DFC, a veteran Typhoon man, was killed on 13th January. He had been a pilot with 56 Squadron in the early days and gone on to command 183 Squadron before being Wing Leader, 123 Wing. After flying a weather sortie he landed at Eindhoven but caught his wheels on a snow bank, turned over and died in the resulting crash. His place was taken by Johnny Button DFC who had commanded 193 Squadron in Normandy.

On 22nd January, Flying Officer Frank Skelly of 438 RCAF Squadron was shot down by flak and Squadron Leader R.G. 'Bing' Crosby, CO of 439, was hit and his Typhoon blew up. He was thrown out and dislocated his shoulder but managed to pull his rip-cord with his left hand. Upon landing he lay in his 'chute in a wood for 36 hours, then made for the Allied lines. He received the DFC in March.

By 15th January, Ronnie Sheward was senior flight commander on 263 Squadron. Leader Martin Rumbold had recently taken command of the squadron. On the 15th, Sheward was detailed for an army support mission to Wisk, on the Maas.

> I taxied out to lead eight aircraft to support the army who wanted a raid across the Maas to find out the strength of the opposition. As we moved along the perimeter towards the take-off point some aircraft from another squadron flew across the aerodrome, one trying to get rid of a bomb which was stuck. He did, right over our heads. It exploded near my last four Typhoons. I called up my aircraft on the R/T to find out who was OK and who had been hit. Half had got away with only slight damage. Control told us not to go but the army were expecting us so felt I had to go. We strafed gun positions in houses and on the roads with good results. I was hit by flak in the starboard mainplane spar and Flight Sergeant Richardson hit in the cockpit.
>
> *Flight Lieutenant R.E.G. Sheward, 263 Squadron*

*

Long Range tanks continued to cause problems even at this stage of the war.

Squadron Leader L.H. Lambert, OC 168 Squadron
> Changing fuel tanks was very nasty because you had to fight the damn cock, which was right down at the bottom of the cockpit. Our drill, especially at low level where we didn't have time to muck about was to get rid of the tanks a little early compared with most people. Once we'd switched tanks there was generally some spare fuel sloshing about in the tanks, and if they got scratched they'd go up, so we generally got rid of them. I've seen one or two Typhoons hit with empty fuel tanks still on – not at all funny. The

two change cocks were quite difficult as you had to lean right forward to reach them and had to loosen your straps, which was not amusing when flying at low level. If they were a bit tight the aircraft began to wobble about. To jettison the tanks we had two levers at the bottom of the cockpit. They were quite long so you'd have plenty of leverage and you'd feel them go.

Flying Officer T.T. Hall, 175 Squadron
For long range ops, one or two LR tanks would be carried which would be switched off and dropped just before they ran out of petrol. Many a twitch was had by all when in trying to get as much endurance as possible, they would be left on just that little bit too long and the engine would cut. What a wonderful feeling when, after frantically switching to mains, slight throttle back, nose down, a cough or two and the Sabre engine would burst into life again.

*

Lennie Lambert's squadron flying low level Armed Recce at long range, had a varied number of interesting targets to go for, including V2 sites.

Very often we were sent on roving commissions. For example when the V2's were being fired from the marshes at the edge of the Ijsselmeer, they were so well camouflaged that nobody really knew where they were; even high altitude photography had failed to locate all of them. Then, our job was to try and find them, attack and try to hit something that would either destroy or at least mark them. If we could find any of the fuel tanks for example, whose explosion would certainly leave a mark for other fighter-bombers to see.

On one occasion we found them actually fuelling a rocket – we managed to get that and the V2 went up with the fuel – an incredible sight! On another trip we were trying to locate a particular V2 site. We knew approximately where it was as it had been spotted previously. It was a very clear day and we were at 10,000 feet and twice we'd covered the area but couldn't find it. We were looking for tell-tale signs, such as vehicle tracks through fields etc, when I saw what looked like a brown mushroom developing on the ground and there was a spot in the middle of it. I quickly realised it was a V2 rocket actually coming up just beneath me! It came straight up so I broke the squadron in all directions and it passed between me and my No 2. I had an incredible view of it before the turbulence hit us and threw us all over the sky.

We then went down and blew up the site and got the fuel tankers which were still there, not having got back into the woods. Some newspaper reporters were at Eindhoven when we got back, but I didn't know it. Our Intelligence Officer asked me what it had looked like, as I had been closer to a V2 rocket than any man alive on the Allied side. It had passed within yards of me and it had big black and white checkered markings on its sides. I replied that if anything, it was pretty, very pretty! Shortly afterwards there was a newspaper story with the headline, 'Squadron Commander says V2 pretty!'

We later were told that there were a number of technician people on the site who had fired it despite the fact that there were Allied aircraft overhead. It must have been a special test, and of course, in our subsequent attack we wrote a number of them off.

Squadron Leader L.H. Lambert, OC 168 Squadron

Lambert and Flight Lieutenant R.M. Mackenzie MBE were both rested on 3rd February. 168 Squadron's ORB says 'on completion of first tours'. As Lambert had joined the squadron in 1942 and Mackenzie soon afterwards it would seem a mighty long tour. Mackenzie had been shot down by a FW190 when he and Lambert had been out on an op back in September 1943 while still on Mustangs. He had evaded and returned to the squadron. An Australian, he received the MBE for his escape and, like Lambert, received the DFC in 1945.

The squadron was taken over by Flight Lieutenant E.C.H. Vernon-Jarvis DFC, who had been with the squadron for some weeks following ops with 175 Squadron. Just before mid-day on 3rd February, his first day of command, V-J led eight Typhoons on an armed recce and attacked a train near Osnabrück. His Typhoon (RB270) was hit by flak, its tail was blown off and he crashed to his death. Lambert had to remain in command until a new CO could be appointed but in the event 168 was disbanded on 26th February.

Another squadron that was disbanded was 257 Squadron, commanded by Arthur Todd DFC:

I took over 257 on 1st January 1945 and it was disbanded in March. They had calculated that the war was going to be finished but of course it didn't, but they had already closed down some of the OTU's in England. So they had to start them up again. I disbanded 257 and went back as CFI at the OTU at Milfield. I left there in May and went on to Mustangs.

Squadron Leader A.G. Todd, OC 257 Squadron

*

Flight Lieutenant J.G. Simpson, 193 Squadron
We had a Belgian chap, Guy Plamondon, when Zip Button went off. I think 'Plum' took over just as we moved up into Antwerp so he was on his home territory. When he went on rest we had Rastus Erasmus from 266 Squadron. He lasted right through till 9th March 1945 when he was lost on a show which I was on. He was leading the squadron and I was leading the other flight. We were attacking railway lines and a goods train and it appears the train had some V2 refuelling tanks on board. It exploded and that was the end of him. I then led the squadron until I went on rest on 9th April, and it was taken over by Don Taylor, who had commanded 195 and 197 Squadrons. I must say our Intelligence boys did a fairly good job because quite often when you attacked a HQ or something you didn't really know what success you'd had and it was quite some days afterwards that we might get pictures back from the recce boys and get the assessment.

We bombed a petrol dump south of Deventer on 21st March. It was just an ordinary show, maximum effort, bombing was good but no fires. Actually we got a little photo cutting afterwards which read: 'Photo recon showed that the largest petrol and oil dump supplying the German forces facing the 21st Army Group, was completely destroyed by RAF 2nd TAF 'planes yesterday.' So that used to encourage us a bit.

Squadron Leader R.E.G. Sheward, OC 266 Squadron
On the way back from a sortie to Bestmenline in bad viz. I was attacked by two hostile Spitfires. No squadron markings. I turned inside one of them and the pilot didn't seem very good at his job. I could have shot him down but I called control and they said no Spitfires should be in the area. The two Spits then turned tail and

Top: Pilots of 197 Squadron before the invasion. On wing: P/O J. Watson DFC (KIA 17 June). Standing (l to r): S/L J. C. 'Zip' Button DFC (OC and later OC 123 Wing), P/O D. I. Fee (PoW 24 Dec), F/O H. W. Coles (KIA 24 May), F/L W. C. Ahrens RCAF (later CO 257 Sqn, KIA 16 July), F/L R. N. G. Allen DFC, – ? –, Bunny Oury. Kneeling: F/Sgt J. Kyle DFM, F/Sgt (P/O) D. E. Tapson (PoW 10 Feb 1945),

F/O K. J. Harding DFC (OC 197 Sqn 1945). Note flying helmet on the control column and the aircraft's serial number on the edge of the cockpit door – JP928.

Bottom: 266 Squadron on Antwerp aerodrome late 1944. From left: F/L J. 'Snowy' Harrison RAAF, G. Henderson, F. N. Laing, unknown, A. P. Knoesen, F/L C. D. 'Rastus' Erasmus DFC, who later commanded 193 Squadron and was KIA 9 Mar 1945.

fled and I think they were captured Spits being flown by Hun pilots and were scouting. This was 14th March.

Ronnie Sheward was now the boss of 266 Rhodesian Squadron, having taken command on 7th March. On the 18th March, Group Captain Johnny Wells and Wing Commander Johnny Deal led 146 Wing to attack the HQ of General Blaskowitz, known as Army Group 'H'. Although no longer in command of 146 Wing, Denys Gillam continued to fly on ops whenever he could borrow a Typhoon. Officially he was Group Captain Ops at 84 Group HQ, but that didn't stop him.

On the 19th, 146 Wing took out a German Repair Depot and Factory at Doetinchem, near Emmerich, Germany. 266 Squadron was led by Ronnie Sheward:

The weather was good and visibility excellent. I led 266 and we went in first with 1,000 lb bombs at low level – 11 seconds' delay.

Johnny Wells and Wing Commander Johnny Deal came along to keep an eye on things and to have a go and also to report on the results.

I easily found the target and was getting my lot into position to attack the longest part of the main building when the Group Captain called me up and said, 'Get a move on, Shewy; we all want to have a go!' I still kept on a bit longer to reach my desired position, then down we went in a shallow dive to zero feet and pressed the tit just before the target was lost from sight; we scored some direct hits.

The other squadrons followed and dive-bombed the smoking target. 263, 197 and 193 were the other squadrons and they used a mixture of HE and incendiary bombs and rockets. I took my squadron out and beat it for home which was at B89 – Mill in Holland. Reports from the Group Captain and Wingco were excellent and the photographs showed the damage. We did hear that the photographs were displayed at Churchill's HQ so that he could see the results.

Squadron Leader R.E.G. Sheward, OC 266 Squadron

*

In most Typhoon wings there was no fixed period for an

Right: The German repair depot at Doetinchem, before 146 Wing's visit on 19 March 1945.

The same depot after the Typhoons had left.

Left: A close-up view of the depot a few days later, taken by David Ince with his forward-facing F24 camera installation which he pioneered.

operational tour either in number of ops flown or operational flying hours. (However, just over the 100 ops seemed to be a yardstick.) With 124 Wing for example, Kit North-Lewis and his squadron commanders kept an eye on their pilots and could usually tell when one had done enough. There was a sort of operational curve and after a pilot had reached the apex of that curve, his aggressiveness began to drop away.

When a man who, it was felt, had the potential to be a flight or squadron commander was singled out, the secret was to pull him out of combat and send him back to England, and arrange with HQ that he should get the next vacancy. This way he could return to ops still full of pep, the adrenalin flowing well, and provided he survived, became an effective leader.

But when finally a man had done enough, he was posted home. In 124 Wing they had their own way of doing that.

Flight Lieutenant G. Clubley, 137 Squadron
When I landed one day after a sortie (11th March 1945) Kit North-Lewis said, 'Well, did you enjoy your last trip?' which is, I think, the best way to do it.

Flying Officer H.G. Pattison, 182 Squadron
Having passed the magic 100 operational sorties mark (I suppose) one became a little invincible. Having got through with very little damage, certainly none to my person, just a bit to the aeroplane, you'd got to a stage where you thought you could go on forever. Of course, we didn't know that the end was very nearly in sight but it did come out of the blue. Suddenly they said right, you're tour-expired and told me where I was going. My departure from the squadron coincided with its move on into Germany and I retired to Eindhoven to command 426 R & R Unit which looked after the aircraft which were being sent home for repair or overhaul, and also for re-mounts which were coming from the UK to the squadrons.

Flight Lieutenant S.J. Eaton, 257 Squadron
Toddy was a very nice chap and I got on well with him. In fact the only time I was cross with him was on 28th January 1945. We went out for a particular target – a railway north of Hilversum and we were diverted to Apeldoorn. This was a German convoy

heading towards our lines and we searched and searched but found nothing so eventually we just looked for a target and found a small bridge on which we dropped our bombs, then flew home. Todd was waiting at dispersal and said to me, 'Jerry, how did it go?' I said, 'Oh, bloody awful.' He replied, 'Too bad, that was your last trip, you're going on rest!' And that's how my tour ended.

Squadron Leader H. Ambrose, OC 181 Squadron
We were all tired. I shouldn't have gone on myself; I had done my 100 trips by November 1944, but I went on and was then promoted so I kept on. No one seemed to take much notice or check up, but I know at the end of the war I was really tired. I finally did 389 ops and I still can't believe I did it.

Flying Officer T.T. Hall, 175 Squadron
I completed 122 operational sorties and was posted on rest to 83 Group Support Unit at Dunsfold on 14th March 1945. I had been awarded the DFC on 23rd February. Whilst on the squadron I had seen a lot come and go. If you could gain experience by graduating from Blue Four – last in the attack – your chances of survival improved quite a lot. On looking back I recall Flight Sergeant Hurrell, who arrived on the squadron on 17th September 1944 and was shot down nine days later!

Squadron Leader G.J. Gray, OC 182 Squadron
I always had a sixth sense about some chaps, that they were going to 'buy it' within a week, however good a pilot he appeared to be. He might be accident prone or something, I didn't know what it was. He might be an exceptional aerobatic pilot, exceptional in air-firing, exceptional something else, but somehow he had the mark of death on him and I knew he wouldn't last. You couldn't fault him on anything but on his first sortie he was the sort of chap who'd get shot-up by an 88, and the next trip he'd run out of glycol and I'd think, well there's only one more time, and sure enough, next trip he'd buy it. It was an incredible thing, but you could almost see the mark of death on a chap.

There were occasions when the odds were just too great. In Gerry Gray's 182 Squadron in the autumn of 1944 for instance the casualties were varied and quite often a pilot would make it back only to fail to return from a later op. Flying Officer J.A. Spellman was shot down in September, got back but was shot down again in March 1945. Pilot Officer S.T. Byer was shot down on 18th October (MN248) only to be shot by the Germans when he gave himself up. Flight Lieutenant Geoff 'Hawkeye' Kinsey was shot down on 29th October, got back, then was shot down on 25th March 1945. Flying Officer J.A. Patterson was shot-up but managed to fly back to the Allied lines before crash-landing. He was reported missing on the last day of 1944.

Others like Gerry Gray himself survived several crash-landings and bale-outs and so too did Pat Pattison, the last on the day the Rhine was crossed. The first show was led by Flight Lieutenant D. 'Slug' Murray, 182 attacking enemy guns as related later by Gerry Gray. Other anti-flak sorties were flown during the day, Pat leading a four-man anti-flak op at 10.15 am into the Isselburg area. Light flak hit his Typhoon and although he made it back he had to crash-land on Eindhoven aerodrome.

Perhaps the saddest loss was that of Jack Taylor and his wingman. Flight Lieutenant J.H. Taylor had been a CAM pilot earlier in the war, flying Hurricane fighters off merchant ships on sea convoys. Later he was with a Hurricane IV squadron flying rocket-armed Hurricanes, before joining 182 Squadron. The war had only eight weeks left to run when he was shot down, and his fiancée was waiting in England for his return.

On 28th February, not a very good morning, Slug Murray led six pilots out at 8.45 am to fly an armed recce into the Bremen-Osnabrück area. Jack Taylor was leading Blue Section, his No 2 being Warrant Officer F.W. Cuthbertson, who himself had been shot down the previous October but had got back. Near Osnabrück they spotted a train but in the attack Taylor's Typhoon was hit by flak and he had to make a rapid forced landing. This he managed successfully, Cuthbertson circling all the while to see that he got down safely. As Taylor slid to a stop he called up on the radio to say he was OK and unhurt, but then Cuthbertson was hit by flak and had also to force land.

Exactly what happened next is not known but some time later the squadron and his fiancée received official word that both men had been taken prisoner and then shot by the Germans.

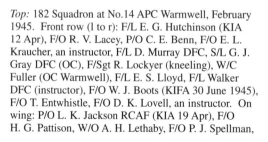

Top: 182 Squadron at No.14 APC Warmwell, February 1945. Front row (l to r): F/L E. G. Hutchinson (KIA 12 Apr), F/O R. V. Lacey, P/O C. E. Benn, F/O E. L. Kraucher, an instructor, F/L D. Murray DFC, S/L G. J. Gray DFC (OC), F/Sgt R. Lockyer (kneeling), W/C Fuller (OC Warmwell), F/L E. S. Lloyd, F/L Walker DFC (instructor), F/O W. J. Boots (KIFA 30 June 1945), F/O T. Entwhistle, F/O D. K. Lovell, an instructor. On wing: P/O L. K. Jackson RCAF (KIA 19 Apr), F/O H. G. Pattison, W/O A. H. Lethaby, F/O P. J. Spellman, W/O J. A. Howard (KIA 23 Feb), F/L J. H. Taylor (killed 28 Feb), F/Sgt L. S. Phillips on prop, T. G. Garrett, P/O K. Grassett, F/Sgt R. Price, F/Sgt R. F. Whicker, P/O I. Ladley, F/O D. White.

Bottom left: Flying Officer Jack Taylor, 182 Squadron, brought down with his wingman on 28 February 1945 and shot by the Germans.

Bottom right: Squadron Leader A. G. Todd DFC, OC 257 Squadron 1945.

CHAPTER SIXTEEN

Victory

Once the winter weather lessened its grip and spring was making its appearance, so the final push came into Germany itself. Everyone on the Allied side fully expected the Germans to fight desperately for their homeland. And they did.

The first obstacle was the River Rhine, Germany's first natural defence line in the west. The attacking Allied ground forces would have to secure the far bank as quickly as possible, then bring their main force across by boat and later by pontoon bridges. 2nd TAF would be fully occupied supporting the assault and the Typhoon squadrons would have their tasks. One of the first was to knock out the German flak so airborne troops could be flown over. The deadly 88 mm flak guns, which could also be used as field artillery and anti-tank weapons, were a priority target. The date for the attack was 24th March.

Squadron Leader G.J. Gray, OC 182 Squadron
  Just before the Rhine crossing, before the gliders went in, from about 48 hours before, we went along the Rhine in pairs in line astern, three pairs. The first pair would just fly along, and as soon as you saw the 88 mm firing at this first pair, who were really sitting ducks, you'd go down and try to rocket the gun underneath them. God, that was a lethal game. You were literally flying as a target for the 88s. You could see them firing on the ground as we'd seen them in the Ardennes show, they were good shots. We would normally be weaving about and if you looked back where you had been, there were the black puffs.

  So, as the Rhine do came, we tried this game to get the 88s. We would keep 2 or 3,000 yards between the pairs, so we were looking for the flash of the gun on the ground, then see the bursts around the pair in front. Having kept your eye on the position, you'd dive straight down on it, though you'd rarely see the actual gun it was so well camouflaged. We were lucky if we didn't lose at least one aircraft each time. We only did it for the 48 hours before the crossing and I think it was the nastiest job I had to do in the whole war.

Squadron Leader H. Ambrose, OC 181 Squadron

Kit North-Lewis had all the pilots together for a briefing and put foward the theory that we were going to fly up and down at 2,000 feet to bait the German flak. The section above us would then go down and attack the gun and knock it out, then we'd change positions after twenty minutes. Of course, the whole idea was a bit like a Kamikaze pilots' briefing – chaps started laughing, thinking, hold on a minute, this is a bit hair-brain. However, it was decided this was going ahead and in the event it was Kit North-Lewis who was in the first section off that morning and he was the first chap the Germans clobbered and shot down.

Wing Commander C.D. North-Lewis, OC 124 Wing

On the morning of 24th March, I led an attack on a defended strongpoint at Krudenberg to the east of Wesel in support of the crossing of the Rhine by the 2nd British Army which had been launched at dawn that day. We dived from about 12,000 feet but my Typhoon was hit as we pulled out and I immediately set off for the Rhine to try and make the British lines. Unfortunately, when I was over Wesel my engine stopped and I had to crash land on the first open space I could see. I made an almost perfect crash-landing – wheels up, and came to rest on Gravel Isle just to the north of Wesel. Climbing out of my aircraft I found I had landed within a few hundred yards of a German Parachute Regiment manning trenches on the banks of the Rhine. A German paratrooper shouted something at me and without more ado I put my hands up.

I was taken along trenches which were quite extensive and had a field of fire across the Rhine, to the Command Post where the German Company Commander was. I stayed here all day but unfortunately they had no food so I remained hungry for the whole of my stay. That evening, after a day in which these Germans were not engaged, the Commander intimated that I was to be sent to his Battalion HQ under escort, but then they learned

Right: Flying Officer D. G. Evans, 137 Squadron 1945. Later Air Chief Marshal Sir David Evans.

Left: Wing Commander Kit North-Lewis DSO DFC and Bar, leader of 123 Wing 1944-45, with his personal Typhoon (RB208) in which he was shot down on 24 March.

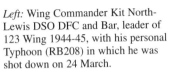

Right: Wing Commander J. C. Button DFC with 'Zippy IX'. One of his later Typhoons was named Zippy XI (RB431), marked JC-B in wing-leader fashion.

Wing Commander C.D. North-Lewis, OC 124 Wing (continued)

they were cut off, as British paratroops had landed to the east of his position. He then intimated that if his position didn't change he would surrender the next morning. I was much relieved as it seemed I should soon be back with our side. During the night I was woken by a sudden disturbance when another officer arrived. He was a most determined looking man with a mass of decorations including the Iron Cross and with a large scar on his face, and stick grenades in his belt. He obviously wanted to break out and to take me with him. Fortunately, after a heated exchange, my officer prevailed and the stranger, to my great relief, departed.

At dawn on 25th, I began to wonder how I could get back, then around 8 am a British artillery spotter light aircraft flew over and I managed to attract his attention. I requisitioned a number of German towels, tore them into strips and laid them out to read, 'Have Hun prisoners send help'. But although the 'plane acknowledged, I had no idea when help would arrive. Meantime I was shown around and it was then that I spotted a canoe complete with paddle. Although I had never paddled before I decided to use it and the Germans carried it down to the Rhine. I then set off across the river, hoping the Germans would not shoot me from the back nor the British from the front. Nearing the British side I could see troops in a firing position so I took out my handkerchief and shouted, "Don't shoot I'm a British officer." The troops were a Highland Regiment whose main interest was in the prospects of loot! Had the Germans any watches, I was asked.

I was quickly taken to Brigade HQ and given a meal. I saw the Divisional Commander and was then flown back by light aircraft to my base at Helmond. Here I was greeted by Harry Broadhurst who informed me I had been awarded an immediate DSO and also forbade me to fly on operations again for some time. As events turned out, this had been my last operational trip. I had flown 175 ops since February 1944.

Of the Germans North-Lewis had been with, 120 handed themselves over to British troops sent across by him shortly afterwards. North-Lewis had other claims to fame. He was the first British pilot to land in Belgium, Holland and Germany, the latter occurring on 19th March 1945. The RE Lieutenant Colonel in charge of No 13 Construction Group gave him a Certificate to the effect, confirming him as the first pilot of a fighter aircraft to land at B100, the first British airfield built in Germany by the Royal Engineers and the Pioneer Corps.

> Airborne landings Wesel area. We acted as anti-flak and any German gun that opened fire was pounced on with cluster bombs. Flight Lieutenant Snowy Harrison and Flight Lieutenant Dusty Miller got shot down but returned a few days later.
>
> *Squadron Leader R.E.G. Sheward, OC 266 Squadron*

*

In April 1945, Flying Officer David Evans joined 137 Squadron with whom he was to fly till the war's end. He just missed flying with George Clubley who had just gone on rest. One of 137's flight commanders was Captain Buster Watt, the South African who had often flown as Gerry Gray's No 2 in 182 Squadron. Evans was a Canadian, trained in Canada but flew with the RAF. In the next few weeks he was to cram in a wealth of experience but he recalls his early limitations:

> I wish I'd had the experience that one acquired subsequently, at the time one was on operations. One was terribly inexperienced, I realise that now. You were really not very expert I suspect, although we seemed to get results but maybe because there were a lot of targets.
>
> We flew a number of armed recce sorties at that time or we got specific targets – shipping strikes, barges, MT, trains – you name it.
>
> *Flying Officer D.G. Evans, 137 Squadron*

Most of the contributors to this book had, by this final stage of the war, been either tour-expired or guests of the Germans, but we can see these last weeks through the eyes of two men. One, the new arrival – David Evans, the other, the experienced pilot and squadron commander – Ronnie Sheward.

During the first half of April, Sheward's 266 Squadron flew, like the other Typhoon squadrons, a whole variety of sorties almost daily – and often more than one sortie a day. In his log book and diary he recorded:

Top: 266 Squadron 1945. Front row from left: I.O., F/L D. C. Borland DFC (South African), S/L R. E. G. Sheward DFC, F/L D. L. Hughes DFC, F/L L. S. Miller, F/O H. H. Wheeler. Sitting on the prop is G. D. Godley.

Bottom: Ronnie Sheward's personal Typhoon ZH-Q (RB478), 266 Squadron 1945.

7th April – Interdiction Zwolle-Meppel. Beat up a train – the whole length.

7th April – Train Recce – Assen. We found 20+ trucks in the marshalling yard. Direct hits. Something went up in a huge bang, and smoke rose to 2,500 feet.

8th April – Armed Recce with long range tanks after lorries and staff cars – two hour trip. [In his diary he recorded 'racks off, LRTs on – Germany here we come! Did two hour A/R – 3 MET. Good fun.]

9th April – Armed Recce west of Emden. Passing a wood the sun flashed on a windscreen which made me take a closer look to find that many transports were hiding under the trees. [All this is recorded in his diary.] We attacked and came in again and left many in flames.

10th April – In his diary Ronnie recorded. 'Armed Recce. Got two lorries one staff car, one horse drawn vehicle. Doug got a train. Bags of flak!

Doug was Flight Lieutenant Douglas Borland DFC, whose brother Flying Officer Noel Borland joined the squadron early in 1945. Noel was shot down and killed in mid-April when Ronnie Sheward was on leave. Not unnaturally, Doug just wanted to get into a Typhoon, fly out and kill every German he could find, but he was restrained and sent on rest.

On 11th April, 266 went airfield strafing as did other squadrons in 146 Wing, Sheward flying his usual Q-Queenie. They hit Varrelbusch aerodrome. In his log book he recorded:

11th April – N. of Cloppenburg. 1 Ju88 exploded, FW190 destroyed, Me109 damaged – shared on the ground. Lots of light flak.

His squadron also got one lorry, two trailers, one big bus, one van. The wing in total claimed five Ju88s, one Me262, one He111, one FW190, one Me109 and one unidentified aircraft; three Ju88s and a Me262 damaged, plus one train, 233 MRT, three HDT and two tanks also damaged.

Alex Shannon, had now left 257 Squadron when it disbanded, received a commission and joined 197 Squadron. He also recalls 11th April, when he was one of four men on an armed recce that evening.

We were being led by Jock Ellis; it was a very quiet evening and we had long range tanks. There were four of us, Jock Ellis, Paddy Byrne, another chap and myself. It was a two hour trip and we overflew Ardorf where there were some Ju88s parked. Jock said, let's go down and have a bash here and see what we can knock out, so down we went. It was as though everybody was waiting for us and the whole sky lit up with flak. I'd never seen so much in my life and really I thought we were lucky to get out of that alive!

Pilot Officer A. Shannon, 197 Squadron

The town of Arnhem was finally taken by the Army on 13th April and 2nd TAF helped.

They called for us to support the Army and they briefed us not to go in until we saw yellow smoke. They kept us hanging about and the Germans were shooting at us all the time, it was most uncomfortable. Eventually we got the yellow smoke and went in. My log book records: 'Bombed and strafed strongpoints with direct hits. Intense light and medium flak. I got one in the rad:' I don't remember much about that flak hit. So that's when the town of Arnhem was eventually taken.

Squadron Leader R.E.G. Sheward, OC 266 Squadron

Bill Speedie flew his 100th sortie just a few days earlier to this. He raised this total to 105 before he was rested:

On 10th April I flew my 100th sortie with the squadron. It proved to be eventful from my personal point of view. It was a close support operation which meant when leaving base we had no specific target but R/T communication during the flight would supply a map reference and details of the target. This required the necessity to map read in considerable detail whilst leading a formation of six Typhoons at a speed in excess of 300 mph. We located and attacked the target – a battery of heavy guns which was holding up the Army's advance. Following my individual attack I was climbing up to observe the attacks made by the remainder of the formation when a flaming red piece of steel (shell) passed over the top of my canopy no more than a foot away. Not only did it rock the Typhoon but it also rocked the pilot! I located the offending gun, installed in a gun emplacement, and having already fired my eight rockets, I gave it my special attention with my 20 mm cannons during a vertical dive. No further action was observed from that offending gun. The Army reported our attack had proved successful and I for one returned to base a rather shaken mortal.

Flying Officer W.R. Speedie, 175 Squadron

*

During the beginning of April, just before I went on rest, I did five shows that were all bombing railway lines and shooting up anything we found. We even chased a motorcycle combination which was great fun. But really what we were trying to do was to stop their trains running and bringing in supplies.

My very last show was on 9th April and it was something we hadn't done before. It took an hour and 20 minutes so that means it was something like 40 minutes each way, to drop supplies to types operating behind the lines. We actually found the field and we got the right signals to show the blokes were there. We did one run round and dropped our stuff and saw them all come rushing out of the woods, pick it up and carry it back. They seemed to have their own transport and everything else, and it was quite rewarding to think that we were actually helping some types miles behind the lines.

Flight Lieutenant J.G. Simpson, 193 Squadron

The pilots of 164 Squadron, now commanded by Squadron Leader P.L. Bateman-Jones, were still very active in April 1945. German flak and ground fire never failed to be a major adversary for the low flying Typhoons, claiming victims almost daily. On the 25th for example, Flight Lieutenant M.E. Jones led a four-man armed recce against trucks and trains around Neumünster and only two came back. Flying Officer R.J.M. Wilson (MN896 'F') was hit by debris and force-landed. Jones called up to say he had to go down but then his Typhoon burst into flames and he was not seen to get out.

The next day eight Typhoons attacked a minesweeper near Wilhelmshaven which they hit with R/P and cannon. Flying Officer W.T. Lawton (RB264) was hit and baled out. Bill Lawton got back on 8th May having been a POW for the last few days of the war. He was badly burnt when he baled out but got into his dinghy, paddled for six hours before reaching land – near a hospital! Two days earlier Dicky Wilson got back from his op on the 25th. He had knocked himself out when he force-landed and woke up a prisoner.

Meanwhile David Evans was doing his share with 137 Squadron. On 14th April, he was on Operation Winston, an attack on SS troops and Hitler Youth. There was some flak and '. . . Flight Sergeant Johnny Pennant went straight into the deck.' The Army sent a 'Good show' signal to the wing for its support.

> We had quite a lot of cloud towards the latter stages of the war, layered cloud at about 2,000 feet and we were flying just below it. That was not a very smart height to fly. At that stage the Germans could predict the height of the cloud too, but again, on an armed recce you couldn't do it successfully from higher altitudes. So we were having to fly these ops at around 1,000-1,500 feet. However, these ops were in the closing weeks of the war and people who had come up from Normandy, and right through France, might have flown these things very differently. But cloud was the trouble and we had to be below it to see the targets.
>
> I remember occasions coming back from ops, screeching along on the deck, literally hedge-hopping where one felt invulnerable. Terrifically exhilarating and fun, great fun. Then the trouble was your navigation probably wasn't all that hot, but that didn't matter because you were flying for one of the railways or one of the rivers, then funnelling in. Once you got back over the bomb line then of course you could pull up. So it was line features really that one was using, rather than pin-point navigational accuracy.
>
> *Flying Officer D.G. Evans, 137 Squadron*

However the end in Germany was near. On 28th April 124 Wing were given an Army target – an SS Headquarters at Friedrichsruh. Four squadrons set out but because of poor weather, only 137 Squadron and one section of 182 Squadron got there. It was enough, however; the target was destroyed amid a terrific explosion. Even so, the pilots generally had no real idea how long the Germans would continue to resist, and although tactics had been a feature of the Typhoon's war, David Evans recalls that it was not such a feature as far as he was concerned in this final phase:

> I never felt there were any great discussions on tactics, although

Flying Officer D.G. Evans, 137 Squadron (continued)

perhaps it was because I was only in at the end of the war. With us it was left very much to the Section Leader to call it as he saw it. Particularly on armed recces, you'd see something and you'd go for it, you wouldn't necessarily have a pre-arranged plan. At the end of the war I was just leading a section and you would just go in and it was up to your No 2 to stay with you. It was the same as the attacks on the ships in Kiel Bay, I rather feel that in the end it was just down to you and your No 2. You were picking your target then trying to form up again for the return, into sections of four, or six, etc. With a lot of flak and a lot of aeroplanes there wasn't time for working out tactics, or you didn't get your attack in at all – you were shot down! So one had to relate everything to that as well.

I cannot recall anticipating the finish of the war at all, I really can't. Maybe I'd been in it for too short a time from the point of view of operation. In fact the operational flying was absolutely superb, it really was great at that time. The sense of exhilaration hadn't left me, I don't think. Sounds a hard thing to say about war but I felt you were living from one attack to the next. The main thing you wanted to do was to get on the next operation. Whether, if you were coming near to the end of the tour – 100 ops, counting the days, and you'd seen so many people lost on the way, one wouldn't have been so enthusiastic, I don't know. I never got to that stage. The keenness to participate increased because the more you flew the more experience you acquired and the smarter you became. Of course, the arrogance of youth or maybe the arrogance of inexperience, I'm not sure which, is that you never thought anyone was going to shoot you down, you're smarter than they are! We didn't, of course, have too many worries about enemy fighters, we were far more worried about being attacked by American aircraft as they so often mistook the Typhoon for FW190s. On one occasion I got a Fieseler Storch with rockets – I couldn't get the thing with cannon. He was literally going round the trees and things, and when he eventually force-landed, I fired the rockets, missed, but the explosion got him.

I remember the heavy flak, especially at dusk when you could see so much of it – tracer, etc. I had several nicks by flak. One thing I recall well of the Typhoon was it had tubular control rods whereas the Spitfire had cables. You could get a nick with flak which would cut a cable but a similar nick on the tubular rod wasn't a problem – it would still hold and bring you home again.

It was a bloody fine aeroplane, built like the proverbial ... For ground attack it was superb – ideal! Its only trouble was the vulnerability of the radiator – if you flew it through any of your debris, or you got anything in your radiator and you lost the glycol, that was it. It glided like a brick, but it was a magnificent airframe for taking flak, and I don't think you'd ever improve on it.

Flying Officer D.G. Evans, 137 Squadron

It was on 3rd May that David Evans got the Storch. 137 flew an armed recce to Neumünster area. They met intense flak over any sort of ground target, but he chased the Storch, then later shot up a convoy of 30 trucks, David destroying seven and damaging six (JR322). The next day, 124 Wing flew out to attack a big 60-ship convoy in Kiel Bay.

We thought the Germans were evacuating to Norway to make a stand there and it was essential to sink the ships. Essentially we attacked in pairs. It was a very big raid for us, 48 Typhoons from our wing plus another wing. We went in at medium level as opposed to very low level on the transit flying up there. There was very heavy defensive fire – 10/10ths flak! I hit the stern of a 6,000 ton ship and stopped it, which was lucky as I had aimed for the ship's bridge!

Flying Officer D.G. Evans, 137 Squadron

The other wing had been 146. Its former Group Captain, Denys Gillam, had flown his last war mission a few days earlier, on 25th April. It had been a shipping recce and he damaged a boat, then a truck on land. He should have come off ops at the end of February 1945 when he was posted to 84 Group HQ but he virtually ignored that and continued to fly with the wing although Johnny Wells was now the Group Captain.

Gillam now had the DSO and two bars, the DFC and bar, plus his 1938 AFC. He had been operational since 1939, flown in the Battle of Britain, led two Czech squadrons in 1940-41, been on anti-shipping Hurricanes during the Channel Stop campaign in 1942, then on Typhoons virtually ever since. When, after the war, he applied for

Above: Shipping attacked by 146 Wing off Lubeck and Neustadt, 3-4 May 1945. Unknown to the pilots was that the ships were carrying concentration camp prisoners from near Hamburg, to be disposed of by the SS. Many died in the attack on three ships, the *Deutchland, Cap Arcona* and the *Thielbek.*

Left: The *Deutchland* hit by 146 Wing's Typhoons, 3 May 1945. As far as the RAF pilots knew, the ships were full of SS troops retreating to Norway. Both pictures were taken by David Ince with his forward-facing F24 camera.

his campaign medals, he was refused the Defence Medal. The letter from Air Ministry read:

> With reference to your claim for a Defence Medal, I must inform you with regret that you do not qualify for it, for your non-operational service does not amount to either three years non-operational service in the UK, or one year non-operational service overseas.

Obviously Denys Gillam had been too operational!

*

Squadron Leader H. Ambrose, OC 181 Squadron

The targets did get very hot. In 1943-44 when we were flying across to France we got wary of really hot targets and tried to skirt round them, but with the war going on as it was then, a target was a target and you had to go in and cope with it. It wasn't too clever.

I remember we put a piano on the back of a 3-ton lorry when we were on the move, and at the end of the war we held a service for my own 181 Squadron. We'd lost 22 pilots from Normandy to the end, apart from chaps shot down and who were prisoners, or wounded. It was very sad really.

On the last day of the war I led two Typhoon wings against a Baltic shipping convoy with the aid of a Mustang wing led by Mike Donnet – a gallant Belgian. A chap rushed up to me and said could we take Sergeant Brown on this op. I asked who was he and was told he had just arrived. I said no, we shouldn't take him on this one, this being his first operational flight. But apparently he was on his bended knee to go, thinking that if he didn't get on this one, the war might end. So I relented and said yes, but only if his flight commander was happy to let him fly as No 2 to him, which we did. Sergeant Brown was the only pilot we lost on that raid. So he came and vanished on the very last day. When you compare that to people like myself, having done four tours on fighters and survived, you just can't beat the law of averages, which dictates that a chap gets killed on his first op while others go on for ever with a charmed life. I suppose you could add about 10% skill to 90% luck!

Squadron Leader H. Ambrose, OC 181 Squadron (continued)

Brian Calnan and I had been great friends since our time in 257 Squadron together. Later when I got a squadron I had him posted to it. I put him up for a commission but the day he was due to see the AOC, Harry Broadhurst, he was shot down near Hamburg and we thought he'd been killed as no one saw him get out. I thought I'd lost a good friend, wrote to his parents and had his gear sent to them.

Then, at Luneburg Heath in May 1945, just before we left to go up to Lübeck, I got a message to go out to a Dakota on the airfield. When I got to it I found Calnan, in plaster from neck downwards. Both arms broken, both legs broken, both collar bones broken – but I kissed him. He then looked at me and grinned. 'Do you see that WAAF, Boss?' and I said yes. 'Well, if she thinks she's safe with me going back across the English Channel, she's well mistaken!' I could have hugged him – that is morale!

Recollections

I have added three new recollections to this reprint, one by David Ince DFC, another by Robert van Zinnicq Bergmann DFC and a third by Robert Allen DFC. David Ince sent me his piece soon after the original book was published so I am pleased to be able finally to use it. It gives us a new look at the versatility of the Typhoon, with the use of napalm and in addition, David's innovation with the F24 camera, whilst flying with 193 Squadron. Group Captain Gillam was keen to see early photographic results of the attacks by his Wing. He had earlier flown with 257 Squadron:

> I first encountered the Tac-R Typhoon on 2 July 1944, whilst ferrying one from No.84 GSU at Thruxton to 35 Wing at Odiham. Later when we were at Antwerp-Deurne, 35 Wing on the opposite side of the airfield were re-equipping with Spitfire XIVs and we found ourselves with three of their discarded FR Tiffies. I understand that these were acquired by 146 Wing to speed up target photographs after an attack.
>
> The Tac-R Tiffies had been fitted with extra armour which had been removed without (as I subsequently discovered) removal of an appropriate amount of extra tail ballast. As a result they were not very pleasant to fly – they tightened up in turns and unlike the standard product, were quite difficult to land neatly. The port inner cannon and its ammunition tank had been removed too and two F24 reconnaissance cameras, one oblique and one vertical, had been installed instead.
>
> Having been seconded from the Army to the RAF for army co-operation duties I had been through a fighter recce OTU and was an obvious candidate for 146 Wing's part time photography team when it was being formed in November 1944. Shortly afterwards, when Jerry Eaton went on rest, I took charge of this activity and it soon became apparent that fighter/ground-attack pilots untrained in photo-reconnaissance were having considerable difficulty in producing satisfactory results and, more to the point, were putting themselves and their aircraft unnecessarily at risk.
>
> I therefore decided to try an experiment. The two existing F24 cameras were removed and replaced with one F24, fitted with the longest available focal length lens, mounted in the camera bay facing forward and harmonised with the gunsight to photograph through the inboard cannon aperture in the wing leading edge. The camera was operated normally by a type 35 Controller or the Bomb/RP push on the top of the throttle. Although this system only came into full use in the last months of the war it was an immediate success.
>
> The run-in was made in a shallow dive to the target – with cannon if so desired to keep opposition heads down! Excellent results were obtained by pilots totally unversed in aerial photography. The bottom photograph on page 228 and the two on page 245, I took with the forward-facing camera installation.
>
> My encounter with napalm began on the first of April 1945 when I accompanied a Typhoon carrying 2 x 1,000 lb napalm bombs from our airfield at Mill, south-west of Nijmegen, to the s'Hertogenbosch ranges in order to photograph the results – the photographs were good but both bombs failed to explode! Later, on 9 April, as part of Operation Jap, I dropped two similar bombs which spread their flaming petroleum jelly very satisfactorily over the top of and into a replica Japanese bunker.
>
> On 12 April, 193 Squadron with eight aircraft, delivered a napalm attack onto a German strong-point south-east of Arnhem, which was followed up later in the day with a conventional low-level bombing and strafing attack. Although the napalm attack could have been better – there was thick artificial smoke and some

aircraft bombed from too high – we understood that the Germans manning the strong-point were still very shaken and that it was over-run by our ground troops with less difficulty than expected, shortly after the second sortie.

After the war I gave a napalm demonstration to British army units south of Hildersheim on 5 September 1945, and in my final personal curtain to the Typhoon, dropped napalm at the 84 Group Battle of Britain display at The Hague that same month.

Apart from napalm tests at A&AEE, Boscombe Down, I am not aware that any other unit was evaluating it at that time. To the best of my knowledge our 12 April attack was the first and only example of napalm in operational use in Europe during the last war – another first for the Typhoon. Actually, we were pretty apprehensive about napalm. The containers were large, barrel-shaped and painted bright red with very visible external pistols. Their aerodynamics were nil, and aircraft handling was very noticeably affected – much more so than with 1,000 lb bombs – and they tumbled immediately on release. As a result napalm had to be dropped at very low altitude and the sight of a shower of flaming liquid chasing one's tailplane immediately after release was quite something.

*

Robert J.E.M. van Zinnincq Bergmann received the Dutch DFC and the British DFC for his war flying, having escaped from The Netherlands, arriving in England in 1942. Coincidentally he was born in s'Hertogenbosch, the town David Ince mentions above. Having then trained in Canada, he returned once more to England, and was then posted to 181 Squadron at B6, Normandy, in August 1944, and later flew with 182 Squadron as a flight commander.

Having flown twice on 16 September, it was a rude awakening by my batman the next morning as he announced the news that there was a 'Wing Show' on and that everybody had to be at the ops room in an hour's time. An hour later we were all standing in front of the maps of Belgium and The Netherlands. The WingCo, North-Lewis, told us what the target was. He explained the set-up and the importance of our task. Later that day the biggest parachute operation of the war would take place in The Netherlands – Arnhem. Our task was to eliminate the flak belt around the town and the WingCo would lead the show with our 181 Squadron.

It did not often happen that the ack-ack itself was the target. On most operations you went for tanks, locomotives, headquarters, etc. The defending guns seldom got our special attention. This time, however, they were the target and it seemed a good chance to take revenge on our arch enemy.

I was detailed as No.2 to the WingCo. On pressing 'tits' hour I saw the propeller of K-NL turn and started my engine. A deafening noise roared over the field when the four squadrons started up. In sections of four we took off and it was a mighty sight to see the aircraft forming up – 64 of us, the biggest formation I ever took part in – setting course and climbing.

We were over Nijmegen, some fifteen miles from our target zone. The three other squadrons left us and went over like we did in echelon starboard. The flak which had interrupted my thoughts when we passed the Volkel area opened up now with all it had. 'Yersey going down,' came over the intercom and the CO winged over and started his attack. The flak was frightening but it also gave the Germans' positions away. When white puffs appeared from behind the CO's plane I let my rockets go a few seconds later at a gun pit and then started to climb fast.

All around us Typhoons were diving or climbing up in their target zone.

Rockets gone, the WingCo went in again firing his cannons and I followed suit. Climbing up my stick was nearly kicked out of my hand as the aircraft was hit. Luckily it kept climbing. I called up that I was hit and climbing in a southern direction. The stick was very heavy to handle and the vibration of the plane was awful. I heard the CO give an order to one of the Yersey pilots to go after me and escort me as far as possible. The Wing was going home.

Bergy, as he was called, was escorted home by Jack Rendall and despite a badly damaged tail, landed safely. It remained a mystery to him why this was their only operation during the Battle of Arnhem.

Kit North-Lewis, on page 216 mentions John Derry and Bergmann's efforts, and Robert Bergmann records his own recollections:

John Derry asked me to come along on a trip to finish off a Typhoon which had belly-landed in the Paderborn area and which might well be recovered by the Germans for further use. We were too late. The track was quite visible but the Typhoon had gone. On the way back John thought it might be a good idea to attack the railway marshalling yard in the town of Münster. Never have I seen more flak than when we got there. But targets galore. Diving very steeply, we let the eight rockets go in pairs. The pulling up caused a blackout and gave us a few seconds of seeing no flak but then it was there again and remained all around us until we were finally out of range. At the debriefing John said that we had attacked some railway carriages and we claimed moderate success. What we did not know, however, was that John's aircraft had been equipped with a camera. When the film was developed we were called in by Wing Commander North-Lewis and got a terrible rocket for attacking such a target.

From time to time there were typically Dutch targets and I was offered the opportunity to come along. One such op was a big square building of the Royal stables in Apeldoorn [Dutch Royal Summer Palace] where SS troops were billeted. It was a splendid precision attack. No damage was done to the building's annex, as I could assess after the war. HM Queen Wilhelmina thought it a pity that there were no SS soldiers lodged in her palace in The Hague which she disliked very much.

Von Seyss-Inquart's headquarters [Reich Commissioner of the Netherlands, executed for war crimes in 1946] was another operation I was asked to take part in. I came back with part of the front door in my radiator, which was not appreciated by maintenance. On 29 March, John Derry became CO of 182 Squadron and took me along as a flight commander.

Later Robert Bergmann became the Air aide-de-camp to Her Majesty the Queen of the Netherlands, and also received the KCVO to add to his many WW2 decorations from his native country and Britain. He also rose to Air Commodore.

*

Group Captain R.N.G. Allen CBE DFC first flew with No.1 Squadron, at one time being wingman to Squadron Leader Colin Gray DFC (later Group Captain DSO DFC & 2 bars). Bob also flew with 128 Squadron in Sierra Leone, West Africa, before serving on Typhoons, firstly with 197 Squadron as a supernumerary, then with 266 (Rhodesian) Squadron in 1944, as a flight commander.

A number of pilots were Rhodesian and while at Hurn it was often the case that two or three of them would go off onto Lord Beaulieu's estate to shoot pheasants which they roasted to supplement lunch rather than going to the Mess, much to the consternation of his Lordship's gamekeeper.

Bob's last wartime operation is recalled by him, taking place on the first day of Operation Cobra – the American break-out from the Normandy beach-head. The Squadron was operating from B3 – Ste Croix-sur-Mer – commanded by Squadron Leader J.D. Wright.

Early on the morning of 25 July we were awakened from our tents and, after a hurried breakfast, were briefed for a squadron attack of eight aircraft, armed with rockets, against a concentration of armoured vehicles, including tanks. They were reported to be hidden in woods on high ground overlooking the River Orne, near Thury Harcourt, south of Caen.

We took off from our dusty airstrip and began to climb steeply to cross the front line above the range of light flak. We flew as two sections of four aircraft and as a flight commander, I was leading the second section while our Rhodesian CO, 'Barney' Wright, led the first. We were soon in the target area flying at about 10,000 feet, but no vehicles were visible. However, the woods, where they were reported to be, were easily pinpointed because of their distinctive shapes.

The order came from the CO to adopt echelon starboard formations as a prelude to peeling off for individual attacks. However, much to my concern, he continued a slow left-hand turn above the target area, quite contrary to the maxim of 'get in and get out as soon as possible'. Before he actually began the attack heavy flak began bursting around us. I was to learn later that it came from a battery of 88 mm guns sited on high ground guarding the river bridges at Thury Harcourt, over which the orbit must have taken us.

To my relief the slow orbit ceased and the first four Typhoons began their attack and I followed with my section, diving at about a 40-degree angle, aiming in the general direction of the target area, whilst firing our 20 mm cannon indiscriminately to deter any light flak defences. Whilst in the dive, at about 5,000 feet, there were further bursts of heavy flak, one of which was quite close and it became obvious some damage had been sustained. By this time the speed had built up but the aircraft was not responding properly to the elevator controls. As I eased the control column back to check the dive, my Typhoon [MN624] began to roll on to its back, increasing the speed still further. The situation was obviously serious – and getting worse!

My first reaction was to release the rockets to lighten the aircraft, which I did into the general target area. My next concern was to jettison the cockpit hood in order to facilitate baling out, if and when control was lost. I reached for the jettison handle which immediately detached the hood and a side panel of the cockpit. After that no further action was possible, as the slipstream roared in and pinned me back against the armour plate, preventing any further movement on my part.

By then the crisis escalated to a point where recovery was out of the question and survival was the order of the day. The ground was getting alarmingly close and in a last desperate effort, I released the seat harness. Almost immediately I was pulled out of the cockpit by the slipstream like a cork from a bottle. My helmet with its connecting R/T lead and oxygen tube attachments were torn off and so, I quickly discovered, were my flying boots, which were trapped in the rudder pedals and left behind.

I found myself with my parachute harness thankfully intact, hurtling earthwards at a terrifyingly low height. I reached for the release handle and, as soon as I pulled it, the canopy deployed and slowed my descent. Almost at once I landed on my feet in a cornfield which appeared empty.

My first thought was that escape might be possible. It was then I appreciated that I was without boots and socks and the corn stalks were very sharp and painful to my feet, and that at least one of my ankles was bruised and probably sprained. Furthermore, from across the field came German troops, some firing their guns in order to deter me from moving.

I was soon surrounded by some surprisingly young soldiers, who took my revolver and marched me into the nearby woods where, in a caravan, I was interrogated by an SS colonel wearing the badge of the *Toten Kopf* [Death's Head] Division. After a short exchange, he asked questions about attacks made by Typhoons against ambulances on the road to and from the front at Caen. Using my schoolboy German, I was able eventually to satisfy him that my squadron had not been responsible. I was then taken in a military Volkswagen, to a flak battery where I was exhibited to its Luftwaffe crews as a trophy.

By this time I was thoroughly exhausted and weakened by my experience. My lack of footwear was also a severe embarrassment but one of the Germans gave me a pair of well-worn French-looking boots, which, although at least one size too small, restored a little of my dignity and mobility. Having been handed over to the Luftwaffe I became their responsibility and I was soon on my way out of Normandy, via Paris, and on to Germany, to spend the last ten months of the war in Stalag Luft III.

I was to learn later that I had been posted as 'killed in action' and my logbook was endorsed in red to this effect. Nobody had seen me escape from my crashing Typhoon.

Epilogue

The zenith of the Typhoon came in late 1944 when 2nd TAF had no less than 21 ground attack squadrons and two fighter reconnaissance squadrons equipped with this powerful machine. Two squadrons were disbanded early in 1945 and after the war ended most units moved into Germany with the occupation forces. As 1945 progressed these Typhoon squadrons were gradually disbanded or re-equipped. By September the Typhoon had gone from 2nd TAF, squadrons still in being having converted to the newer Hawker Tempest fighter.

In total, 3,317 Hawker Typhoons were built, the last being delivered to the RAF in November 1945. Some Typhoons survived for a time at Nos 5, 20 and 51 Maintenance Units before all Typhoons were removed to the scrap yards during 1946-47. Like many aeroplanes once held in quantity they disappeared totally almost overnight. The aeroplane that only a few months before was the terror of the German Wehrmacht, and had been, in some respects a more efficient and deadly 'Stuka' for the RAF, was simply erased from the face of the earth.

Visitors to London's Imperial War Museum can see a cockpit of a Typhoon, but the only complete example to survive is MN235. This had been sent to America in March 1944 for evaluation and after the war it was stored by the Smithsonian Institute. In 1968 it was returned to England for display at the RAF Museum, Hendon.

The Typhoon has gone. Yet for the men who flew them it survives – in the memories of their war.

Index

Abbott, F/O C 45, 48
Ahrens, S/L W 129, 130, 145
Ainsley, P/O 221
Allan, P/O J 71, 73
Allan, F/L R N G 248, 250-2
Ambrose, S/L H 37-8, 63-4, 74, 75,
  86-7, 128, 135, 146-8, 156, 158-9, 182,
  185, 195, 197, 200-1, 219, 230, 234,
  246
Appleton, G/C C H 216
Ashman, F/S R W 221
Atcherley, AVM R L R 96-7

Baker, W/C E R 63, 124
Baldwin, W/C J R 41, 45-6, 48, 70, 73,
  124, 129, 130, 132, 145, 152
Barlow, Maj D H 141, 142, 145
Barraclough, S/L R G V 180
Bateman-Jones, S/L P L 241
Beake, S/L P H 106, 118, 148
Beamont, W/C R P 23, 26
Bean, W/O R F 182
Beardsworth, G/C H I T 16
Beaulieu, Lord 250
Bell, F/O B E 185
Benn, P/O C E fn166
Bergmann, F/L R J E M van Zinnicq
  216, 248, 249-50
Bitmead, G/C E R 183, 185, 216
Blacklock, F/O N P 68
Bonar, E W 96
Booker, W/C R E P 118
Borland, F/O V N 239
Borland, F/O N 239
Bowman, F/O K 48
Broad, F/O F 154, 197
Broad, F/O N 239
Broadhurst, AVM H 16, 25-6, 120,
  156, 216, 236, 247
Brown, Sgt J A 246

Bryan, W/C J M 39, 40-1, 42-3, 45,
  70-1, 73, 94, 104, 116, 118, 123, 145
Button, W/C J C 221, 225
Button, W/O K E 219
Byer, P/O S T 231
Byrne, F/O K 240

Calnan, F/S B C J 38, 247
Camm, Sydney 11, 15, 18
Campbell, S/L R W 221
Capstick-Dale, Lt 156
Catterns, F/O J B C 192
Clarke, F/O R W 158
Clift, F/L T 219
Clubley, F/L G 74, 81-2, 108, 114, 120,
  134, 147, 149, 153, 156, 163, 170,
  180, 194-5, 203-4, 208-9, 229
Cole, F/O R W 28, 39, 49-52, 54, 56-8,
  60-3
Collins, F/O E H 82-3
Collins, S/L J R 51, 119, 146
Colvin, Sgt J A 42
Coombes, P/O W E 25
Cotes-Preddy, S/L D V C 94
Crisford, F/S C 54
Crosby, S/L R G 222
Crowley-Milling, S/L D 74
Cryderman, F/L F 174
Cumming, F/O D H 182
Cuthbertson, W/O F W 231

Daix, F/O G J G 70
Dall, F/L R J 70, 71, 94
Davidson, W/C R T P 69, 102-3
Davies, F/L 166
Davies, F/O A 94
Davies, S/L I J 70, 106, 126
Davoud, G/C P Y 141
Dawson, F/L R H L 23
deCallatay, F/O J G P 51, 52

deSelys Longchamps, F/O J M P 51-2
de Soomer, S/L L F 49, 52
de Spirlet, F/L F X E 20
Deall, W/C J H 227
Derry, S/L J 183, 216, 250
Detal, P/O C F J 48, 70
Deugo, P/O R H 21
Donnet, W/C M G L M 246
Downes, F/O J M 55
Dredge, W/C A S 56, 61
Dring, W/C W 123, 221
Dryland, P/O R 62
Dundas, S/L H S L 14, 15, 16, 18, 21, 24, 25, 26, 27
Dunkell, F/O W T 182
Dykes, J 94

Eagle, F/O W G 71
Eaton, F/L S J 78-9, 83, 102, 107-8, 115, 122, 124, 137, 145, 149, 154, 159, 164-5, 169, 175, 177, 197, 199, 206, 212, 219, 229-30, 248
Edwards, F/L 182
Ellis, F/L J 240
Entwhistle, F/L T 186
Erasmus, S/L C D 225
Evans, F/O D G 205, 211, 237, 242-4
Ewan, F/S W H 130

Feldman, F/S S B 55
Figg, LAC K F 76, 78, 86, 119, 122, 136-7
Fisher, Sgt G M 106
Fittall, F/L V C 29-30, 39, 40-1, 42-3, 45, 46, 48, 93, 94, 96, 145
Flood, F/L A 141
Fokes, S/L R H 123-4
Foster, F/L J L 55
Freeman, F/O H 48, 71, 73
Frost, F/L J E 111

Gear, F/L K F 163
Geerts, S/L L L E J M 48, 70
Getty, F/O R C 126
Gillam, G/C D E 15, 16, 19, 21, 23, 25, 65-6, 78, 101-2, 107, 151, 156, 174-5, 177, 188, 198, 199, 200, 202-3, 209, 211-2, 213-5, 244, 246, 248
Gilland, F/S B F 41-2

Gilroy, S/L G K 13, 15
Gonay, S/L H A C 124, 126
Gower, S/L A V 25, 63
Grandy, G/C J 13, 21, 25, 27
Grant, W/C F G 182
Gray, S/L C F 250
Gray, S/L G J 88, 90, 93, 136, 140-1, 145, 150, 163-4, 179, 180, 182, 185, 186, 193-4, 202, 205-6, 208, 217, 230, 231, 233-4, 237
Green, G/C C L 15, 66, 120, 139, 146, 147, 179, 180, 183, 185, 208, 216

Haabjoern, W/C E 21, 26
Hall, F/O T T 97, 111, 116, 127, 135-6, 151, 153, 168-9, 170-1, 173-4, 182-3, 221, 223, 230
Handley, F/S W S 68
Hanks, S/L P P 13, 14, 23
Hardy, P/O 73
Harrison, F/L J 237
Harwood, F/O C F 182
Hawkins, S/L P 54, 55, 56
Henrion, Sgt L L 48
Hillock, W/C F 69
Hopkins, Capt M C 158-9
Howarth, F/L J D 197
Hunter, F/O R C 69
Hurrell, F/S R W 158-9

Ince, F/L D H G 80, 248-9
Ingle-Finch, S/L M R 25, 80, 111

James, F/O 188
Jensen, S/L F W M 64, 82-3
Jenvey, F/L D E 186
Johnson, S/L W J 145
Johnson, W/C J E 27, 208
Jonas, F/O A R F 39, 42-3
Jones, F/L K 203
Jones, F/L M E 241
Judd, W/C M T 103

Kaufman, Capt G H 141
Kay, F/L J M 191
Keep, S/L J G 80, 106
Kelsick, F/L O R 219
Khin, F/L S 219
King, F/O W R 82-3

Kinsey, F/L G 231
Kluge, FM G von 146

Lao, F/L H Y 219
La Rocque, W/O 55
Lallemant, S/L R A F 20, 73
Lambert, S/L L H 91, 159-60, 190-2,
   201, 205, 207-8, 212-3, 222-4
Lamon, P/O M 45, 71
Laurence, F/O F H 182, 186
Lawton, F/O W 241-2
Lee, F/L R G E 146

Macdonald, F/O J A 45, 48, 71
Macdonald, LAC D N 100-1, 122-3,
   153-4, 174
Mackenzie, F/L R M 224
Manak, S/L J 39-40
Marriott, F/S M E 129
McCaw, F/L J 94
McConnell, S/L W W 66
McLaughlin, P/O J G 70
Merlin, W/O H E R 182-3
Merrett, F/L N L 178
Merrett, F/L W K 178
Millar, F/L R G 237
Miller, F/O C W 48
Mogg, F/O D E G 68
Montgomery, FM B L 132
Munro, P/O 23
Murphy, F/O F 32, 34-5
Murray, F/L D 231

Niblett, S/L J 69, 71, 73, 106
Noble, F/O T B 192
North-Lewis, W/C C D 79-80, 102,
   106, 108, 134-5, 149-50, 155-6,
   179-80, 198-9, 202, 204, 216-7, 229,
   234, 236, 249-50

Ortmans, F/O C C A 20
Osborne, F/S E L 41

Patterson, F/O J A 186, 231
Pattison, F/L H G 88, 91-3, 97, 108-9,
   110-1, 114, 141, 142, 144-5, 150, 166,
   182, 194, 204-5, 210, 213, 229, 231
Patton, Gen G S 146
Pennant, F/S J 242

Pentland, S/L W H 161
Petherbridge, Sgt F 70
Phillips, S/L 94
Plamondon, S/L J M G 71, 73, 128,
   225
Plows, F/L L 104
Pottinger, P/O R W 39, 49, 52, 55-6,
   58-62, 99-100, 171-2
Price, F/S R 109, 141
Proddow, F/O B F 66

Racine, F/L G G 68, 69
Read, S/L M E 80
Rendall, F/L J 250
Reynolds, F/L W S 120
Richardson, F/O 154
Richey, S/L P H M 12, 13, 15, 18-19,
   20-1, 23-5, 26, 28, 73
Roberts, F/O A E 118
Roberts, S/L C L C 29
Rommel, FM E 132, 146
Roper, F/O B 69
Ross, F/O A S 48
Ross, S/L D 108, 115
Rumbold, S/L M 222
Rundstedt, FM G von 179
Russell, S/L H A B 103, 104, 106
Rutherford, F/O A 142
Rutter, S/L R D 175, 177
Ryan, Sgt 126

Sage, F/L K 182
Saville, F/L J 107
Scarlett, S/L F H 128
Schaefer, F/S 135
Schwarz, F/O R 51
Scott, F/L L S B 40
Scott, W/C D J 35, 36, 148
Scrambler, F/L J 70
Seyss-Inquart, A von 250
Shannon, P/O A 76, 99, 116, 129,
   130, 165, 200, 209, 239-40
Shepherd, LAC D C 78, 83-4, 90, 119,
   136
Sheward, S/L R E G 66, 68, 76, 175,
   177, 178, 195, 222, 225, 227, 237,
   239, 240
Sholto Douglas, ACM Sir W 12, 13,
   26

Short, S/L H P 180
Sievwright, F/O N G 186
Simpson, F/L J G 80-1, 98-9, 108, 130,
    132, 137, 139, 147, 165-6, 173, 197-8,
    204, 209, 215, 225, 241
Sinclair, S/L G L 103
Skelly, F/O F 222
Smith, S/L A H 29, 30, 32-7, 132, 148,
    151-3, 161-2, 186, 188-9
Smith, F/L V 39, 40-1, 45, 48
Smith, F/L W 119-20
Snell, P/O R W 197
Sopwith, T O M 18
Speedie, F/O W R 111, 113, 156,
    158-9, 166, 168, 170, 240-1
Spellman, F/O J A 231
Spragg, F/L B J 24, 75, 93, 100, 102,
    115, 116, 124, 130, 154, 169-70, 175,
    177, 197
Stanley, W/O A 46, 71
Stapleton, S/L B G 148
Stark, S/L L W F 70, 126
Stuart-Turner, Sgt K M 21
Stubbs, F/L J D 190-1
Steib, F/O P F 38

Tallala, F/L C L F 142fn
Tallala, W/O H C B 142-144
Taylor, F/L J H 231
Taylor, S/L D M 68, 225
Thomas, S/L S R 52, 54
Thornton-Brown, S/L P G 48
Todd, S/L A G 75, 91, 93-4, 103, 104,
    118, 219, 221, 224-5, 229-30
Tough, F/O R B 69
Trafford, F/L G R 148
Trott, F/O K A J 130

Vernon-Jarvis, F/L E C H 111, 191,
    224

Waddy, S/L I 148
Walker, Sgt L 30
Walker, W/C P R 24
Walmsley, F/O R M 60
Warnes, S/L G B 68, 69
Washburn, F/O D J 182
Watkins, F/O A A 106
Watkins, P/O W E 69

Watson, W/O R A 142
Watt, Capt J I A 185, 237
Watts, F/O W F 70
Weir, P/O L 30
Wells, W/C J C 70, 178, 188, 227, 244
West, F/O P G 104, 106
White, F/S R A E 148
Whitman, Sgt G A 55
Whitmore, P/O W B 219
Williams, F/S G 69
Williams, F/L J F 45, 48, 129, 145
Wilson, P/O N B 96-7, 113, 126, 139
Wilson, F/O R J M 118, 241
Wright, S/L B 94
Wright, S/L J D 251
Wright, F/S W A 182

Yi, F/L M H 219